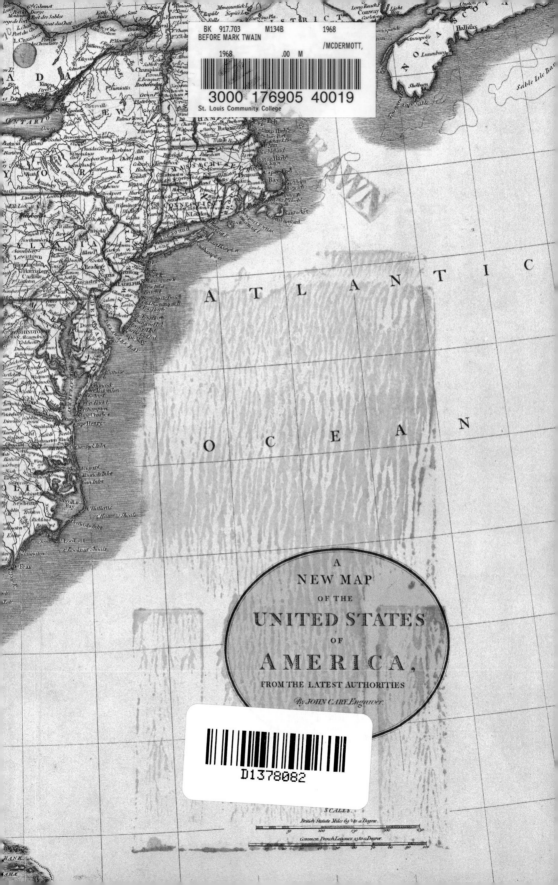

A
NEW MAP
OF THE
UNITED STATES
OF
AMERICA,
FROM THE LATEST AUTHORITIES

By JOHN CARY, Engraver.

SCALES.
British Statute Miles 69 ½ to a Degree.
Common French Leagues 25 to a Degree.

TRAVELS ON THE WESTERN WATERS

Travels on the Western Waters

John Francis McDermott, *General Editor*

BEFORE
MARK TWAIN

A Sampler
of Old, Old Times
on the Mississippi

EDITED BY

John Francis McDermott

SOUTHERN ILLINOIS UNIVERSITY PRESS

CARBONDALE AND EDWARDSVILLE

FEFFER & SIMONS, INC.

LONDON AND AMSTERDAM

To
NICHOLAS JOOST
Colleague and Good Friend
this volume
Before Mark Twain
and
this series
Travels on the Western Waters

━━━━

FOREWORD

With the close of the Revolution the spilling over the Alleghenies of thousands of Americans and of many foreign visitors and observers led to an untold number of diaries, travel accounts, and reminiscences of voyages through the wilderness in which men detailed the adventures of their youth, the development of their business enterprises, their share in military actions, their work in carrying the Word to the Indian, their wanderings in the cause of science, or their plain curiosity as tourists. The firsthand reports of this flood of travelers of every persuasion, afloat on the "western waters" for every conceivable reason, are documents of prime value to the social and cultural historian as well as narratives of perennial interest to those who delight in reading of man and his ways.

Many of these early accounts of life and scene on the rivers of the Mississippi Valley were printed by the traveler-author in small editions and in time have become quite scarce, accessible only in rare book collections. A few of them were reprinted by Reuben Gold Thwaites in his model series of *Western American Travels* in 1904. Others have since found their way back to a new audience in a new dress. But many of the narratives describing the new world beyond the Alleghenies have remained out of common reach.

To make such treasures of vivid, on-the-spot reporting once more available to students of American history and to all who delight in reading it the Southern Illinois University Press is undertaking to reprint under the general title of "Travels on the Western Waters" many which cannot be readily obtained or which have never been reissued in an annotated edition.

The series opens with a sampler to illustrate what life on the Mississippi was like in the days before Mark Twain took it over as a literary property, a reader which focuses attention on many facets of the river world. The selections from many sources each contribute to a panorama which unrolls before the onlooker displaying "old, old times" on the river from the levee at St. Louis to the water front of New Orleans.

For the second volume we have chosen the well known and valued *Recollections of the Last Ten Years in the Valley of the Mississippi (1815–1825)* by Timothy Flint, a frequently petulant and prejudiced but always sharp observer of this western country. Published in 1826, this book has been reprinted only once (1932) and that issue has been long out of print. Now it is once more available, this time with illuminating annotations by George R. Brooks, director of the Missouri Historical Society.

These publications will be followed by Francis Baily's *Journal of a Tour in Unsettled Parts of North America in 1796 & 1797*, edited by Jack D. L. Holmes, Associate Professor of history at the University of Alabama at Birmingham, originally published in England in 1856 and virtually unknown today, although it is the earliest detailed account we have of travel down the Ohio and the Mississippi. Christian Schultz, Jr.'s *Travels on an Inland Voyage performed in the years 1807 and 1808* (published in 1810) is being edited for the series by Richard E. Oglesby, Assistant Professor of history at the University of California at Santa Barbara.

Later publications will include such varied work as Albert Koch's *Reise durch einen Theil der Vereinigten Staaten von Nordamerika in den Jahren 1844 bis 1846* (Dresden, 1847); Zadok Cramer's *The Ohio and Mississippi Navigator* (1804); *Lloyd's Steamboat Directory and Disasters on the Western Waters* (1856); W. Aitken's *A Journey up the Mississippi River from its mouth to Nauvoo, the City of the Latter Day Saints* (1845); G. H. DeVol's *Forty Years a Gambler on the Mississippi* (1887); S. W. McMasters' *Sixty Years on the Upper Mississippi* (1893); J. C. Beltrami's *Pilgrimage in America to the Sources of the Mississippi River* (1828); Ralph Keeler's *Vagabond Adventures* (1870). Hitherto unpublished diaries will also be printed.

It is thus intended to include a wide variety of travel narratives presenting many phases of life on the western waters. No rigid scheme will be followed in developing the series. Each volume will be chosen for its inherent value as an eye-witness travel document, of interest and importance alike to students of history and to river buffs. Each will be a complete reprint of the original text, edited and annotated in the manner most suitable to it. Each will be accompanied by a block of pictures, themselves contemporary documents.

John Francis McDermott
GENERAL EDITOR

Southern Illinois University
Edwardsville

PREFACE

What was it like in the old, old times on the Mississippi before *Huckleberry Finn* came into being, before "Old Times on the Mississippi" charmed the readers of *Harper's Magazine* in 1874, even in that dim, dark day before young Sam Clemens was born? Long before Mark Twain took out his copyright on it, the river was there, a carrier of commerce and chicken coops, princes, prelates, and paupers. Businessmen and lawyers and missionaries and artists, soldiers, newspapermen, eager-eyed and sour French and English and German tourists, botanists, politicians, peddlers, emigrant families, musicians, actors, and gamblers floated patiently or impatiently down the great river, risked the hazards, enjoyed the pleasures, suffered the discomforts, delighted in the bustle of steamboat travel. They filled their notebooks and sketchbooks with friendly approval or sharp reproval, with coolly distant comment or warm enthusiasm. They crowded their letters with the sights of the Western World viewed from the decks of the boats and the wharfs and levees of the towns and with the experiences shared with fellow passengers. And they went home, a multitude of them, to write about it.

From their books this one has been made. No one at all could crowd between the covers of one volume anything more than a sampling of the lively record of the river. Here have been brought together a representative lot of day-by-day notations and calm or stormy retakes developed in leisurely contemplation which build up a picture of what life and travel on the Mississippi between St. Louis and New Orleans was like in those long ago days "before the war."

The selections presented have been drawn almost entirely from materials in print in the days before Mark Twain began writing about the Mississippi and those few actually printed later were recorded before his time. All are offered without annotation, for this is not a source book for Mark Twain but a reader for those who love the river. It is a sampler of old, old times on the Mississippi. If some chuckling or crabbed reviewer would rather call it a crazy quilt, let him do so—let him have as much fun in his way with this volume as I have had in mine.

As always, of course, I am happily grateful for the more than usual courtesies shown me by the Mercantile Library of St. Louis, Ridgeley (now Olin) Library of Washington University, and the Missouri Historical Society. The Western Americana Collection at Yale has been good enough to let me quote a few passages from the diary of Nathaniel Hobart (1838) and the Minnesota Historical Society from a letter written by Nathaniel Whiston, Jr. (1847). Franklin J. Meine of Chicago lent me one or two items from his fine library of rare Mississippi River books. My own university has generously encouraged my interest in this as in other projects. Vernon Sternberg and his staff at the Southern Illinois University Press have been uncommonly patient and forbearing. So, too, has been my ever helpful wife, Mary Stephanie McDermott.

I take particular pleasure in dedicating this volume—and the series it introduces—to my colleague and good friend Nicholas Joost, for he unwittingly became its sponsor when he invited me several years ago to the research professorship I enjoy.

John Francis McDermott

Southern Illinois University
Edwardsville, 7 February 1968

CONTENTS

FOREWORD   *vii*

PREFACE   *xi*

SKETCHES OF THE MISSISSIPPI   (*between pages 158–159*)

INTRODUCTION   *xvii*

No Craft So Whimsical — No Shape So Outlandish
     TIMOTHY FLINT   *3*

Flatboat Fleets in 1808
     CHRISTIAN SCHULTZ, JR.   *13*

Episode on a Flatboat: *the Death of Banks Finch*   *20*

The Western Steamboat
     CHARLES JOSEPH LATROBE   *26*

From New Harmony to New Orleans, 1826
     DONALD MAC DONALD   *40*

Time Passes Tranquilly, If Not Pleasantly
     THOMAS HAMILTON   *48*

Joe Cowell Recalls a Voyage in the *Helen McGregor* in 1829; *or, Twelve Days Confinement in a High Pressure Prison*
     JOSEPH L. COWELL   *58*

A Lady Writer Reports Some Incidents of Steamboat Travel
     MRS. ELIZA STEELE   *70*

Deck Passage to Natchez, 1838
HENRY B. MILLER 83

The Little Steamboats of the Mississippi
T. B. THORPE 87

Concerning the Conduct of the Captain of the *Casket* 91

Steamboat Manners
M. DE GRANDFORT 103

"Never Such a Collection of Unblushing
Degraded Scoundrels"
G. W. FEATHERSTONHAUGH 107

Adventures of the Artist
JOHN BANVARD 112

Description of Banvard's PANORAMA
JOHN BANVARD 126

ARROWSMITH's Panorama of Western Travel 140

On Board a Keelboat During an Earthquake
JOHN BRADBURY 148

A Little Difficulty with Ice
CHARLES AUGUSTUS MURRAY 155

Hurricane at Natchez 159

A Storm Scene on the Mississippi
T. B. THORPE 161

A Severe Time on the Mississippi
CODDINGTON C. JACKSON 166

The Burning of the *General Pratte* 170

Explosion of the Steamer *Pennsylvania*   *178*

Fever, Fatigue, and Death
        TIMOTHY FLINT   *187*

The "Pilgrims"
        TIMOTHY FLINT   *191*

Reminiscence of Natchez "Under-the-Hill":
  "*My Grandmother's Trick*"
        WILLIAM C. HALL   *196*

Gamblers and Suckers
        JONATHAN H. GREEN   *200*

Thimblerig, The Riverboat Gambler
        DAVID CROCKETT   *209*

The Big Bear of Arkansas
        T. B. THORPE   *222*

The Disgraced Scalp Lock *or Incidents on the
  Western Waters*
        T. B. THORPE   *235*

Sketches from the Saga of Jack Pierce: *Flatboatman
  and Ram-Butter*
        MENRA HOPEWELL   *248*

The Steamboat Captain Who Was Averse to Racing
        GEORGE P. BURNHAM   *257*

Stopping to Wood
        JOSEPH M. FIELD   *261*

The Second Advent! Tom Bangall, the Engineer,
  and Millerism
        JOHN S. ROBB   *264*

Glimpses of New Orleans in 1819
        BENJAMIN H. LATROBE   *270*

Ten Days in New Orleans, 1826

      DONALD MAC DONALD   *278*

Carnival in New Orleans, 1846

      CHARLES LYELL   *287*

Index   *295*

INTRODUCTION

"Never since St. Louis was a 'place,' never since broadhorns and flatboats hid their diminished heads before the introduction of mighty steam upon the vast tide of the Mississippi, has this city presented so lively an aspect as at the present moment. The expansive Levee is so narrowed by the rising river that the boats stand opposite to the store doors, so near as to present the singular appearance of a contracted street with very queer houses, having tall chimneys all along one side. What is left of the Levee is literally piled up with produce and merchandise. It is with the utmost difficulty that drays can move about, and passengers have enough to do to elbow their way along the sidewalk. All is bustle and activity. The steamer Eclipse, I am told, went off the other day with a freight barge in tow, and the value of the cargo taken down was estimated at the enormous sum of seventy-five thousand dollars! Boats are starting now every day loaded down with produce, and yet the Levee continues heaped with it. Steamers from above report that it will take all the boats in the trade a full two months to bring down the cargoes that are now ready and waiting for them.

"The winter has been very severe . . . but the reaction has burst out very suddenly and with singular effect. The town seems to have jumped out of passive slumber into raging excitement. . . . Three new hotels are now open. . . . numbers of fashionable strangers are here, as well as officers of the army and many of the prominent citizens. . . ."

So Matt Field wrote from St. Louis to the New Orleans *Picayune* on April 25, 1843.[1] Every day the levee was crowded with people, coming and going. A month earlier John James Audubon and his four friends on their way to the Upper Missouri

[1] New Orleans *Weekly Picayune*, May 8, 1843.

had arrived from Louisville aboard the steamboat *Gallant*, "the very filthiest of all filthy old rat-traps" the ornithologist had ever traveled in. On the very day that Field had stepped ashore from the *Missouri* Audubon had departed in the *Omega*, the American Fur Company boat, for Fort Union. The bird-painter had sketched the scene in his journal. A few Indians, who were being taken home, squatted on the highest part of the steamer, "tranquil lookers-on." One hundred and one engagees "of all descriptions and nearly a dozen nationalities" shoved each other roughly as they poured onto the deck. When the boat pushed off shore, leaving behind a crowd of loafers, the men on board "congregated about the hurricane deck with their rifles and guns of various sorts, all loaded, and began to fire . . . a very disorganized kind of salute, which lasted for something like an hour." [2]

Sir William Drummond Stewart was yet in town, stopping at the Planters House. (The hotelkeepers charged outrageously, Audubon thought: board at the Planters, the newest and finest hotel in St. Louis—"much larger than the Astor House"—cost ten dollars a week or more.) The Scottish sportsman, no stranger in this western city, had arrived April 1 on the *Julia Chouteau*, dampened but not discouraged. He had been "on the point of losing his Life and that of all on Board the steamer J. M. White" when it had struck a rock forty miles above the mouth of the Ohio on the 28th and had sunk in four minutes. Luckily, every person but one and almost all the baggage had been saved. Matt Field himself had journeyed up from New Orleans to be a member of this huge hunting party which Stewart was taking to the Wind River Mountains, a prospect, thought the reporter in advance, "of a most exciting and truly delightful travel." When the Stewart party left aboard the *Weston* on the first stage of their excursion, "thousands of friends and curious spectators congregated on the Levee to cheer." [3]

Captain John C. Frémont was in town, signing up men for

[2] Maria R. Audubon and Elliott Coues, eds., *Audubon and his Journals* (2 vols., New York, 1893), I, 450–52, 455–56; John Francis McDermott, ed., *Audubon in the West* (Norman, The University of Oklahoma Press, 1965), 30–35, 72.

[3] McDermott, *Audubon in the West*, 47. For the Stewart expedition see Matthew C. Field, *Prairie and Mountain Sketches*, edited by Kate L. Gregg and John Francis McDermott (Norman, The University of Oklahoma Press, 1957).

his second pathmarking expedition to the Rocky Mountains.[4] The day after the *Omega* carried the famous Audubon away, the steamer *John Aull* took its departure for Weston, Missouri, opposite Fort Leavenworth, carrying three officers and their families, one hundred and thirty-seven privates from Jefferson Barracks, one hundred cabin passengers, seventy-eight deck passengers, three hundred tons of freight, twenty-three wagons and carts, nine mules, and five Catholic missionaries—practically a payload for a boat one hundred and sixty-one feet long and twenty-one wide, announced as two hundred and forty tons burden.[5]

But stop awhile on the St. Louis levee—any day—any year. Take your stand with a *Reveille* reporter on an April afternoon in 1848. Watch that conceited-looking fellow, that dandy levee clerk with the tightly knotted cravat. A rough deckhand brushes against him. He stays a moment to see if his coat has been smirched, looks with great complacency at his boots, and walks on. Striding by is a man with his coat off, a lard trier in one hand, and a proof glass in the other. Him you will meet "every where, and in all weathers; when it rains you will see him wrapped up in a warm coat, and carrying a cotton umbrella in his hand, always in a hurry, always busy." He is a levee salesman. Here is an odd fellow "in brown jeans pants and coat, with his whip in his dexter hand, and a 'section' of gingerbread in the other. He is stopping to look at those 'fixins' in that shop."

A steamer is ringing a bell "just as if she were about to leave. How sober the Captain looks in his dignified occupation of swinging the clapper. What a resigned expression pervades a countenance which says, 'I'm sorry to leave so soon, but I'm bound to get off this evening.' He is done ringing now, and is speaking to his clerk. He is telling him to go up to the Reveille office, and have his departure continued over until to-morrow, at 10 A.M., *positively.* A man walks up the gangway, and addresses him—'Capt., are you certain to leave this evening?' 'Yes sir-e, we ain't going to do anything else. . . . We are the only boat that leaves for Cincinnati this evening.' The man muses a little while,

---

[4] John C. Frémont, *Report of the Exploring Expedition to the Rocky Mountains in the year 1842 and to Oregon and North California in the year 1843–44* (Washington, 1845), 105; Theodore Talbot, *Journals of Theodore Talbot, 1843 and 1849–52,* edited by Charles H. Carey (Portland, Oregon, The Metropolitan Press, 1931), 3–4.

[5] St. Louis *Daily Evening Gazette,* March 13, April 26, 1843.

then the Captain takes him by the button and talks confidentially. There he's gone in and registered his name. He's caught, sure." The boat will undoubtedly leave before noon the next day—unless the captain holds back just a little longer to pick up a few more passengers.

Watch the boys and girls with little tin buckets in their hands, crowding around those molasses barrels. They have seen the molasses oozing out the vent holes and are scraping it into their buckets. One boy leans against a pile of coffee bags. He watches to see if anyone is looking, then holds a small empty sack behind him and lets it fill from a hole in one of the bags. "Now he has thrust the sack under his coat and walks toward that woman, who stands at a distance; she is his mother, and encourages him in his rascality." A noise up the levee. What are those men hallooing about? The road is blocked with drays, and every driver is bawling at the top of his voice. What cursing, swearing, and cracking of whips! Yonder is a wharf-rat, lying back on some sacks of produce. Every day he is to be seen in that same position for months at a time. Some people think he sleeps his time away in the winter only to reappear, as soon as warm weather comes, to take that same position on the sacks. The moving of freight is the only thing that disturbs him but he soon finds another pile and has settled down again. The man you see yonder with restless eye, dressed so extravagantly, wearing many chains and jewels and walking with a slow and lounging gait—he is a river gambler who will probably take the boat that "leaves" this evening—just now he is watching to see if there are any going aboard whom he can swindle.

A New Orleans boat comes in. How swiftly she approaches the landing, rings her bell to stop. What a crowd is gathering near to board her! The hotel runners hasten from boat to boat, to be the first to offer the card of the houses they represent. Look at that club-footed fellow—in spite of his deformity he will be first aboard. Go on with the crowd but be careful or you will be knocked overboard by the deckhands—they are not very particular. In the cabin, mistaken for a passenger, you will have runners thrusting cards in your face: Planters' House, sir? Virginia Hotel, sir? City Hotel, sir? "The Virginia man will tell you that they haven't anything to eat at the City Hotel, the 'City' man will swear lustily that the Virginia ain't worth a d——n; and the Planters' House runner will call them both common houses and not fit for a white man." Newspapers will dun you for the latest news, draymen and baggage wagon drivers for a fare.[6]

Anything can happen on the levee–everything does–sooner or later everybody passes. Prince Paul Wilhelm of Württemberg, gentleman amateur of science, the Duke of Saxe-Weimar-Eisenach, the Prince de Joinville, Prince Maximilian of Neu-Wied (traveling more simply as the Baron von Braunsberg) with his staff artist Karl Bodmer, Washington Irving, Lafayette, Frederick Marryatt (who found St. Louis in the summer worse than the Black Hole of Calcutta), Charles Dickens, the Maréchal Simon Bertrand, the notorious and often furious journalist from Washington, D. C., Mrs. Anne Royall, Daniel Webster (one of the bad debts in Pierre Chouteau's estate in 1849 was a note of Webster's for $5,000), the Count d'Otrante (son of Fouché, Napoleon's chief of secret police), Jenny Lind, Thackeray, the Earl of Selkirk, Lord William Lennox on a sporting venture up the Missouri, America Vespucci seeking to capitalize on her ancestor, Jonathan Green, "the reformed gambler," Father Mathew, temperance crusader, and an endless stream of immigrants–English, Irish, French, German–pour off the boats which pull into the mile or two of shipping on the water front.

That rowdy keelboatman Mike Fink decides to improve the shapeliness of a Negro's foot by "trimming" his heel with a rifle shot. A mulatto prisoner being brought ashore by a sheriff's officer turns on him and kills him: the colored man is seized by a mob and lynched a few blocks away. Out on Bloody Island Thomas Biddle and Spencer Pettis settle their difficulties permanently with pistols at five feet. William Cullen Bryant, come out to visit his brother in Illinois, writes home about a whorehouse riot. Jack Pierce wins a butting match with Nigger Jim from New Orleans. Noah Ludlow, Sol Smith, their acting company, and their guest stars, Mr. and Mrs. Charles Kean, arrive from New Orleans. To greet them, "At least four or five hundred people were assembled when she [the steamboat] reached the landing, and a rush was made on board her, that more resembled

---

[6] These paragraphs about the Levee are compressed from "A Glimpse at Our Landing," St. Louis *Weekly Reveille*, April 3, 1848, p. 1641. This feature story was not signed but quite likely was by John S. Robb (Solitaire), an assistant editor.

an attack on a hostile ship than any thing else. One unlucky keelboat, laden with flour and wheat, that happened to be between the enormous hull of the Missouri and the wharf, was crushed in an instant." [7]

Any day when the river is open you may join an excursion party on an outing to Jefferson Barracks or to bustling Alton, you may take a little trip to Nauvoo to see what is going on among that strange lot, the Mormons, or you may start on the tour which Easterners so often come west to make from St. Louis to Fort Snelling and the Falls of St. Anthony. When the river is high in the spring, you may even have the sport of a "sail *over the prairies* of the American Bottom" to Cahokia and the Illinois bluffs eight or ten miles away, "skimming through the streets of villages and over barn-yards and cornfields in a *steamboat*," the "enthusaism and hilarity" of the party in no way dampened by unfavorable weather. You may learn at breakfast that the steamer *Shepherdess* at half past eleven last night struck a snag three miles below the Market Street wharf and sank so quickly that more than forty passengers went down with it. (One of those saved was the "Fat Girl of Ohio.") You may waken in the night to discover the city ablaze: twenty-three steamboats, three barges, a canalboat, and block after block of the waterfront buildings flaming to ruins. You may go some week to see two giant moving panoramas of the Mississippi painted by St. Louis artists: "between the *two* 'rivers,'" declares the *Reveille*, "we shall have a rise which will make the whole town turn out." [8]

Every kind of accommodation is to be found on the steam-

---

[7] The Mike Fink story was published by Solitaire in the St. Louis *Weekly Reveille*, January 25, 1847, p. 1147. The lynching in May, 1835, was reported in the St. Louis newspapers. A full report of the duel is to be found in the New York *Observer*, September 17, October 8, 1831. For Bryant's letter see *Prose Works of William Cullen Bryant*, edited by Parke Benjamin (2 vols., New York, 1884), I. 10–11. The story of Jack Pierce is printed below. For the enthusiastic reception of the Keans consult the St. Louis *New Era*, April 23, 1846.

[8] The flood story is from the St. Louis *Daily Evening Gazette*, June 29, 1844. The wreck of the *Shepherdess* was reported in the St. Louis press January 4, 5, 6, 1844; estimates of death ran as high as seventy; see also *Lloyd's Steamboat Directory and Disasters on the Western Waters* (Cincinnati, 1856), 137–40. The great fire at St. Louis (May 17, 1849) was, of course, reported in great detail in the local newspapers. For the moving pictures see John Francis McDermott, *The Lost Panoramas of the Mississippi* (Chicago, The University of Chicago Press, 1958); the quotation is from the *Weekly Reveille*, August 30, 1849.

boats that line the wharfs of St. Louis. Not merely had the *Gallant* been filthy and its captain far from gallant, but the fare provided was worse, Audubon declared, "certainly much worse and so scanty withal that our worthy commander could not have given us another meal had we been detained a night longer. . . . Our *compagnons de voyage*, about one hundred and fifty, were composed of Buckeyes, Wolverines, Suckers, Hoosiers, and gamblers, with drunkards of each and every denomination, their ladies and babies of the same nature, and specifically the dirtiest of the dirty. We had to dip the water for washing from the river in tin basins, soap ourselves all from the same cake, and wipe the one hundred and fifty with the same solitary one towel rolling over a pin. . . . My bed had two sheets, of course, measuring seven-eighths of a yard wide; my pillow was filled with corn-shucks, Harris fared even worse than I, and our 'state-room' was evidently better fitted for the smoking of hams than the smoking of Christians. When it rained outside, it rained also within, and on one particular morning, when the snow melted on the upper deck, or roof, it was a lively scene to see each person seeking for a spot free from their many spouts overhead." [9]

Avoid, if you can, such a miserable tub as Audubon's *Gallant*, though you may be lucky to get even such passage so early in the season. But there are grander steamboats afloat on the western waters. The *General Bernard Pratte*, built in 1840 at Pittsburgh for St. Louis owners, with a deck length of two hundred and five feet and a width of twenty-seven, can carry five hundred tons downstream. "Her cabins are by far the most elegant and tastefully furnished of any boat in the west. The gentlemen's cabin has forty state rooms with two large berths, spring bottoms, in each. The doors [are] of beautifully cut glass with ventilators overhead. . . . Two elegant chandeliers shed their lustre over the centre, and on either side are large French mirrors. The ladies' cabin, which is eight feet longer than any on the western waters, is still more elegantly furnished and fitted up. In fact, both cabins contain all that could be added for taste or luxurious ease; fine pier tables, splendid Brussels carpets, rocking chairs, sofas, and last, though not least, there is in the ladies' cabin a splendid well-toned piano. . . . Nor has the captain been unmindful in other respects. He has on board an ice house capable

[9] See Note 2, above.

of containing four or five tons of ice, an indispensable article in the warm weather, but which frequently gives out on a long voyage, a large laundry, &c., &c." Alas, this magnificent steamboat is doomed to have no longer life than most: when it is bound upriver from New Orleans in November 1842 a fire will break out a few miles above Memphis and the boat will be completely destroyed, though without loss of life.[10]

Or look in on the *Missouri*, not the one Matt Field had traveled on in 1843 but a yet more elegant boat, the third or fourth of its name. "In a walk through her spacious cabin it is hard to divest one's self of the idea that the foot is treading the hall of some regal palace, so finished is every thing around—elegant carpets, splendid chandeliers, and sumptuous furniture. . . . Her saloon, when thrown open from the office in her bow to the stern windows, is one of the most imposing on any vessel in the world. Its extreme length is three hundred and five feet, by eighteen wide and twelve high. . . . Seventy-three feet of this length shuts off with beautiful folding-doors, separating the ladies' saloon from the gentlemen's cabin, and is furnished with an elegant piano. In this apartment Captain Twitchell has recently made a pleasing improvement; he has removed the bulk head in the rear of the ladies' saloon, supplied its place by curtains, and constructed large stern windows, of beautiful colored plate glass, through which a soft and mellow light falls into the ladies' apartment. When the heat is oppressive, these windows can be thrown open, leaving a free passage of air through the entire length of the cabin. Her sleeping apartments are furnished with every comfort which can be found in the best regulated hotels—are well ventilated and kept scrupulously neat. Bath houses for ladies and gentlemen, supplied with hot and cold water, gentlemen's barber shop, servants' apartments, and, indeed, every necessary and luxury which can tend to pleasant travelling, comfort of invalids, pleasure of the tourist, or ease of the man of leisure, is here concentrated in a floating palace. Her cook is a prince of the culinary art, and her steward is an epicure in taste; so, of course,

---

[10] St. Louis *Missouri Republican*, March 10, 1840. For an account of one upriver trip see *Tixier's Travels on the Osage Prairies*, edited by John Francis McDermott, translated by Albert J. Salvan (Norman, The University of Oklahoma Press, 1940), pp. 85–94. The newspaper reports of the burning of the *Pratte* are printed below.

the table abounds in everything that can tempt the appetite." [11]

Board any steamer and see the world of the Mississippi. As you step on deck, boys selling books rush you "with great bundles under their arms, singing out, 'Last Lecture of Mrs. Caudle' only one half-penny; No. 20 of the 'Wandering Jew,' and all of Bulwer's and James' novels, at a shilling each!" A lively boy in this trade, Thomas Horton James found out, "could drive a lucrative trade in these wares"; one youth told him that on a capital of ten dollars he could clear ten dollars a week. [12]

Once aboard you see any and every kind of person. You may have occasion to fill your diary with details about them as Nathaniel Hobart did the letters he was writing home on a trip west late in 1837. "The passengers aboard this boat [the *J. Gilman*, bound to St. Louis from Louisville] are a different sett from those on board the Monarch" in which he had voyaged down the Ohio to Kentucky. "Those were stylish people—here are 'Tom, Dick & Harry.' One pedlar of prints & jewelry has tables spread all over with prints of the strangest kind—Political caricatures—scenes of murder &c. &c. asks a dollar for a common print—does not appear to sell any. Two men have been shooting at a mark with pistols, their mark a piece of wood thrown into the water." The *Gilman* stopped to wood. "A coloured man came down through the woods to the river, with milk, eggs and apples to sell to the Capt. of the boat. A coloured woman brought a tin pail of cider, and offered to let our deck passengers drink as much as they could at one time without stopping for a 'picaune.'" On your boat you may enjoy, as Hobart did, the company of "thirty or forty great oxen on board going down to New Orleans. . . . On the upper deck, over all our heads, are long rows of cages, which go clear round the boat; these are filled with turkies, geese & hens. The cocks make a proper great crowing in the morning. Last night the boat stopped . . . to take in some hogs, and you never heard such a squeeling as they did make. That set the hens, geese & turkies to cackling and gobbling, and the oxen mowed." [13]

[11] *Weekly Reveille*, June 8, 1846, p. 886. An earlier *Missouri* had burned at the foot of Pine Street on August 9, 1841; an account of this disaster was published in *The Family Magazine* (Cincinnati 1841), p. 398.

[12] Rubio [Thomas Horton James], *Rambles in the United States and Canada during the year 1845* (London, 1847), p. 40.

[13] Ms. Letter-journal of Nathaniel Hobart, 1837–38, Western Americana Collection, Yale University Library.

Faster and faster the boats make the river trip but traveling alone can be tedious. "It is possible," an observant voyager writes with mild irony in his notebook, "that you may meet with a few well-bred, intelligent travellers—the steamboat may have an engine that works smoothly and without jarring; you may have contrived to keep a few books in your travelling equipage." But you will spend a good many idle hours watching the deck passengers below you, you will make your own notes about the mania for whittling and the American sprawl so noticeable in the lounge. The gamblers at work, the inevitable race with a rival boat, the hour stuck on a sandbank, the stops for wooding, the excitement of "man overboard," the rush and discomfort of mealtimes at tables spread with profusion and variety, the picturesque sight of the firemen, "almost invariably athletic negroes or mulattoes," performing their labor "amid bursts of boisterous merriment, jests, and songs . . . while with a thousand grimaces they grasp the logs and whirl them into the blazing throat of the furnaces"—these are the daily incidents of travel for the business man rushing about his concerns up and down the river, for the curious tourist from Europe or the eastern states, for the vacationing family of St. Louisans or Louisianians.[14]

Perhaps, like Henry Miller, you will find that this lazy life aboard a steamer will make you dull and sluggish. "This is one of the effects that travelling on Steam Boats will have on a person used to active exercise; the table is filled with the luxuries of life, and all things fitted up in an inviting manner; you sit down with a great variety before you; you are paying well for it and have every encouragement to eat (with the exception of a keen appetite sharpened by active exercise); breakfast over, you sit and lounge about or walk the deck if you see fit; about 11 o'clock comes a lunch; here again is eating for you, cakes, raisins, Almands, &c., &c.; dinner about 2; still very little exercise; dull and drowsy, you may retire to your birth and sleep an hour or two to drive away a heavy hour or more; supper comes, and after drinking a good portion of tea or coffee, you are ready to go to sleep quite tired with dullness and eating; thus time is too frequently spent on board the Steamers." [15]

---

[14] Compressed from a chapter in Charles Joseph Latrobe's *The Rambler in North America* (2nd edition, 2 vols., London, 1836). See the extended

Watching from the deck of your steamer as you slip rapidly downriver to New Orleans, you may well conclude that Matt Field has been a little too hasty in writing in his breezy journalistic fashion about the "diminished" heads of broadhorns and flatboats. Hundreds of steamboats do crowd the waterways, but in a day or two of travel you see more kinds of river craft than you thought could exist—timber rafts, skiffs, barges, keelboats, flatboats of every size and style. Traffic has steadily increased in volume and comfort ever since Jolliet and Marquette with their five men paddled down the Mississippi from the Wisconsin to the Arkansas in their birchbark canoes in 1673. But in these decades "before the war" the capacious pirogue cut from the trunk of a huge cottonwood poplar, used by traders and travelers in the eighteenth century, is still seen. Mackinaw boats laden with furs come down the Missouri to St. Louis warehouses. Keelboats such as those in which Mike Fink roared his unglamorous way downstream are still freighting to New Orleans. Even yet Kentucky arks are being hastily put together at Brownsville on the Monongahela or Pittsburgh or Wheeling for the one-way trip to the great valley as they have been ever since the Americans first came pouring over the mountains into the western country. A man can still load his family, his livestock, and his plunder on one of these broadhorns and float away to settle in Kentucky or the Yazoo Delta or a merchant can carry a cargo to New Orleans.

Look at this ark you are about to pass, a huge flatboat possibly a hundred feet long, with sweeps at each end and a pair at the sides—all the sweeps are used for is to keep her in the stream; the current will do the work. In the forward part of the boat the family housekeeping is going on. There is the resolute-looking mother stirring the big pot and a girl of eighteen setting a table. Near the fire is an old and bent white-haired couple. Numerous children of various sizes are helping in the work, some of them lolling about on the heaps of hay and provender in the center of the boat. Two or three little ones are sleeping beneath a canvas tent which protects the bedding of the travelers. Stacked in piles you see the household furniture—chairs, tables, pots,

description of steamboat travel reprinted below.
[15] Henry B. Miller, "Journal," *Missouri Historical Society Collections*, VI (1931), 242. Miller was returning (June, 1838) to St. Louis from a trip to Galena.

kettles, bedsteads, cupboards, churns, spinning-wheels, a store of
quilts and blankets, barrels most likely filled with flour and pork,
a heap of cabbages. In the stern, horses, cattle, chickens, dogs,
goats, farming tools. What cheaper and easier way to move your
family to new farming lands and to have a supply of ready lumber
when you arrive and dismantle your broadhorn? [16]

In an earlier day you might have seen, as Timothy Flint tells
us, sometimes a hundred boats landed on a single day at New
Madrid, first port below the mouth of the Ohio. "The boisterous
gaiety of the hands, the congratulations of acquaintances, who
have met here from immense distances, the moving picture of life
on board the boats, in numerous animals, large and small, which
they carry, their different ladings, the evidence of the increasing
argriculture above, and, more than all, the immense distances
they have already traversed," indeed could "afford a copious fund
of meditation." There were boats put to every use: a floating
tinner's shop, a blacksmith's, dram shops, produce boats, family
boats, shipments of planks, whisky, hemp, cotton, lead, pork,
"cider royal," and "floating mansions of iniquity." The coming of
steam has changed this but little. Steamboat passengers see less
of it because they go faster on their way, but there is more
flatboating and keelboating than ever. A passenger on the
J. Gilman in December 1837 told Nathaniel Hobart that he had
counted ninety-four such craft during the first eighteen hours
after the steamer had passed the mouth of the Ohio. [17]

From the shore, at least, this floating down the stream is a
tempting life. "All the toil, and danger, and exposure, and moving
accidents of the long and perilous voyage, are hidden" from those
who "contemplate the boats floating by their dwellings on beautiful spring mornings. . . . The boat takes care of itself. . . . one
of the hands scrapes a violin, and the others dance." To the girls
on shore "rude defiances, or trials of wit, or proffers of love" are
thrown. These scenes and the notes of the ever-present bugle
echoing from the bluffs "have a charm for the imagination . . .
that almost inspires a wish, that we were boatmen." The flatboats
passed by the steamers look "so picturesque . . . there is some-

[16] This paragraph compressed from "A Winter in the South," *Harpers
New Monthly Magazine*, XVII, 297 (August, 1858).
[17] This paragraph compressed from the section of Timothy Flint's *Geography and History of the Western States* (2 vols., Cincinnati, 1828) printed
below. For Hobart's journal see note 13, above.

thing so fanciful in the canopy of green boughs under which the floating voyagers repose during the heat of the day" that a traveler is led to half propose "building a flatboat and floating down to New Orleans at leisure." Tranquil jolly flatboatmen thus seem to take their way with calm romantic ease.[18]

It is, however, a world of trials and hazards you share in when voyaging on the Mississippi. Whether you travel in flatboat or keelboat or on the finest of midcentury steamers, the snags and the sawyers and the sandbanks lie in wait for you. High water, low water, roaring floods, crevasses, tornadoes, hurricanes, the bursting of boilers, fire, explosion, collision are commonplace. Hardly a steamboat is in service for more than two or three years, however powerful its engines, however lauded its safety. Many are the minor accidents. "In the afternoon we ran over a log," writes a traveler; "the vessel trembled to her centre; the ladies raised their heads from their work; the gentlemen looked overboard; and I saw our yawl snagged as she was careering at the stern. The sharp end of the log pricked through her bottom as if she had been made of brown paper. She was dragged after us, full of water, till we stopped at the evening wooding-place, when I ran to the hurricane deck to see her pulled up on shore and mended." [19] Not infrequent are disasters. The steamboat *Prairie* is wrecked by a hurricane at Natchez and fifty flatboats in harbor at the moment are engulfed by the river waves.[20]

It is not uncommon for a young fellow on his travels to be able to report nonchalantly to his "Dear Father, Mother, Sister and Brother" that "we lay aground 1½ days, run aground in a fog, so we all got aboard of another boat, I could mention several little items, which occured coming up but time will not permit of much, for instants, Felix Grundy, snag'd, sunk, total loss, passengers and crew came up on our boat, same day past the Ambassador burnt to the water, and was smoking, same day passed the duke of Orleans aground, strugling hard to get off, and in course of two hours after we passed her, some sparks caut in some hemp

[18] The first part of this paragraph is from Flint (note 17); the last quotation is from Harriet Martineau, *Retrospect of Western Travel* (2 vols., New York, 1838), II, 15.

[19] Martineau, *Retrospect of Western Travel*, II, 15.

[20] Captain Freligh's account of this disaster is printed below. According to Lloyd's *Steamboat Directory and Disasters on the Western Waters* (pp. 140–42) 116 flatboats at the landing were wrecked and 200 men lost.

which she had a board and was burnt to the water, passengers and crew, making there escape with only the close on there persons, by a flat boat being dropped to there assistance, the river down from Natches down was very high, in many places covering whole plantations, the stock wading about the barns in water up to there belly and a skift fasten to the door to convey wood, from the pile to the house, such was the sight of things below." [21]

There is an even greater hazard predicted by Parson William Miller for April 25, 1843, though he is to be proved wrong in his calculations of the end of the world. Matt Field, on his way to St. Louis, reported how on that "last day" he had awakened "as people usually do on board steamers, with the clattering of machinery and the blowing off of steam, and to our very great wonder the Mississippi seemed rolling onward much in the same manner as it has rolled heretofore. . . . no symptom of spontaneous combustion either on water or land. We looked to see the Mississippi turned into a roaring cataract of lurid flame, but it seems Parson Miller has not set the river on fire after all. Many waited in great fear and trembling until noon day, expecting to hear the grand 'crack of doom' as the clock struck twelve, but it became apparent that . . . the performance was not to come off." Some, he added, "expected to see a burning flood of lard oil come pouring down the Ohio from Cincinnati; but here again was disappointment, and *La Belle Riviere* came bounding into the bosom of the Father of Waters with the same chrystal purity that has been her characteristic of old." [22]

But life afloat on the western waters is not all disasters. You may chance upon a showboat. William Chapman, long known as a Covent Garden actor, has been in the practice of building a theater "upon a raft at some point high up the Mississippi" from which he takes his departure "early in the fall, with scenery, dresses, and decorations, all prepared for presentation. At each village or large plantation he hoists banner and blows trumpet, and few who love a play suffer his ark to pass the door, since they know it is to return no more until the next year. . . . Sometimes a large steamer from Louisville, with a thousand souls on board, will command a play whilst taking in fuel. . . . The *corps drama-*

[21] Nathaniel Whiston, Jr., St. Louis, May 6, 1847, to Nathaniel Whiston, ms., Minnesota Historical Society.
[22] New Orleans *Weekly Picayune*, May 1, 1843.

tique is . . . principally composed of members of his own family, which is numerous, and, despite of alligators and yellow fever, likely to increase and flourish. When the Mississippi theatre reaches New Orleans, it is abandoned and sold for firewood; the manager and troop returning in a steamer to build a new one. . . ." By 1836 Chapman has come to devising an engine to bring the boat back up river.[23]

If Shakespeare and other regular theatrical fare is not for you, perhaps you may pass Spalding & Roger's Floating Circus Palace, "a most curious, original and interesting affair." The interior of this craft is "a most commodious amphitheatre. The 'dress-circle,' as it is termed, consists of eleven hundred cane-bottom arm-chairs, each numbered to correspond with the ticket issued. The 'family-circle,' comprises cushioned settees for some five hundred persons, while the residue of the accommodations are comprised in the nine hundred gallery seats. The amphitheatre is warmed by means of hot water pipes or steam. . . . The interior is lighted by over a hundred brilliant gas jets, forming a great ornament in their construction, and supplied by gas apparatus on board—this furnishes the entire light for vestibule, the halls, offices, saloons, green rooms, dressingrooms and the stable. A chime of bells is attached to the structure, and discourses most eloquent music previous to each performance, while Drummond-lights render the neighborhood of the floating palace brilliant during the exhibition." [24]

Visits ashore will alleviate the tendium of many days on the river. You can break your voyage as Christian Schultz did at Ste. Genevieve, a place, he found in 1808, "that does not seem to be in want of amusements, if eternal dancing and gambling deserve the name." None of this was too bad until Schultz discovered that in return for the many parties to which he had been invited in carnival season he was expected to give one himself.

Like many another traveler from the very days of the found-

[23] Tyrone Power, *Impressions of America* (2 vols., Philadelphia, 1836), II, 120; this comment was dated February 1835. See also the New York *Spirit of the Times*, VIII, 298 (November 3, 1838) for a letter by Charles H. Eaton, dated Cincinnati, May, 1836 reprinted from the Cincinnati *Daily News*. Philip Graham, in *Showboats. The History of an American Institution* (Austin, The University of Texas Press, 1951, p. 9) gives 1831 as the date for the beginning of Chapman's enterprise.

[24] *Gleason's Pictorial Drawing Room Companion*, IV, 128. See also Harold E. Briggs, "Floating Circuses," *Egyptian Key*, III, 19–23 (1951).

ing of Natchez, you may enjoy a glimpse—horrifying or exciting, depending on your temperament—of the village-under-the-hill, with its gambling hells and whorehouses where the keelboatmen so often are played for the dull suckers they are, but sometimes, aroused by their losses, go on a rampage and tear the place to pieces. There you could have overheard with Christian Schultz a dispute between two boatmen which arose "over a *Choctaw lady*." One, declared Schultz, shouted: "I am a man; I am a horse, I am a team. I can whip any man *in all Kentucky*, by G——d.' The other replied, 'I am an alligator; half man, half horse; can whip any *on the Mississippi*, by G——d.' The first one said again, 'I am a man; have the best horse, best dog, best gun, and handsomest wife in all Kentucky, by G——d.' The other, 'I am a Mississippi snapping turtle: have bear's claws, alligator's teeth, and the devil's tail; can whip *any man*, by G——d.' " Such challenge could only lead to violence and they fought for half an hour until "the alligator was fairly vanquished by the horse."

Hell-hole though it is, Natchez-under-the-hill can offer the traveler such a curious and interesting group as the gang of idle Choctaw, Natchez, and Muskogee Indians Schultz saw early in the century. About forty men, women, and children, they would serenade the arriving boats with a full band of music. Five of the instruments were devised from cane; the sixth was "a two gallon tin kettle, with a drest buckskin extended over its mouth" to make a drum of it. "Their manner of performance was as follows: Having first formed their company under a tree a small distance from the boats, they advance singing short stanzas of 'ho ha.' When near the boats, the captain or leader advances before with a white or striped silk banner, taking long and solemn strides, and then halting a moment for the rest to come up. After reaching the boat he stands as still as a post, not moving his eyes, or any of his limbs. The men approach next, and form a circle round him: then follow the boys; after them the squaws with the girls in the rear. The music now becomes slow and solemn for about five minutes, when it gradually increases to a brisker motion, during which you will first perceive the captain move his eyes, next his lips, then his head and hands, and at last a very curious and pleasing panto-mimical dance strikes up, which continues for about a quarter of an hour. The music is performed in two parts, being tenor and treble: the men and boys composing the former, and the women and girls the latter. The several instruments were used with such accurate time and motion, and so blended with the vocal music, that it rendered the performance far superior to any thing I had anticipated." [25]

If you have an eye for oddities, you may come upon a splinter sect like the "Pilgrims" whom Timothy Flint encountered on their miserable wanderings from Canada to the Arkansas and watch them come ashore, ragged and dirty, led by their Prophet, marching in Indian file, the old men in front, the women next, and the children in the rear, all chanting: "Praise God! Praise God!" [26]

Finally, you pass the great sugar plantations and the French towns of Louisiana. Soon your steamboat is nosing into a vacant place in the almost unending line of steamers and flatboats and ocean vessels that crowd the bustling water front of New Orleans, that always "different" city, half American, half foreign. You stride along the levee, visit the markets, look into the Cathedral, stroll through the French part of the city with its colorful eighteenth century buildings, watch the Carnival crowds, contrast the Sunday customs with those you know at home, walk of a Sunday to Congo Square where the slaves dance, gaze at the curious "cities of the dead" with their above-ground sepulchres, hear French spoken on every side. Your run down the river is over, whatever its pains and pleasures.

This is the Mississippi in the days before Mark Twain.

John Francis McDermott

[25] These quotations from Christian Schultz, *Travels on an Inland Voyage*, are drawn from passages printed below.

[26] Timothy Flint's account of these people is printed below.

BEFORE MARK TWAIN

NO CRAFT SO WHIMSICAL—
NO SHAPE SO OUTLANDISH

TIMOTHY FLINT

[*Timothy Flint, after spending ten years wandering up and down the Mississippi Valley as a missionary, at last settled down in Cincinnati as a writer and editor. Much of what he had observed went into his* A Condensed Geography and History of the Western States, or the Mississippi Valley *(2 volumes, Cincinnati, 1828), from which have been selected these pages (I, 229–42) describing the variety of boats then found on the Ohio and Mississippi Rivers.*]

No form of water craft so whimsical, no shape so outlandish, can well be imagined, but what, on descending from Pittsburg to New Orleans, it may some where be seen lying to the shore, or floating on the river.

The barge is of the size of an Atlantic schooner, with a raised and outlandish looking deck. It had sails, masts and rigging not unlike a sea vessel, and carried from fifty to an hundred tons. It required twenty-five or thirty hands to work it up stream. On the lower courses of the Mississippi, when the wind did not serve, and the waters were high, it was worked up stream by the operation, that is called 'warping,' a most laborious, slow and difficult mode of ascent, and in which six or eight miles a day was good progress. It consisted in having two yawls, the one in advance of the other, carrying out a warp of some hundred yards in length, making it fast to a tree, and then drawing the barge up to that tree by the warp. When that warp was coiled, the yawl in advance had another laid, and so on alternately. From ninety to an hundred days was a tolerable passage from New Orleans to Cincinnati. In this way the intercourse between Pittsburg, Cincinnati, Louisville, Nashville and St. Louis, for the more important purposes of commerce, was kept up with New Orleans. One need only read the journal of a barge on such an ascent, to comprehend the full value of the invention of steam boats. They are now gone into disuse, and we do not remember to have seen a barge for some years, except on the waters above the mouth of the Ohio.

The keel boat is of a long, slender and elegant form, and generally carries from fifteen to thirty tons. Its advantage is its small draft of water, and the lightness of its construction. It is still much used on the Ohio and upper Mississippi in low stages of water, and on all the boatable streams, where steam boats do not yet run. Its propelling power is by oars, sails, setting poles, cordelle, and when the waters are high, and the boat runs on the margin of the bushes, 'bush-whacking,' or pulling up by the bushes. Before the invention of steam boats, these boats were used in the proportion of six to one at the present time.

The ferry flat is a scow-boat, and when used as a boat of descent for families, has a roof, or covering. These are sometimes, in the vernacular phrase, called 'sleds.' The Alleghany or Macki-naw skiff is a covered skiff, carrying from six to ten tons; and is much used on the Alleghany, the Illinois, and the rivers of the upper Mississippi and Missouri. Periogues are sometimes hol-lowed from one very large tree, or from the trunks of two trees united, and fitted with a plank rim. They carry from one to three tons. There are common skiffs, canoes and 'dug-outs,' for the convenience of crossing the rivers; and a select company of a few travellers often descend in them to New Orleans. Hunters and Indians, and sometimes passengers, make long journeys of ascent of the rivers in them. Besides these, there are anomalous water crafts, that can hardly be reduced to any class, used as boats of passage or descent. We have seen flat boats, worked by a wheel, which was driven by the cattle, that were conveying to the New Orleans market. There are horse boats of various constructions, used for the most part as ferry boats; but sometimes as boats of ascent. Two keel boats are connected by a platform. A circular pen holds the horses, which by different movements propel wheels. We saw United States' troops ascending the Missouri by boats, propelled by tread wheels; and we have, more than once, seen a boat moved rapidly up stream by wheels, after the steam boat construction, propelled by a man, turning a crank.

But the boats of passage and conveyance, that remain after

the invention of steam boats, and are still important to those objects, are keel boats and flats. The flat boats are called, in the vernacular phrase, 'Kentucky flats,' or 'broad horns.' They are simply an oblong ark, with a roof of circular slope, to shed rain. They are generally about fifteen feet wide, and from fifty to eighty, and sometimes an hundred feet in length. The timbers of the bottom are massive beams; and they are intended to be of great strength; and to carry a burthen of from two to four hundred barrels. Great numbers of cattle, hogs and horses are conveyed to market in them. We have seen family boats of this description, fitted up for the descent of families to the lower country, with a stove, comfortable apartments, beds, and arrangements for commodious habitancy. We see in them ladies, servants, cattle, horses, sheep, dogs and poultry, all floating on the same bottom; and on the roof the looms, ploughs, spinning wheels and domestic implements of the family.

Nine tenths of the produce of the upper country, even after the invention of steam boats, continues to descend to New Orleans in Kentucky flats. They generally carry three hands; and perhaps a supernumerary fourth hand, a kind of supercargo. This boat, in the form of a parallelogram, lying flat and dead in the water, and with square timbers below its bottom planks, and carrying such a great weight, runs on to a sandbar with a strong headway, and ploughs its timbers into the sand; and it is, of course, a work of extreme labor to get the boat afloat again. Its form and its weight render it difficult to give it a direction with any power of oars. Hence, in the shallow waters, it often gets aground. When it has at length cleared the shallow waters, and gained the heavy current of the Mississippi, the landing such an unwieldy water craft, in such a current, is a matter of no little difficulty and danger.

All the toil, and danger, and exposure, and moving accidents of this long and perilous voyage, are hidden, however, from the inhabitants, who contemplate the boats floating by their dwellings on beautiful spring mornings, when the verdant forest, the mild and delicious temperature of the air, the delightful azure of the sky of this country, the fine bottom on the one hand, and the romantic bluff on the other, the broad and smooth stream rolling calmly down the forest, and floating the boat gently forward, present delightful images and associations to the beholders. At this time there is no visible danger, or call for labor. The boat

takes care of itself; and little do the beholders imagine, how
different a scene may be presented in half an hour. Meantime one
of the hands scrapes a violin, and the others dance. Greetings, or
rude defiances, or trials of wit, or proffers of love to the girls on
the shore, or saucy messages, are scattered between them and the
spectators along the banks. The boat glides on, until it disappears
behind the point of wood. At this moment, perhaps, the bugle,
with which all the boats are provided, strikes up its note in the
distance over the water. These scenes, and these notes, echoing
from the bluffs of the beautiful Ohio, have a charm for the imagination, which, although we have heard them a thousand times
repeated, at all hours and in all positions, even to us present the
image of a tempting and charming youthful existence, that almost
inspires a wish, that we were boatmen.

No wonder, that the young, who are reared in these remote
regions, with that restless curiosity, which is fostered by solitude
and silence, who witness scenes like this so frequently, no wonder, that the severe and unremitting labors of agriculture, performed directly in the view of such scenes, should become taste-
less and irksome. No wonder, that the young, along the banks of
the great streams, should detest the labors of the field, and embrace every opportunity, either openly, or, if minors, covertly to
escape, and devote themselves to the pernicious employment of
boating. In this view we may account for the detestation of the
inhabitants, along these great streams, towards steam boats,
which are continually diminishing the number of all other boats
and boatmen, and which have already withdrawn, probably, ten
thousand from that employment. We have seen, what is the character of this employment, notwithstanding all its seductions. In
no employment do the hands so soon wear out. It is, comparatively, but a few years, since these waters have been navigated in
any way. Yet at every bend, and every high point of the rivers,
where you go on shore for a moment, you may expect to see the
narrow mound, and the rude monument, and the coarse memorial
carved on an adjoining tree by a brother boatman, to mark the
spot, where an exhausted boatman yielded his breath, and was
buried.

The bayou at New Madrid has an extensive and fine eddy,
into which boats float, almost without exertion, and land in a
remarkably fine harbor. It may be fairly considered the central
point, or the chief meridian of boats, in the Mississippi valley.

This bayou generally brings up the descending and ascending boats; and this is an excellent point of observation, from which to contemplate their aspect, the character of boating, and the descriptions and the amount of produce from the upper country. You can here take an imaginary voyage to the falls of St. Anthony, or Missouri; to the lead mines of Rock river, or Chicago of lake Michigan; to Tippicanoe of the Wabash, Oleanne point of the Alleghany, Brownsville of the Monongahela, the Saline of the Kenhawa, or the mountains, round whose bases winds the Tennessee; or, if you choose, you may take the cheap and rapid journey of thought along the courses of an hundred other rivers; and in the lapse of a few days' residence in the spring, at this point, you may see boats, which have arrived here from all these imagined places. One hundred boats have landed here in a day.

The boisterous gaiety of the hands, the congratulations of acquaintances, who have met here from immense distances, the moving picture of life on board the boats, in the numerous animals, large and small, which they carry, their different ladings, the evidence of the increasing agriculture above, and, more than all, the immense distances, which they have already traversed, afford a copious fund of meditation. In one place there are boats loaded with pine plank, from the pine forests of the southwest of New York. In another quarter there are numerous boats with the 'Yankee notions' of Ohio. In another quarter are landed together the boats of 'old Kentucky,' with their whiskey, hemp, tobacco, bagging and bale rope; with all the other articles of the produce of their soil. From Tennessee there are the same articles, together with boats loaded with bales of cotton. From Illinois and Missouri, cattle, horses, and the general produce of the western country, together with peltry and lead from Missouri. Some boats are loaded with corn in bulk, and in the ear. Others are loaded with pork in bulk. Others with barrels of apples and potatoes, and great quantities of dried apples and peaches. Others have loads of cider, and what is called 'cider royal,' or cider, that has been strengthened by boiling, or freezing. Other boats are loaded with furniture, tools, domestic and agricultural implements; in short, the numerous products of the ingenuity, speculation, manufacture and agriculture of the whole upper country of the West. They have come from regions, thousands of miles apart. They have floated to a common point of union.

The surfaces of the boats cover some acres. Dunghill fowls

are fluttering over the roofs, as invariable appendages. The piercing note of the chanticleer is heard.

The cattle low. The horses trample, as in their stables. The swine utter the cries of fighting with each other. The turkeys gobble. The dogs of an hundred regions become acquainted. The boatmen travel about from boat to boat, make enquiries and acquaintances, agree to 'lash boats,' as it is called, and form alliances to yield mutual assistance to each other on the way to New Orleans. After an hour or two passed in this way, they spring on shore, to 'raise the wind' in the village. If they tarry all night, as is generally the case, it is well for the people of the town, if they do not become riotous in the course of the evening; in which case, strong measures are adopted, and the proceedings on both sides are summary and decisive. With the first dawn all is bustle and motion; and amidst shouts, and trampling of cattle, and barking of dogs, and crowing of the dunghill fowls, the fleet is in a half an hour all under way; and when the sun rises, nothing is seen, but the broad stream rolling on, as before. These boats unite once more at Natchez and New Orleans; and although they live on the same river, it is improbable, that they will ever meet again on the earth.

In passing below, we often see a number of boats lashed, and floating together. In travelling over the roofs of the floating town, you have a considerable walk. These associations have various objects. Boats so united, as is well known, float considerably faster. Perhaps the object is to barter, and obtain supplies. Perhaps to kill beef, or pork, for fresh provisions. Apples, cider, nuts, dried fruit, whiskey, cider and peach brandy, and drams, are ratailed; and the concern is for a while one of great merriment and good will. Unforeseen moral storms arise; and the partnership, which began in a frolic, ends in a quarrel. The aggrieved discharge a few mutual volleys of the compliments, usually interchanged on such occasions, unlash, and each one manages his boat in his own way.

The order of things in the western country naturally fosters a propensity for a floating life on the water. The inhabitants will ultimately become as famous, as the Chinese, for having their habitancy in boats. In time of high waters at the mouth of the Ohio, we were on board an immensely large flat boat, on which was 'kept a town,' which had figured in the papers, as a place, that bade fair to rival the ancient metropolis of the Delta of the Nile. The tavern, the retail and dram shops, together with the inhabitants, and no small number of very merry customers, floated on the same bottom. We have seen a large tinner's establishment floating down the Mississippi. It was a respectable manufactory; and the articles were sold, wholesale and retail. There were three apartments, and a number of hands. When they had mended all the tin, and vended all, that they could sell in one place, they floated on to another. We have heard of a large floating blacksmith's establishment; and of another, in which it was contemplated to work a trip hammer. Beside the numerous periogues, or singular looking Spanish and French trading retail boats, commonly called 'chicken thieves,' which scour the rivers within an hundred leagues of New Orleans, there are on all the waters of the West retail trading boats. They are often fitted up with no inconsiderable ingenuity and show. The goods are fancifully arranged on shelves. The delicate hands of the vender would bear a comparison with those of the spruce clerk behind our city counters. Every considerable landing place on the waters of the Ohio and the Mississippi has in the spring a number of stationary and inhabited boats, lying by at the shores. They are too often dram shops, and resorts of all kinds of bad company. A severe enquiry ought to be instituted at all these points, respecting the inmates and practices of these floating mansions of iniquity.

There is no portion of the globe, where the invention of steam boats ought to be so highly appreciated, as in the valley of the Mississippi. That invention ought to be estimated the most memorable era of the West; and the name of the inventor ought to be handed down with glory to the generations to come. No triumph of art over the obstacles of nature has ever been so complete. But for this invention, this valley might have sustained a nation of farmers and planters; and the comforts, the arts, refinements and intelligence of the day would have made their way slowly from New Orleans to the lakes, the sources of the Mississippi, and the Rocky mountains. Thousands of boatmen would have been slowly and laboriously warping, and rowing, and poling, and cordelling their boats, in a three months trip up these mighty and long streams, which are now ascended by steam boats in ten days. It may be safely asserted, that in many respects, the improvements of fifty years without steam boats, were brought to this country in five years, after their invention. The distant points of the Ohio and the Mississippi used to be separated by distances and obstacles of transit more formidable, in the passing, than the Atlantic. These points are now brought into juxtaposition. Distances on the rivers are not indeed annihilated; but they are diminished to about an eighth of their former extent; and their difficulties and dangers are reduced even more than that. All the advantages of long rivers, such as variety of soil, climate, productions, remain, divested of all the disadvantages of distance and difficulty of ascent. The day, that commemorates this invention, ought with us to be a holiday of interest, only second to that, which gave birth to the nation.

It is, perhaps, necessary to have something of the experience, which we have had, of the slowness, difficulty and danger of propelling boats against the current of these long rivers, fully to estimate the advantages of this invention.

We have ascended the Mississippi in this way for fifty days in succession. We have had but too much of the same kind of experience on the other streams. We considered ten miles a day, as good progress. It is now refreshing, and it imparts a feeling of energy and power to the beholder, to see the large and beautiful steam boats scudding up the eddies, as though on the wing. When they have run out the eddy, and strike the current, it is a still more noble spectacle. The foam bursts in a sheet quite over the deck. The boat quivers for a moment with the concussion, and then, as though she had collected her energy, and vanquished her enemy, she resumes her stately march, and mounts against the current five or six miles an hour. We have travelled ten days together, between New Orleans and Louisville, more than an hundred miles in a day against the stream. The difficulty of ascending used to be the only one, that was dreaded in the anticipation of a voyage of this kind. This difficulty has now disappeared, and the only one, that remains, is to furnish money for the trip. Even the expense, considering the luxury of the fare, and accommodation, is more moderate, than could be expected. A family in Pittsburg wishes to make a social visit to a kindred family on Red river. The trip, as matters now stand, is but two thousand miles. Servants, baggage, or 'plunder,' as the phrase is, the family and the family dog, cat and parrot, all go together. In twelve days they reach the point proposed. Even the return is but a short voyage. Surely we must resist strong temptations, if we do not become a social people. You are invited to a breakfast at seventy miles distance. You go on board the passing steam boat, and are transported, during the night, so as to go out in the morning, and reach your appointment. The day will probably come, when the inhabitants of the warm and sickly regions of the lower points of the Mississippi will take their periodical migrations to the north, with the geese and swans, and with them return to the south in the autumn.

We have compared the most beautiful steam boats of the Atlantic waters with those of the Mississippi; and we have seen none, which in splendor and striking effect upon the eye, and the luxury and comfort of accommodation, could equal the *Washington*, *Philadelphia*, *Lady of the Lake*, *Florida*, and some others, on these waters. We have been amused in observing an Atlantic stranger, who had heard us described by the phrase 'backwoods men,' taking his first survey of such a steam boat. If there be any ground of complaint, it is, that so much gorgeousness offends good taste, and seems to be in opposition to that social ease and comfort, which one would desire in such a place. Certainly, there can be no comparison between the comfort of the passage from Cincinnati to New Orleans in such a steam boat, and a voyage at sea. The barren and boundless expanse of waters soon tires upon every eye, but a seaman's. And then there are storms, and fastening of the tables, and the necessity of holding to something, to keep in bed. There is the insupportable nausea of sea sickness, and there is danger. Here you are always near the shore, always see the green earth; can always eat, write, and study undisturbed. You can always obtain cream, fowls, vegetables, fruit, fresh meat, and wild game, in their season, from the shore.

A stranger to this mode of travelling would find it difficult to describe his impressions upon descending the Mississippi for the first time in one of these steam boats, which we have named. He contemplates the prodigious construction, with its double tiers of cabins, and its separate establishment for the ladies, and its commodious arrangements for the deck passengers and the servants. Over head, about him, and below him, all is life and movement. He contemplates the splendor of the cabin, its beautiful finishings of the richest woods, its rich carpeting, its mirrors and fine furniture, its sliding tables, its bar room, and all its arrangements for the accommodation of eighty cabin passengers. The fare is sumptuous, and every thing in a style of splendor, order, quiet and regularity, far exceeding that of most city taverns. You read. You converse, or walk, or sleep, as you choose. Custom has prescribed, that every thing shall be 'sans ceremonie.' The varied and verdant scenery shifts about you. The trees, the green islands, the houses on the shore, every thing has an appearance, as by enchantment, of moving past you. The river fowl, with their white and extended lines, are wheeling their flight above you. The sky is bright. The river is dotted with boats above you, beside, and below you. You hear the echo of their bugle reverberating from the woods. Behind the wooded point you see the ascending column of smoke, rising over the trees, which announces, that another steam boat is approaching you. The moving pageant glides through a narrow passage, between an island, thick set with young cotton woods, so even, so beautiful, and regular, that they seem to have been planted for a pleasure ground, and the main shore. As you shoot out again into the broad stream, you come in view of a plantation, with all its busy and cheerful accompaniments. At other times you are sweeping along for many leagues together, where either shore is a boundless and pathless wilderness. A contrast is thus strongly forced upon the mind, of the highest improvement and the latest pre-eminent invention of art with the most lonely aspect of a grand but desolate nature—the most striking and complete assemblage of splendor and comfort, the cheerfulness of a floating hotel, which carries, perhaps, two hundred guests, with a wild and uninhabited forest, it may be an hundred miles in width, the abode only of bears, owls and noxious animals.

FLATBOAT FLEETS IN 1808

CHRISTIAN SCHULTZ, Jr.

[*Christian Schultz, Jr., one of the earliest tourists from the eastern states to make a personal examination of Thomas Jefferson's hopeful purchase of Louisiana, ventured from his home in New York State in 1807 down the Ohio, up the Mississippi to St. Louis, and thence in 1808 down to New Orleans. His many interesting impressions, sampled here, he published in two volumes in New York in 1810. His* Travels on an Inland Voyage, *which has never been reprinted, is being edited for issue in the present series. The passages below are from the second volume, pages 96–98, 100–101, 134–36, 140–46, in letters dated New Madrid, March 9, and Baton Rouge, April 13. The injury to which he refers was from a splinter which he had run under his finger nail.*]

It was nearly sunset when we passed this stream [the Bayou de She]. Our pilot therefore thought it prudent to land on the farthermost shore, as there was no other safe landing-place within five or six miles below us. He gave orders accordingly; but the hands being all engaged in listening to some interesting story, the orders were not given quite early enough to attain our object; as the wind, which was off that shore, and the velocity of the current, soon carried us beyond our mark. In consequence of having been sheltered under the land by the trees for the last two hours, we had not noticed any change in the weather; but as the current now swept us past the point, which had covered us, and which we intended to make, into the middle of the river, we found a considerable swell, and every appearance of a heavy blow on a lee-shore. It had now become quite dark, nor was it long before the wind and current had carried us over into the bend of the river on the opposite shore, which was full of sawyers and planters; and it was so dark, that we could not distinguish an object at the distance of fifty yards from the boat. We sent one of our men ahead with the small boat, to notify us of any danger, as likewise to discover a spot where we might possibly land. But the whirling of the water among the sawyers, and the dashing of the swells against the banks, prevented us from distinguishing the warning voice of our companion. We were by this time blown so close in with the shore, that we expected every moment to be wrecked. We already had several narrow escapes from the sawyers; some we just grazed; others were so near as to be touched with the hand, and all of them strong enough to have shivered our boat to pieces, had we been so unfortunate as to come in direct contact with either of them. For three miles did we run in this perilous situation after dark, expecting every instant to be dashed to pieces, when we discovered a considerable number of lights ahead, and shortly after heard some voices calling to us to pull in for the shore. This we immediately began to do, and at last effected, but not without great risk to ourselves, as well as to part of a fleet of fourteen Kentuckians, who had made a harbour here for the night, and against whom we were driven with so much violence as to break four pair of their sweeps by endeavouring to keep us from dashing their boats to pieces. After so many narrow escapes, and being withal exhausted by the violent exertions we had made, we were not a little pleased to find ourselves in a safe harbour for the night, surrounded by fourteen vessels and their crews, of the hearty lads of Kentucky. . . .

As the moon arose soon after, I had an opportunity of examining the fleet; which, although it did not quite equal that of Agamemnon before Troy, yet made a very respectable appearance in the wilderness by night. The two first were loaded with tobacco from Green River; four with flower [*sic*] and whiskey from Cincinnati; two with horses from Limestone; four with families and household stuff removing to the river Amitié [Amite]; two with cotton and tobacco from Cumberland; and two with lime in bulk from Virginia.

After having visited most of the fleet, I went on board the family boats, and was most agreeably surprised at the neatness and order displayed in every part of them; far surpassing, in point of cleanliness and convenience, one half of the settlements on shore. The boats were of the largest size, and the floors covered with rough sawed boards. In the rear a partition had been run across, in which they had stowed away all their present useless furniture. Through the middle was a passage about five feet wide; on each side were small bed-chambers of about twelve feet long and six wide, divided and surrounded by clean white cotton curtains; while in front there was a large open space for the general use of the boat. Three of the four boats had each three charming girls on board; who, although plainly dressed, yet appeared equally neat with every thing else on board. They informed me, that excepting our boat, their present fleet consisted of four divisions, all strangers to each other, having met at this place by mere accident. While conversing with these agreeable strangers, the notes of a violin from one of the boats struck our ears, when a lively little girl exclaimed, "O, if we could get it on board we might have a dance!" Although from the violent pain of my finger, I was much better disposed for crying than dancing, yet my disposition to oblige the girls impelled me to give them a promise to find out the musician, and, if possible, to bring him, with some other company, on board. I found no difficulty in succeeding; and had it not been for my wound, should have enjoyed a very agreeable evening.

The next morning at day-break we prosecuted our voyage, and had another very narrow escape from a sawyer, which all of a sudden showed itself so near as to touch the side of the boat as it arose. This is one of those dangers which no human prudence can either foresee or prevent. The river was as smooth as glass, and most of us on the look out; yet we had no notice of this until the moment it arose, nor did we see it again as long as we remained in sight of the place. Had our boat been ten inches more to the left, we must have been wrecked. Having thence descended thirty-two miles, and passed four islands, we arrived at the village of New Madrid, where we found the peach-trees in blossom. . . .

From the eminence on which the city stands [Natchez], which is about one hundred feet above the present level of the river, you have a very pleasing prospect of the river both above and below; but in front your vision is lost in tracing the immense forests which cover the low grounds, extending in one uniform horizontal line before you. One evening, as I was enjoying the cool refreshing breeze from this charming situation, I was agreeably surprised with the sight of a fleet of eleven Kentucky boats, which just came in sight, and were making for the landing. This is situated in a bend of the river, where the projecting point above causes a very extensive eddy along the shore below, and makes it very convenient for a landing-place. The current of the river is so strong, that the boatmen always make a proper allowance for the drift of the vessel while making in for the shore. But here the eddy setting up with nearly equal velocity, carried the most of them far above the town, where they had to take the channel once more, before they could effect a landing at the Levee. The next thing that afforded us amusement, was a long raft of boards and shingles, which was intended for this place. The owners expected its arrival, and were on the Levee to see it landed in safety, but it was soon discovered that it would not be able to reach even the eddy. They accordingly mustered all the ropes and boats which could be readily collected, and while those on the raft sent their boats and ropes ashore, these went off with theirs; but the power of the raft was so great, and the current so strong, that the ropes all snapped like threads; nor were they able to make a landing before they had drifted five miles below the city.

I had the curiosity the next morning to count the number of boats then lying along the Levee, and found they amounted to eighty-three, all loaded with the produce of the upper country as far as the 42d degree of north latitude. When I went on board of my own boat, (which was very early, and before the sun had risen,) I discovered that my visit was as unwelcome as it was unexpected. I was so unfortunate as to disturb the morning slumbers of exactly one quarter of a dozen of the copper-coloured votaries of the Cyprian queen, who it seems had undertaken to enliven the idle hours of our Canadian crew. The *ladies* really seemed ashamed; but whether from a conviction of their being the intruders, or considering me as such, I am unable to say. Suffice it, I took my leave until they had time to decamp. . . .

There is a gang of idle Choctaw, Natchez, and Muskogee Indians, who stroll about the city, or rather are settled down on the Levee, which being the landing-place of the cargoes of whiskey and provisions that continually arrive, has attracted them to that spot. They are about forty in number, of both sexes, and of every age. They are provided with a full band of music, with which they serenade the different boats as they arrive morning and evening, or as often as they want a little money, whiskey, or provisions. You would no doubt have been surprised, if you had inspected the band, with their instruments, before the beginning of the performance; but you would have been satisfied, after hearing the music, that a given quantity of discord may produce harmony. I must certainly do them the justice to say, that I never was more agreeably disappointed in my life, and the harmony produced by such an unpromising collection of instruments and performers, exceeded all my expectations.

As I was very particular in examining the instruments used on this occasion, I must not omit giving you a description of them. The first and largest was a joint of thick cane, open at both ends, which, when applied to the mouth, and sung or blown through with a strong voice, served as a bass to the whole. The next was also a joint of cane with both ends closed, containing a few small pebbles: this was used by shaking it to the time and motion of the piece. The third was two separate joints of cane, each of which were cracked in several places, and used by suspending the one between the fingers of the left hand, and striking the other upon it with the right; producing a kind of rattling jarring sound. The fourth was likewise a joint of cane open at one end, having a small slip of cane inserted directly across the aperture. This was held in a perpendicular direction, when by contracting the lips, and blowing or singing through the aperture upon the slip, it produced a hollow hissing sound. The fifth was another joint of cane closed at both ends, with a narrow strip out from end to end, over which was extended a strong deer sinew; which being set in vibration by the thumb, produced a dull monotonous sound, something like the lowest string of the African jumbo. The sixth and last instrument was a two gallon tin kettle, with a drest buckskin extended over the mouth, not unlike a drum, which it was intended to represent. This was carried under one arm, and beat with a stick held in the hand, producing a dull sound like a drum.

The first five instruments were of various sizes, according to the age of the persons using them, those of the children being always the smallest. Their manner of performance was as follows: Having first formed their company under a tree a small distance from the boats, they advance singing short stanzas of "ho ha." When near the boats, the captain or leader advances before with a white or striped silk banner, taking long and solemn strides, and then halting a moment for the rest to come up. After reaching the boat he stands as still as a post, not moving his eyes, or any of his limbs. The men approach next, and form a circle round him; then follow the boys; after them the squaws with the girls in the rear. The music now becomes slow and solemn for about five minutes, when it gradually increases to a brisker motion, during which you will first perceive the captain move his eyes, next his lips, then his head and hands, and at last a very curious and pleasing pantomimical dance strikes up, which continues for about a quarter of an hour. The music is performed in two parts, being tenor and treble: the men and boys composing the former, and the women and girls the latter. The several instruments were used with such accurate time and motion, and so blended with the vocal music, that it rendered the performance far superior to any thing I had anticipated. The burthen of the song was the same throughout, consisting of a single stanza, and, as near as I can remember as follows: "Ho, hoa, ho; ho, al, hoa; hoa, ho, ho; ho, hoa, ho."

In traversing the city, I had noticed leopard skins hanging at the doors of several stores, which I concluded had been brought from the Atlantic ports, to be used in making military housings, as I knew that animal was not an inhabitant of our continent. I happened to mention this circumstance to a number of gentlemen at the hotel one evening, when I was informed they were the skins of animals killed in that country. One of the gentlemen told me that he had the skin of one at his house which had been killed the week before, within twenty miles of that city. He invited me to examine it, which I did the next morning, and found that it measured five feet three inches in length, and four feet in breadth. I thought it as beautiful a spotted tiger or leopard skin as I had ever seen. The only remarkable difference that I could recollect was, those I had seen from Africa generally had a darker stripe along the back from the head to the tail; in other respects they appeared to me as skins of the same kind of animal. They are called the spotted tiger in this country, and although not numerous, yet of late years they are frequently met with.

Wild horses are likewise sometimes seen on the west side of the river. It requires great dexterity to take them, but when once broken they become very useful animals. The sugar-cane is sometimes planted as high up as the Natchez, but only in small patches for curiosity or medicinal purposes, as the frosts are too severe to insure a crop; but from Point Coupee, one hundred and forty miles below, the cane becomes the staple quite down to New-Orleans. Natchez Heights is the tenth bluff or ridge of the highlands which you pass on that side of the river, and is about one hundred and thirty miles in length, and twenty-five in breadth, and the soil of a most excellent quality. This country likewise exhibits signs of having formerly cherished a population far exceeding any thing which has been known in our time. A considerable variety of ancient mounds are found here, some of which are round, others oval, but most of them square, with a small platform on the top. Some of these have been opened, and a single skeleton discovered near the top. Several very curious specimens of their ancient earthenware have likewise been discovered, with singular figures and characters well traced upon them.

The evening preceding that of my departure from Natchez being beautiful and bright, I walked down to the Levee, in order to give some directions to my boatmen. In passing two boats next to mine, I heard some very warm words; which my men informed me proceeded from some drunken sailors, who had a dispute respecting a *Choctaw lady*. Although I might fill half a dozen pages with curious slang made use of on this occasion, yet I prefer selecting a few of the most brilliant expressions by way of sample. One said, "I am a man; I am a horse; I am a team. I can whip any man *in all Kentucky*, by G——d." The other replied, "I am an alligator; half man, half horse; can whip any *on the Mississippi* by G——d." The first one again, "I am a man; have the best horse, best dog, best gun, and handsomest wife in all Kentucky, by G——d." The other, "I am a Mississippi snapping turtle: have bear's claws, alligator's teeth, and the devil's tail; can whip *any man*, by G——d." This was too much for the first, and at it they went like two bulls, and continued for half an hour, when the alligator was fairly vanquished by the horse.

EPISODE ON A FLATBOAT:

The Death of Banks Finch

———

[*This file of documents reporting a not very rare kind of incident on the river is reprinted from the Franklin* Missouri Intelligencer *of September 24, 1819.*]

A Copy

Of the depositions of sundry witnesses, taken before Thomas G. Davison, Esq. a justice of the peace for Madison county, state of Illinois, at the house of Mr. Isom Gillham, at the mouth of Missouri, to establish and explain a transaction that took place about seven miles above St. Genevieve, on the bank of the Mississippi, in which the death of Banks Finch took place, the 26th July, 1819, viz:

OTHA BATMAN, being of lawful age, and being duly sworn, deposeth and saith, that he was present when Banks Finch was killed, on the 26th July, 1819; that the deponent and also Banks Finch, the deceased, were employed by captain I. D. Wilcox, at Fort Masaac, to work as hands on board of the keel boat of the same name; that in a very short time he discovered said Finch to be a very overbearing, troublesome man, and particularly so when intoxicated; that said Finch, the deceased, would have whiskey when and where he could get it; that he would sometimes leave the boat to purchase whiskey elsewhere; that on account of the frequent practice of drinking to excess, and disorder and confusion on board the boat, an order was given the passengers in the cabin not to allow whiskey to be drawn and used, as it had been almost without limit; that Finch, after this order, went to the cabin to draw whiskey as usual—captain Stubbs, being in the cabin, forbade it, and informed said Finch that it was contrary to orders. From this period the said Finch, the deceased, appeared to have a settled and constant enmity towards the passengers, and would frequently threaten to whip them; that he would whip two or three of them, and a great deal of very insulting language; that lieutenant Campbell was one of the passengers—when the boat arrived at St. Genevieve, the deceased bought a jug of whiskey on shore; that after going some distance from that place, the said Finch was on shore, in company with other hands, cordelling the boat—upon arriving at the mouth of a run, which was very muddy, he stopped; but the boat being under headway, the bow of it passed on. Capt. Wilcox and the passengers exerted themselves to throw the stern of the boat to shore, that he, Finch, might get on board to pass the muddy place, hallooing at the same time to Finch not to go in the mud and water. The boat had nearly reached shore, when Finch, the deceased, rushed into the mud and water to cross over, when in a minute or two he might have stepped on the boat. Every evertion was making by captain Wilcox, lieutenant Campbell, and others, to get him on board and prevent his wading through the mud and water. As soon as he, Finch, had rushed himself into the mouth of the run, he commenced cursing and abusing all on board, the captain, passengers, and hands. The captain then directed him not to take such liberties any longer. Finch, the deceased, then applied to captain Wilcox to pay him off his wages, for he would not step on the boat, or go with such a rascally set any more. The captain offered him his money in paper bank notes—he refused it. The captain then gave him silver, and made a final settlement with him, and still persuaded Finch to come on board, and offered to let him go to the next town as a passenger free of cost, which offer he refused to accept, swearing he would not be dragged or hauled on a boat by any men. The said Finch then left the boat, and endeavored to get other hands to go with him and leave the boat also, and one hand did leave it, and went with him. The boat being scarce of hands, the passengers went on shore and assisted in cordelling the boat, while, he Finch, and his comrade, came on behind. In going some distance, the boat arrived at a spring, where she stopped for all hands to refresh themselves; and in a short time Finch, the deceased, and his comrade, arrived, and, in this deponent's presence, he, said Finch, swore he intended to whip some person before he left them, but did not state who he intended to chastise. He, Finch, used very insulting language, and most of all the

hands were afraid of him, from his large size and bullying disposition. He then commenced trying to get some of the hands to
fighting one another, and in a very little time succeeded in his
attempt; and while the two men were fighting, Finch, the deceased, interfered and kicked one of them. During the whole of
this period, capt. Wilcox made use of every means, mild and
persuasive, to pacify said Finch, but to no effect. As the deceased
kicked one of the fighting party, captain Wilcox took hold of him
to keep him off. The deceased cursed the captain, and dam'd him
—to take out his dirk or pistol, for he disregarded them, (or
words to this effect,) and at this instant pushed the captain back,
and gave one of the fighting party another kick or two. During
the whole of this affair, captain Wilcox neither drew a pistol, or
dirk, nor any other weapon, neither did he misuse Finch in any
shape.

About the time that Finch shoved captain Wilcox back, this
deponent discovered lieutenant Campbell and the deceased engaged against each other: both appeared to be exerting themselves to injure each other. In a very short time, lieutenant Campbell left Finch and went to the boat, and Finch fell and expired.
In a few minutes after his death, upon examination the said deponent found that the deceased had been dirked in a number of
places; but this deponent does not recollect to have seen any dirk
until after lieutenant Campbell and the deceased were separated;
but immediately after, he saw a dirk in the hands of lieutenant
Campbell.

(*Signed*)   *Otha Batman.*
                                    his
                                    X
                                    mark.

WE, the undersigned, being hands on board the keel boat *Massac*, have carefully examined the foregoing deposition of Otha
Batman, on the subject of the death of Banks Finch, and state
upon oath that it is just & true, we having been spectators of the
whole scene.

(*Signed*)   *John Bennet.*
                                    his
                                    X
                                    mark.

(*Signed*)   *John Robertson.*
                                    his
                                     X
                                   mark.

THE undersigned, Edward M'Ginnis, was not present during the
whole affray with Banks Finch, in which he lost his life; but was a
hand on board the keel boat Massac, but remained on board of the
boat during the rencontre. I further state, that I heard Banks
Finch frequently threaten lieutenant Campbell; and I did warn
said Campbell of said threats, as I did believe said Finch intended
some injury to said Campbell.

          (*Signed*)   *Edward M'Ginnis.*
                                    his
                                     X
                                   mark.

STATE OF ILLINOIS,⎰
Madison County, ss.⎱

                                 August 7, 1819.
This day, personally appeared before me, a justice of the peace
for said county, Otha Batman, John Bennet, John Robertson, and
Edward M'Ginnis; and each of them made oath to the foregoing
statements, or depositions, to which each of their names are re-
spectively subscribed. Given under my hand the date above.

          (*Signed*)   *T. G. Davison*, J. P.

I DO certify, that I was on board the keel boat *Massac*, as a
passenger from St. Genevieve to Belle Fontaine, and that Banks
Finch was killed by David H. Campbell, in a riot, which took
place about seven or eight miles above St. Genevieve, on the 26th
of July, 1819. The riot commenced about two miles below where
Finch was killed. The hands were walking on the bank cordelling
the boat, where they came to a small creek, at which they intended to take dinner. The bottom of the creek was very muddy;
and when the men came to it, captain Wilcox told them not to
wade through—that he would send or take the skiff. Finch, who
was foremost, went on, not paying any attention to what captain
Wilcox said to him; and as soon as he got out of the water and

mud, began cursing the patroon, bowsman, boat, and owner, wishing them in hell—and demanded his wages, saying he would leave the boat. Captain Wilcox paid him his wages, and discharged him. He then got a bottle of whiskey, and, as I thought, took his leave of the boat and crew, though he continued with the hands, who were walking on the bank cordelling and talking—when the hands began to stop, one at a time, until there was not a sufficiency to go on with the boat. Captain Wilcox ordered the boat to put to shore, and came to the cabin and asked lieutenant David H. Campbell, William B. Eddy, and myself, who were passengers, to assist him in getting on to where he could get more hands. Lieut. Campbell and myself went with captain Wilcox and Mr. Harlen, who was the patroon, to the cordell. Mr. Eddy took the place of patroon when we went on shore—Finch, and some of the hands, sitting on a log, talking. We went on with the boat. After going about a mile, we stopped at a spring to take a drink, when Finch and his party came up, and one of them began quarrelling with one of those who had been at work, who refused to quarrel with him. He then went to another, who also refused. Finch encouraged the one, who had been with him, and made him pull off his clothes; and took off his own coat to show fair play, as he termed it. Finch's man, and the other whom he had been quarrelling with, began boxing. Finch attempted, or did assist his friend; when capt. Wilcox, who had been endeavoring to keep peace by talking, took hold of Finch; at which time I heard Finch dare him to draw his dirk or pistol—he disregarded him, or his pistol or dirk either; that he had kicked him, and would kick him again, (meaning one of those who were boxing, as I supposed,) at the same time shoved captain Wilcox from him, and turned into the crowd. Immediately after I saw Finch and lieutenant Campbell engaged. I saw Campbell strike several times. As Campbell turned off from Finch, I discovered he had a dirk in his hand. Finch fell immediately, being stabbed in seven or eight places, one of which was below the left nipple, which to every appearance struck his heart.

There appeared to be a great confusion on board of the boat when I came to her, and I have heard some of the men say Campbell's life was in danger before Finch was killed, though I did not understand whether he was in danger of Finch or not. Captain Wilcox was doing all in his power to keep peace on board the boat, from the time he came on board the boat, which was at St. Genevieve, until Finch was killed, though he was not able to suppress quarrelling and threatening of lives.

(Signed)   G Marshall.

STATE OF ILLINOIS, ⎱
Madison County, ss. ⎰

This day Gilbert Marshall personally appeared before me, T. G. Davison, a justice of the peace for said county, and made oath to the above disposition. Given under my hand this 7th day of August, 1819.

(Signed)   T. G. Davison, J. P.
August 21.   22 2w

THE WESTERN STEAMBOAT

CHARLES JOSEPH LATROBE

―――――

[*Charles Joseph Latrobe, who had sailed to the United States in 1832 with Washington Irving and had visited the Osage Prairies with him, in November of that year went up the Mississippi and the Ohio with his young friend, the Comte de Pourtalès, from the mouth of the Arkansas to Wheeling in (West) Virginia. His observations on this trip, perhaps reinforced by further travel on the Mississippi in the following year, formed the basis for an objective report on the satisfactions and the discomforts, the tedium and the pleasures of steamboat voyaging. The following pages are from the second edition (2 volumes, London, 1836) of his* The Rambler in North America (*I, 281–304*).]

On the evening of the second day, a small cloud of white steam, seen like a star in the dark blue shade of the forests, seven or eight miles off, announced the approach of a steam-boat toiling up the river. In half an hour's time we could distinguish the sonorous breathing of the scape-pipe, and by the time that the wild song of the negro fire-men reached the ear, all was bustle and preparation. The bell on shore was rung to bring the steamer to; and jumping into a wherry, we found ourselves on board the 'Cavalier,' a boat of the second or third class, bound from New Orleans to Pittsburg, and took possession of the berths which we eventually retained, till our arrival at Wheeling a fortnight after. We found that since they had left the city, they had had no case of cholera on board, and thanked God with all our hearts.

You may imagine us then toiling for thirteen hundred miles and upwards against the rapid currents of the Mississippi and Ohio. This, at a season when natural scenery had lost its charm, you will suppose must necessarily have proved a trial of patience. In some degree I grant that it was such, nevertheless not so great as might be argued by those who know the impatience of modern travellers; and now that it is over, I look with interest upon all that we learned or experienced.

No sketch of mine could give you an adequate idea of the steam-boat of the West. From the epoch of the launch of that solitary Wanderer, whose first voyage I have elsewhere recorded, up to the close of 1833, it is computed that about five hundred boats of various sizes, from one to five hundred tons burden, had been constructed or run upon the Mississippi and its tributaries. A very small portion of these were built prior to 1820, and the number of new boats launched yearly, for several years back, is stated to have been upwards of fifty.

There is a great difference between the build and interior arrangement of the Eastern and Western steam-boat, and both are essentially distinct from those unadorned but compact vessels, which, propelled in the same manner, buffet the boisterous and dangerous billows of our narrow seas, straits, and roadsteads.

As to the Eastern steam-boat, the whole of the hold is converted into cabins—the transport of heavy freight being no part of the speculation; they are superior in finish and durability, but not in appearance, to those of the West, and cost much more; being, moreover, almost invariably furnished with low-pressure engines. On the contrary, the whole of the hull of the steam-boat of the West being appropriated for the transport of goods, the cabins are generally constructed upon the main deck. The vessels consequently appear much higher out of the water, and every one must be greatly struck at the first sight of these huge floating palaces, with their double tiers of gay cabins. The boilers, which are cylindrical, and vary from four to double that number, are placed forward on the main-deck, and behind them the machinery is arranged towards the centre of the vessel, enclosed between the huge paddle-boxes and a row of offices on either side. The great cylinder lying in a horizontal position, the piston works on the same plane. Thus in the western boat the whole arrangement and movement of the engine is horizontal, while in the east it is perpendicular. Sometimes a ladies' cabin is constructed on the same deck, in the stern of the boat; but, more generally, this part is given up to the so-called deck-passengers, and the whole range of superior cabins is built upon an upper deck, extending from the stern over that part of the vessel where the boilers are situated, the portion most in advance being called the boiler-deck. Through the latter, the great chimney pipes conducting the smoke from the fires below ascend, and as the range of cabins do not extend quite so far, the open space and view afforded by it, renders it a favourite lounge. Of the disposition of the cabins little need be said. The ladies' apartment is aft, and opens with sliding doors and curtains into the main, or gentleman's cabin, which is frequently fifty or sixty feet in length. Both are furnished with handsome tiers of upper and lower berths, canopied with ample chintz or moreen curtains, and the former cabin is frequently fitted up with staterooms. A gallery runs round the whole exterior. Between the forward end of the great cabin and the boiler-deck, ten or fifteen feet of the deck is ordinarily occupied by a Bar, washing-room, captain's and stewards' offices, ranged on either side of an antichamber. On some of the larger class of steamers, there is yet a third deck and range of cabins before you come to the roof, or hurricane-deck—upon the forward extremity of which the glazed and painted cabinet, containing the tiller, is placed, affording a lofty and unimpeded view of the channel.

As to the question often started with regard to the safety of the principle upon which the machinery is generally constructed in the West, much might be said in favour of high-pressure engines; and in spite of my full consciousness of the great danger attending them, when placed, as they frequently, are under the care of incompetent and careless persons, I think that the reasons given are good. These are chiefly founded upon the character of the waters navigated; their turbid state, their extraordinary swiftness, requiring the application of great power: the far greater simplicity of construction of the high-pressure engine, all the complicated condensing apparatus being dispensed with, which is of great consequence on a navigation where the boat must proceed five or eight hundred miles without the possibility of repair; its superior lightness, and its being calculated to work off all the steam which is generated; and lastly, the mud is not apt to accumulate so fast in the boiler of the high-pressure engine, being blown out at the safety valve, while under the low-pressure system it must continue in the boiler, and by interposing a stratum between the water and the iron, the latter is sometimes burnt through, and explosion takes place.

Yet, though it may thus be well maintained that the high-pressure engine is better fitted for the Western navigation, as long as the accidents upon those waters are so frequent, and the loss of human life so great as it has been for some years past, it is no wonder that great prejudice must exist in the minds of many with regard to the system pursued. It is not, however, the principle which is wrong, it is the careless use of it. The history of steam-boat disaster is one of the most terrible and revolting imaginable; and the disregard of human life which is as yet, generally speaking, a feature of the West, is a sure proof that the standard of moral feeling is low.

I have seen so much during four or five thousand miles of steam-navigation in this part of the country, as to believe, that there are few voyages of more evident peril in the world than that from St. Louis or Louisville to New Orleans, or vice versa; for, leaving out of the question the casualties incident to the navigation arising from snags, ice, rocks, fire, or being run down, in consequence of which numbers have perished, the peril which impends over you from a tremendous power like that of steam, being left under the direction of incompetent or careless men, is a constant and fearful one.[1]

The sketch of a day's proceeding on board will perhaps give you a livelier idea of our position, and of the scenes connected with it, than can be otherwise conveyed.

State-rooms are not always to be had by gentlemen, as they are commonly found to be attached to the ladies' cabin alone—but in case they are unoccupied they may be secured, and your position is so far more than ordinarily a favoured one, as you have private access to them by the outward gallery. Otherwise it must be conceded that nothing is omitted that the known ingenuity of this people can contrive, to render the berths in the main cabin as tidy and ornamental in appearance by day, and as secluded and convenient by night as circumstances permit of. They are so arranged, that when you retire to rest, the thick curtains with their vallance can slide forward upon brass rods, two or three feet

---

[1] By a published list of the steam-boats lost on the Western waters, from July 1831, to July 1833, their number would appear to be sixty-seven; viz.— seven burnt under weigh; nine in port; twenty-two snagged; two sunk by rocks; five by running foul; seven by ice; and fifteen abandoned as unfit: and previous to that time, out of one hundred and eighty-two, which had been on the river, but did not exist in 1831, sixty-six had been worn out; thirty-seven snagged; sixteen burnt; three run down; four or five stove by ice or rocks, and thirty destroyed otherwise.—Latrobe.

from the berth itself, and thus form a kind of draped dormitory for you and your companion.

About an hour before the time appointed for breakfast, after the broom has been heard performing its duty for some time, a noisy bell rung vociferously at the very porches of your ear, as the domestic marches from one end of the cabin to the other, gives notice that the hour of rising has arrived, and it is expected that every one will obey it and be attired in such time as to allow the berths to be arranged, and the whole cabin put in its day-dress, before the breakfast, which like all the other meals is set out in the gentlemen's cabin, is laid upon the table. In vain you wish to indulge in a morning dose and thus to cut short the day; every moment your position becomes more untenable. Noises of all kinds proceed from without. You persevere—shut your eyes from the bright light which glares upon you through the little square window which illumines your berth, and your ears to all manner of sounds. Suddenly your curtains are drawn unceremoniously back, the rings rattle along the rods, and you see your place of concealment annihilated and become a part of the common apartment, while the glistening face and bright teeth of the black steward are revealed, with eyes dilated with well-acted surprise, as he says, 'Beg pardon! Colonel; thought him war up: breakfast almost incessantly on de table.' He retrogrades with a bow, half-closing the curtains; but you have no choice, rise you must. Happy he, whose foresight has secured to him all the enjoyment of the luxury of his own clean towels, as none but the disagreeable alternative of drying his person by the heat of the stove, can be the fate of him who has not done this. As to making use of the common articles, hung up for the accommodation of some thirty citizens in rotation, no one need blush at being termed fantastically delicate in avoiding that. There exist yet certain anomalies, in a position, and under a state of society, like that found on board these boats, which, though they may not surprise a thinking mind, and may be accounted for, are far from being either pleasant, or usual elsewhere. And the arrangements made of the above class are surely of this kind.

But I do not dwell much on these fertile subjects for a traveller's maunderings, for four reasons. First, because they are but blots on the general picture, and as blots they are considered by all those Americans whose opinions are worthy of attention.

Secondly, others more competent to the task, have contrived to make them sufficiently notorious. Thirdly, time and a sense of common propriety may have already produced changes for the better; and, lastly, they are disagreeable both to recollect and to detail.

During the interval which elapses between your being thus unceremoniously ousted from your quarters and forced to begin the day, and the ringing of the breakfast-bell, you may walk forward to the boiler-deck, and satisfy yourself as to the progress which has been made during the hours of darkness; or, if you choose to follow the custom of the country, and the example of a great majority of the passengers, you may linger in the antichamber opposite the bar, and take the glass of wine and bitters, which the prevalence of that common complaint of the United States, dyspepsia, finds a bad apology for. The Americans, as a people, are far from being intemperate; if by intemperance you mean absolute inebriety, of which less is seen, as far as a casual observer like myself might judge, than in any country of Europe. But if by intemperance, you understand a habit of the frequent unnecessary indulgence in stimulants, and dram-drinking, then do they richly deserve the stigma; though the improvement, and the return to sound feeling in this respect, has been so general in many parts of the Atlantic States, that the stricture can hardly be applied to them. But in the West and South, the custom prevails to a degree ruinous to the moral and physical strength of a great part of the male population. And whoever has been witness to the mode and the marvellous rapidity with which the hot cakes and viands of the plentiful tables of steam-boats and hotels are cleared and consigned to the stomach, without the possibility of having undergone the natural process of preparation, which nature has indicated as advisable, both from the number and construction of the human teeth and the original smallness of the swallow—need seek no further into the arcana of natural causes to account for the pale faces, contracted chests, and lack-lustre-eyes of a great number of citizen travellers in all parts of the West. Compared with this, what are the effects of climate or sedentary life—or even the possible hindrance to a natural and easy digestion, consequent upon the internal heat generated by republicanism, and the weight of democratic cares?

But I have anticipated breakfast by alluding to its principal feature. The table is spread with substantials, both in profusion and variety; and considerable impatience is generally observable to secure places, as it frequently happens that the number of cabin passengers is greater than can be seated with comfort at the table, however spacious. The Steward, or his assistant, after many a considerate glance at his preparations, to see that all is right, goes to the ladies' cabin, and announces breakfast—an announcement which is generally followed by their appearance. They take their places at the upper end of the table, and then, and not till then, the bell gives notice that individuals of the rougher sex may seat themselves. The meal I leave to your lively imagination to picture. I have noted its chief characteristic. You might imagine that the beings engaged in it were for the time, part of the engine, which is sighing and working underneath at the rate of one hundred strokes in the minute, so little does their occupation admit of interruption. There is little or no conversation, excepting of the monosyllabic and ejaculatory kind which is absolutely necessary; and instead of the social hour, during which in other lands, the feast of the body is often found to be compatible with the feast of the soul, you spend, in fact, an uneasy ten minutes, in which the necessary act of eating is certainly stript of all the graces under which supercultivation contrives to shroud its sensuality, and is reduced to the plain homely realities of bestial feeding. Woe to the poor gentleman of habitually slow and careful mastication—he who was taught to 'denticate, masticate, champ, chew, and swallow!' Woe to the man of invariable habits —he whose conversational powers are the greatest during repast —the proser—the sentimental bon-vivant who loves to eat and think—or the gentleman with stiff jaw-bones and slow deglutition! Woe to the epicure, whose eye might well else dilate at the sight of the well-covered board, and its crowd of western delicacies. Woe to the hungry gallant, whose chivalry cannot suffer him to enjoy a morsel till he has seen the ladies well-served and attended through the meal. Small credit gets the good-natured soul who deftly carves for all, and ever carves in vain. There is no quarter given. Many of the males will leave the table the moment they are satisfied—the ladies leave it as soon as they well can; and then in come the barkeepers, engineers, carpenter, pilot, and inferior officers of the boat: the table again groans with its load of plenty, and is again stripped and forsaken, to be a third time the scene of feasting for the black steward and coloured servants of both sexes. During these latter scenes of the same act of the same play, I need hardly press you to quit the cabin for the seats on the boiler-deck, or, still better, for the hurricane-deck above.

In fine warm weather, more especially during your first voyage in the West, both curiosity and comfort will lead you to spend by far the greater part of your time in the open air; where the gentle breeze, freshened by the rapid motion of the boat, and the magical manner in which scenes rise and disappear, will always cheer you, while with conversation and reading you while away the monotonous hours of a long morning. Should the boat be one of the first class for power, well commanded and carefully engineered, and the season fine, few situations could be named of an equally exciting character. It is possible that you may meet with a few well-bred, intelligent travellers—that you may be both in good health and good-humour—that the general run of the voyage may be prosperous and without accidents or detention. The steam-boat may have an engine which works smoothly and without jarring, so that the use of your pen may be easy; you may have contrived to keep a few books in your travelling equipage; the cabin may be fully adequate to the comfortable accommodation of those having a claim to its use. Above all, favourable circumstances may have given you friends in the ladies' cabin; by occasional visits to whom at proper seasons, you may please and be pleased. If so, well and good—but you may chance to fare otherwise, and for the sake of illustration we will suppose that the very contrary is the case in almost every particular; that heated in body and mind by confinement and disappointment, you are peevish as a pea-hen; that the society is decidedly ill-bred and vicious —that the boat jars so with every stroke of the piston that you cannot write a line—further that you have no books—the cabin is crowded—the machinery wants constant repair—the boilers want scraping. This hour you get upon a sand-bank, the next you are nearly snagged—drift-wood in the river breaks your paddles—the pilot is found to be a toper, the engineer an ignoramus, the steward an economist, the captain a gambler, the black fire-men insurgent, and the deck passengers riotous. This moment you have too little steam, and hardly advance against the current; another, too much, and the boat trembles with the tremendous force exerted by the power that impels her. To complete your dismay, the captain agrees to take a disabled steam-boat, or a couple of heavily-laden barges, in tow, for the next four or five hundred miles. Instead of accomplished females, such as at another time you might have as fellow-passengers, we will suppose the ladies' cabin to be tenanted by a few grotesque, shy, uninteresting beings, never seen but when marshalled in by the steward to their silent and hurried repast, and never heard, but, when shut up in their own apartment, a few sounds occasionally escape through the orifice of the stove-pipe, making up in strength for what they want in sweetness.

What are you to do in such cases? You may lounge in the anti-chamber, and watch the progress of stimulating at the bar— you may re-enter the cabin and strive to get possession of a chair and a gleam from the store; or you may ascend to a small apartment found in some steam-boats, called Social Hall, in other words a den of sharpers and blacklegs, where from morning to night the dirty pack of cards are passed from hand to hand. For the rest, you may study human nature in many forms, and one thing will not fail to strike you, and that is the marvellous rapidity with which the meals follow, and the world of important preparation which passes before your eyes for an end so little worthy of it.

The time occupied by the supple-limbed black boys, Proteus and William, in drawing out the long table, laying the cloth, and other preliminary preparations, will not be far short of an hour; while a quarter of that time suffices for the demolition of the various courses, the whole meal, as already described, consisting of a shove to the table, a scramble, and a shove from the table. Things are cleared away, and the sliding table pushed together again; William and Proteus placing themselves at either end, twenty feet apart, and straining with might and main till the ends meet. You take a dozen turns across the floor—you read a little, write a little, yawn a little—when before you could have believed it possible, the steward's myrmidons, with looks of infinite importance, enter again, seize on the two ends of the table, strain them once more asunder, and the work of preparation recommences.

The mass of the society met with upon the Western boats is, as far as a transient traveller may be allowed to plead his individual experience, to be designated by the single term, bad. It is one thing to deny the truth of a statement in which I believe most travellers, of any pretentions to education and moral feeling agree, whether they be from the Eastern or Midland States, or from Europe; and another to find palliative reasons why it cannot be otherwise for the present. A man may make up his mind to glance good-humouredly around him, and to look upon the unwonted society into which he is here introduced, with equanimity, studying neither to give nor take offence; but nothing can make him believe that what appears before him as absolute vice, is, in fact, virtue in disguise—or that consummate vulgarity is, in fact, anything else. My impression was, that in these boats we came in contact with much of the scum of the population, and in judging them to be such, I was far from believing that they were a fair sample of the people of the West generally. On the contrary, it was not the uncouth and uncultivated, but honest bearing, of the people 'belonging to the river,' which was offensive—rusticity and vulgarity are far from being synonymous terms—nor that of the young Kentuckian, noisy and intemperate as he might be, stunning your ears with an amusing and fanciful lingo, which, however some who should know better may attempt to dignify and perpetuate, is, after all, nothing but slang. The decidedly worst company was I found invariably made up of those who should, considering their pretensions to education, public employment, or the sober lives and civilization of the stock from which they came, have known better. And to this class belong many of the Americans, who travel on business connected with commercial houses in the large or smaller towns. They are as busy as wasps in a sugar-cask, as long as they are about their business, and the most listless of human beings when not so employed. They have apparently no thought, no reading, no information, no speculation but about their gains—dollar is the word most frequently in their mouths, and judging from them and their numbers, the proportion of men with money and without manners would appear to be greater in this part of the globe than elsewhere.

There is one operation connected with your daily progress, which may be signalized, as it affords some variety, and breaks the monotony of your proceedings. This is wooding, or the hour's halt at one of the innumerable farms or wood-yards, for the purpose of laying in the necessary stock of fuel; the quantity of which that is burned in the course of twenty-four hours on board a steam boat of four or five hundred tons, is almost incredible.

This halt generally takes place twice a day, morning and evening, when the whole of the bow of the boat, and on either side of the furnaces, is covered with regular piles. Besides the opportunity thus afforded of going ashore, the scene is always a busy and lively one, as in addition to the crew being engaged in it, the major part of the deck passengers lend a hand, in consideration of a reduction in the passage money, which it is to the advantage of the proprietors to make as this procedure is productive of a great saving of time. During the night, immense fires are kept blazing at the wood-yards, to direct the boats where to find them, and the scene then presented in wooding is highly wild and picturesque.

Among the beings attached to a Western steamer, there is one class too remarkable to be passed by, and this is composed of the fire-men, the sphere of whose labour is directly on the bow of the boat, upon which the long row of gaping furnaces open. They are almost invariably athletic negroes, or mulattoes. The labour, which would be considered pretty severe by all but themselves, is generally performed amid bursts of boisterous merriment, jests, and songs; and the peculiar character of the latter has often made me hang over the boiler-deck railing to listen; particularly after dark, when the scene was very stroking from the bright ruddy glare thrown upon and around them, while with a thousand grimaces they grasped the logs and whirled them into the blazing throat of the furnaces. Their ordinary song might strictly be said to be divided into a rapid alternation of recitative and chorus—the solo singer uttering his part with great volubility and alertness, while the mass instantly fell in with the burden, which consisted merely of a few words and notes in strictly harmonious unison.

As usual we were not without our quantum of Kentucky boatmen and backwoodsmen on board, that race whose portrait sketched by himself as 'half horse, half alligator, with a dash of the steam-boat,' and filled up by the wondering and awe-struck travellers from the Old World, has been so often the subject of mirth and obloquy. I fear the genuine breed is getting rather scarce; at least, though I saw many boisterous doings, and many an amusing specimen of rough manners, I never saw any one stabbed or gouged. Take, however, the portrait of the extraordinary 'Kentucky Swell,' who was our fellow-passenger for a day or two in the Cavalier. He came up with the boat from New Orleans, accompanied by his father, a fine, hale, sensible old man, clad in a suit of home-spun from the loom of his wife and daughters. He had perhaps also been a 'swell' in his youth, but all had sobered down into an independent, staid demeanour. Every word he spoke was full of good, sound, sense—that kind which age and experience can alone produce; and my slight intercourse with him added to the respect which I feel to those of his class, in whom generous feeling, sound practical sense, and shrewd judgment, are often found united with unassuming manners and simple-heartedness. His maxim, the wisdom of which he upheld, after bringing up a fine family of sons, was—'I give my boys seven years' play, seven years' labour, and seven years' instruction;' and though his youngest, whose figure will be before you anon, evidently showed that a few years more must pass, before all the good fruits of this system were fully developed, I am not at all inclined to dispute it.

They were returning from New Orleans to their plantation. The dress of the parent I have alluded to. That of the son bore no resemblance to it. He was strong and well-built, having what is rather a rarity in the West, shoulders of a breadth proportionate to his height. His countenance, which was good, with a bold aquiline nose, bore a strong resemblance to that of his parent, though it was for the present destitute of the expression of good sense and honest-heartedness by which the latter was eminently distinguished. His whole dress and manner were peculiar. A coat of strong blue cloth of the Jehu cut, with white bone buttons of the Jehu size, the standing collar of which was always pulled up over the ears, and concealed them beneath its shade, served at the same time, in consequence of its being tightly buttoned from throat to waist, to hide the neck-cloth and waistcoat, of the existence of neither of which am I therefore able to make affidavit. This upper garment, which was certainly typical of the horse part of his nature, impended over a pair of full corduroy pantaloons. The legs of the same, though constructed by the artist of amplitude sufficient to reach the ancle if they had been allowed to do so, having apparently been elevated to mid-leg in the act of drawing on a pair of half-boots, remained hitched on the top of the latter during the whole of the first day of my observations, no effort having been made to induce them to descend to the ordinary position. On the second, one descended and the other did not, and in this way Tom Lavender sported his Nimrod-looking person. I never saw his hands; as whether sitting, standing, or walking,

they were always thrust decidedly to the bottom of the large flap
pockets of his Jehu coat.

In the manner in which he disposed his person in the cabin,
when inactive, upon two or three chairs, basking before the fire,
with his nose erect in the air, I thought I detected something of
the alligator part of his origin; while in the impetuous manner in
which, striding forward with outstretched limbs, he perambu-
lated the cabin or the deck to take exercise, alternately inflating
his cheeks, and blowing forth the accumulated air, I could not fail
to detect the steam-boat, by which the purity of the race had been
recently crossed. He was a man of no conversation, but he made
up for it by an incessant hoarse laugh, filling up the pauses in that
of three or four trusty young cronies, who seemed to hold him in
great respect and consideration. I should not forget to mention
that at a later period I was informed that the mode of wearing the
pantaloons hoisted half-leg high as described above, was premeditated, and intended to give an '*air distingué*!'

About noon on the second day, the steam-boat was directed
to the right hand, or Kentucky shore, at a point where the forest
appeared cleared from the bank for many hundred yards in front,
and the long line of fencing peered over the edge, denoting a large
and extensive clearing. As we approached the landing-place, I
noticed a little group gathering at the corner of a pile of cut wood,
ranged on the high bank above. Over the landing place, inclined a
single sycamore, supported by his main, perpendicular root over
the river, with all his leafless branches surrounded by the sweeping folds of a gigantic grape-vine. A fine handsome man stood in
advance, and upon our mooring, came slowly down towards the
boat. His resemblance to the old man on board was too striking to
leave us in doubt as to his relationship to the parties I have
described, being that of an elder son and brother. Our companions had then reached their home. While a knot of negroes and
coloured men descended to the boat, with their teeth displayed in
the broad grin of welcome, and laid officious hands upon the pile
of baggage which lay on the boiler-deck in readiness, I noticed the
wife and daughter of the good old man, half-sheltered by the
woodstack, standing coyly in the rear, till the whole group had
ascended the bank, when they all proceeded in joy and contentment to the house. The dwelling was situated a few hundred
paces in the rear—good and substantial, with an open compart-

ment in the centre, such as I have described elsewhere. I got a glimpse of it by following the party up the bank, for to tell the truth, the meeting was both a pleasant one to see, and one calculated to make travellers like ourselves, thousands of miles from our native countries, feel a little homesick; and, notwithstanding the amusement I had extracted from the 'Swell,' I could have found it in my heart to envy him the snug home and warm welcome which we saw him receive.

But I must draw to a conclusion. Through God's good providence, we escaped dangers and difficulties of every kind, and there were many encountered before we reached Wheeling, just as the river was filling with ice. There we took a stage, and proceeded over the Alleghany into Maryland. We arrived early on Christmas-day, within a few miles of what was to be the termination of a very long and singular ramble; when we got unexpectedly overturned in descending the Catoctin mountain, into a deep ditch; and though we all escaped with limbs and lives, I got a sounder blow on the head than ever fell to my lot before; which was all very well; as it made me, perhaps, think more seriously than I should else have done, of the many dangers which the hand of God had led us through, in peace, health, and safety.

FROM NEW HARMONY TO NEW ORLEANS,
1826

DONALD MACDONALD

[*Donald MacDonald came to the United States to have a look at Robert Owen's New Harmony project. After visiting the town he boarded the steamboat* Columbia *March 5, 1826, to arrive at New Orleans on the 13th. His diary, 1824–26 (edited by Caroline Dale Snedeker for the* Indiana Historical Society Publications, *XIV [1942], 147–379) is plain and factual, giving a good picture of the ordinary travels of a business-like man. This passage is from pages 338–45.*]

Monday night at 10 o'clock—I got on board the *Columbia* steam boat, commanded by Major Miller, and reached New Orleans on the 13ᵗʰ. (tuesday)

The *Columbia* is a large new steamboat handsomely & conveniently fitted up, with the ladies cabin below. The Captain an active & accommodating man. I found a few gentlemen & one lady on board from Louisville. Most of the gentlemen were Kentuckians. They were very fond of playing at cards & backgammon & drinking spirits and water, which custom I found myself obliged to adopt while in their company. Another boat (the *Paragon*) reputed the fastest boat on the river, left Louisville the day before the *Columbia*, which passed her while taking in Cargo at Henderson. The whole of the voyage down the Mississippi, the great object of our Captain was to keep ahead of her and reach New Orleans first. He therefore was constantly forward urging on the firemen, who are in this country negroes, to keep the furnaces well supplied. The rivers, as the northern snows were now melting & heavy rains falling around us, were rapidly rising & bringing in their floods great quantities of drift wood. Immense misshapen logs and trees were overtaken by us in large shoals and in the eddies, and in the night time the wheels lost their paddles which would be splintered to pieces by coming in contact with them. The Pilot at the helm wheel was in the habit of ringing a small bell to stop the wheels whenever he could not avoid these drifts. Snags, sawyers and planters, appellations given to trees & logs aground in the channel of the river, were often seen, but as the river was high and their situations generally known, no alarm was felt at them. The banks of the river with few exceptions were flat, & thickly covered with tall timber. As we proceeded down the Ohio, some rocky hills & ridges little exceeding 100 feet in elevation appeared here & there on the right in the state of Illinois. On them I remarked the cabins of poor settlers, who probably sought the triple advantage of rising land, a little society by river navigation, and a market for cord wood for the steamboats. A cord is 8 f'. long & 4 f'. high & wide. Down the Ohio, except in the immediate vicinity of large towns the price for black & white oak is from 2 to 3$ a cord. On the Kentucky side nothing was seen for many miles before we reached the Mississippi but a tall thick forest in a low swamp; the timber consisting for the most part of Cotton, Peccan, Hiccory, black red & white oak, vine and walnut trees. The mouth of the Ohio is hidden by an island, so that the supposed striking appearance of the junction of the Ohio with the Mississippi river is thus intercepted; and as the land is flat & the trees lofty, the eye does not perceive at first any great increase of water. The first striking indication of our being in a larger stream, was the change in the colour of the water which gradually mingled itself with the blacker water of the Ohio, till the whole river became lime water. Here I could not help gazing with some little degree of novel feeling at the scene. A smooth expanse of water, to all appearance a lake full of Islands, and encompassed by a wild forest luxuriantly growing in an immense marsh, through which I was rapidly passing in an elegant vessel and enjoying the most comfortable accommodations. We occasionally passed keel & flat boats floating on the water, & deeply laden with corn, potatoes or cattle for the Orleans Market. Six or eight tall bony & sunburnt men would be sitting on their tops lounging away the five to eight weeks voyage they were upon. The mouth of the Ohio is somewhere about 400 miles below Louisville. I had left, the southern corner of Indiana two days before, under the influence of a cold & wet spring, its forests bare & its lands black.

I now beheld bright sprouting leaves on all the young trees smiling beneath the yet sappless heads of their tall parents. The lively green of the cane breaks which covered the banks on both sides served as an additional relief to the scene. Here & there some hardy woods man had cleared a small space & built a log cabin on some spot which only the highest waters would cover; contenting himself with having the river open to him, and a plentiful supply without labour from his cows which feed upon the cane at all seasons of the year. But even these hardy beings rarely escape the effects of the marshy atmosphere, their faces & skins denoting that they frequently suffer from ague & fever. Mosquitoes abound in these situations, & even disturb the native woodsman with their numbers and powerful sting.

At the mouth of the Cumberland river, the *Columbia* stopped for 6 hours to take in 200 & odd bales of cotton, each bale being 8 or 9 f'. long, 6 or 8 f'. round & containing from 3 to 400 lbs of cotton. This freight was stowed away below, above & on both sides of the steamboat. The settlement at the mouth of the river bore a lively & thriving appearance, a few low hills gently rising at a short distance in the rear, and being partly cleared and looking green with the young corn shoots. While we lay at this place a fine & fast steam boat, called the *General Jackson* came down the Cumberland, and the *Paragon* passed before us. [It is the fashion to name the steamboats after the most distinguished men.] We met several boats going up the stream, all deeply laden & full of passengers.

From this place to Memphis a neat settlement on the Chicasaw bluffs (sandy ridges which terminate in high falling banks on the left bank of the river) we saw nothing but a flat forest, some feet lower, as you advance a few hundred yards from the river which gradually heightens its banks by the annual deposits of its inundations. [It is at this place that an experiment has lately been commenced to lead to the gradual emancipation of the negroes. Land has been purchased & a village is forming. Slaves are purchased who are to work together with a common stock. The profits of their industry to be employed to purchase their freedom. It is said that La Fayette has subscribed 10000$ to the fund, & that Miss Wright & Mʳ. George Flower are both contributors and managers. As this settlement is made in a slave state, the surrounding proprietors are said to be very jealous of its

interests, & throw obstacles in the way of its progress. Besides all
the white population have so thorough a contempt & mean opinion
of a coloured person, that it is doubtful whether their feelings
may not operate to defeat a practical step towards emancipation.]
At the mouth of White river on the right bank, we stopped to take
on wood & land a passenger. Here there is a small settlement of
two or three families. I entered into conversation with one man
who told me he was born in Georgia, raised in Tennessee, had
lived where he was two years, & intended in another year to go
west into the red river country. He had a wife, or a woman that
acted as such, (for in these countries changes & exchanges are
easily made) and a heap of young children.

In many conversations that I had I found the tide of emigra-
tion, was generally from the southern & eastern states, first to the
banks of the Ohio or Mississippi, then into Illinois, Indiana, or
Ohio state, and thence again west up the Arkansaw or Missouri,
or into the red river country. The steam navigation, & the trade
for the raw materials for manufacturing, ensure the migrating
woodsman a supply of cash & the boundless & fertile soil around
him & the domestic labour of his family, secure to him a full
supply of all which the rude habits of his life give him a desire
for. Whiskey & tobacco are cheap, and powder & lead easily
procured. He therefore freely indulges in these great stimuli,
chewing & drinking at all hours, and rarely passing a day without
his gun in his hand. They have little or no moral feeling in the
composition of their character, and if we except their fear of the
law, and their attachment to the American Constitution, which
they belief (without understanding) to be the safeguard of their
freedom, I should suppose their minds were under no influence
but that of their appetites.

The river winds continually in every direction down this
immense vale which is more or less subject to its inundations in
the months of April, May & June, from two to 300 miles in
breadth, particularly on its western side where there are extensive
lakes. In some places among the Islands and at the bends of the
river its breadth is more than a mile, occasionally nearly two
miles. The banks being of the finest & softest soil is continually
crumbling down, spreading out in tongues on one side & rounding away in hollow places on the other. Large trees are seen with
their heads above the water, denoting their late fall; others with

their bare roots tottering and awaiting their inevitable fate; while tall & slender shrubberies are every where rapidly arising to shade and fortify the newly formed shores of this inland ocean.

In one part we passed what the boatman called the new cut off where the river, after a process of wearing the bank away into a deep elbow forced its way across the istmus into its next bend, shortening its course by a distance of 18 miles and forming another large Island in the midst of its waters. At sunset a thick vapour rises & floats over the surface of the river, frequently obliging the boats to lay too during the night.

The gentlemen on board passed their time at cards & backgammon, and frequently had disputes about the game. One day they abused one another violently, and two of them struck & threw chairs at one another. This dispute however was amicably settled, & tranquility resulted from it during the remainder of the voyage. I got on the best terms with them; so much so that they hoped we should hereafter meet again, and two who left us at Natches, and followed to New Orleans in two or three days, met me there at the Hotel like old friends. This was a pleasant circumstance to a stranger, and I judge from it that a traveller among the western people, particularly the Kentuckians, should he be a man of education but liberal & accommodating in his habits & opinions, will have daily reason to say that they are extremely hospitable. But they have their passions & their prejudices & bad habits. The first they are accustomed to indulge, the second they are less sensible of than a traveller, and they have are privileged at home in the gratification of the third.

It was my custom to seat myself on a bale of cotton on the top near the pilot, and enjoy the current of air, & the unusual scenery around me. We rapidly got into a warmer atmosphere, under a clearer sky and amidst greener forests; but a dead flatness spread in all directions. The variety however was considerable. At one time the shades among the trees caught the eye; at another the immense drifts of wood led the mind to speculate upon the growth & decay of vegetable matter, & the great quantities of timber thus annually sent into the Mexican gulf; at a third the attention was directed to a steamboat approaching, or some solitary flat boats which we were rapidly overtaking and passing by.

Natches is the last place on the river bank which we passed, & which stands elevated above the dead level. The bank is about

100 f'. high, and apparently entirely of sand. The town stands on an extensive flat, and contains a large population. Down by the water side are a miserable collection of wooden houses in which the boatmen reside. There it is that a degraded state of morals is to be found. From the top of the bank the eye has nothing to look at but the winding river and the tops of the trees.

As our stop was short I had not time to see the town, which I am told contains many agreeable inhabitants and good buildings. The negroes & quadroons (or mixed race) were very numerous on the bank. I there fell in with two—carpenter and Tanner who had left Harmony. They told me business was brisk, and the carpenters intended making some money to carry them to New Orleans, & perhaps to visit Scotland & some parts of the Old Country.

I learnt that one of my fellow voyagers was a member of the Kentucky legislature, another the son of a landed proprietor, one a young lawyer going to look out for business in Florida, another, a Virginian from the back parts going to settle there, & another a lawyer (who had been a play-actor), going to Pensacola. The gentleman we landed at White river was going some distance up that river; he was a young doctor.

When least expected settlements spring up, and west of the Mississippi and in the Missouri, there are more white settlers (already there & annually removing there) than in Europe they have any conception of.

Below Natches the river banks on both sides are more thickly settled. As they are more elevated & only covered by the highest waters much more land is in cultivation, and although compared with the extent of country the river winds through the part cleared is but trifling, yet lying on the edge of the water, it serves to vary the scene and gives a slight idea of the richness of the land.

As we advanced the habitations became more numerous, we overtook more boats, the trees looked greener, the corn crops farther advanced, the slaves out in the fields preparing the ground for cotton & sugar. Levees or embankments from 3 to 5 & 6 feet high & as many thick extended on both sides the river. For the last 100 miles before we reached New Orleans the line of communication from one farm or plantation to another was scarcely broken, and in many places were well fashioned stone & brick houses and regularly planned rows of buildings for the slaves employed on the sugar plantations. The usual form was a wide street of small brick or painted wooden houses with the overseer's house at one end & the sugar house at the other, extending towards the river, and about the middle of the plantation, and some distance from the proprietor's house which is usually surrounded by a few trees. The plantation is surrounded by rail fences, and in the marsh or swamp behind, tower the thick forests of Cypress trees which are covered with a brownish weed which thickly spread over their misshapen tops giving a dead appearance to them. This weed is called Spanish moss, and is much used for stuffing mattrasses, being of a soft & cool nature, and supposed to be very wholesome.

By the laws of the State of Louisiana the lands on the river bank are divided into lots of a certain extent of river bank & extending thence straight into the marsh & woods behind, so that each holder of a lot has his proper portion of embankment or Levee to keep in repair.

The vale of the Mississippi seems to have been formerly entirely flooded at the rainy season or in the early summer months when the northern snows & ice melt. But the river bringing in its troubled waters a great quantity of light soil which as it spreads & stagnated over this extensive vale, settled and gradually raised its surface, some seasons left considerable portions of its banks dry. These were occupied & defended by levees by the first settlers, who gradually encreased in numbers, untill their properties were formed into a connected line of embankment; leaving the river to spread through the woods around them.

The channel of the river is very deep, and the working of the currents & eddies below are marked by the boiling up of the water as it rolls on at the rate of from two to three miles an hour. No scheme has yet been thought of which could oppose the progress of the river in washing in its banks, at its different windings, and as this process is very rapid, and in the neighbourhood of New Orleans a small quantity of great value; rich persons have frequently in a few years lost a great part of their fortune by the river changing its course.

The mouth of the red river is about a quarter of a mile wide, having an island near it; but it is very deep. It is navigable for steam boats a great way. It is from a point high up this river, that the land journey to Mexico is commenced, thus avoiding the marshes which extend to the shores of the Gulf.

We passed several boats floating down with cotton, and some ships which had been towed by steamboats up the river to receive the cotton & sugar from the very bank of the plantation.

We passed many steamboats & small towns, and I felt the sensation of coming out of the retirement of the country into the bustle of a city. The weather became warm, the trees were almost in full leaf, and the Cypress & wild herbs of the forest perfumed the evening breezes.

It was becoming dark when we saw the roofs of houses, the masts of shipping & the long iron flues of numerous steamboats, crowding the side of the Levee. The *Paragon* had got in a few hours before, as our paddles had been so broken that we had to stop several times to mend them. The *General Jackson* came in a few hours after us.

It was too late to quit the boat that evening, therefore after a short walk in the dark through two or three narrow streets, I returned on board for the night.

TIME PASSES TRANQUILLY,
IF NOT PLEASANTLY

THOMAS HAMILTON

———————

[*Donald MacDonald was interested in what he saw. Thomas Hamilton, one of the Edinburgh* Blackwoods *group and author of the popular novel* Cyril Thornton, *was concerned with his own reactions, which he set down in a mildly snobbish tone that did not endear him to American readers. It may well have been his own aloofness that was particularly responsible for the dullness he experienced on his slow voyage from Louisville to New Orleans in 1831, as reported in his* Men and Manners in America (*2 volumes, Edinburgh, 1833*), II, 180–200.]

The New Orleans steam-boats are a very different description of vessels to any I had yet seen. They are of great size, and the object being to carry as large a cargo as possible, the whole vessel, properly so called, is devoted to this purpose, and the cabins for the passengers are raised in successive tiers above the main deck. The lower of these cabins is appropriated to the gentlemen. It is generally spacious, and very handsomely fitted up. Three of its sides are surrounded by a gallery and veranda. Over this is the ladies' cabin, equally handsome, though smaller. On the roof of the ladies' cabin is a deck on which the passengers may amuse themselves as they think proper. Near the forecastle, at the same elevation, is the place for the steerage passengers. These vessels have very much the appearance of three-deckers, and many of them are upwards of 500 tons burden. Their engines are generally constructed on the high pressure principle, and one or two generally blow up every season, sending a score of two of parboiled passengers to an inconvenient altitude in the atmosphere.

On the day following we commenced our voyage, of 1500

miles, to New Orleans. The weather was delightful, and I now enjoyed the privilege of reading and writing undisturbed in my cabin. The passengers, though coarse as heart could desire, were at least less openly and obtrusively profligate than those I have already described. There was the same scene of gambling and drinking, but I was now able to remove from the din and the blasphemy.

After leaving Louisville, we were nearly three days in reaching the point of junction between the Mississippi and Ohio. The latter river receives the waters of several large tributaries, the Tennessee, the Cumberland, the Wabash, &c., by which its magnitude is prodigiously increased. We skirted the new and flourishing states of Indiana and Illinois, which I did not visit. With their facilities, agricultural and commercial, their advantages and disadvantages, their soil, their climate, their productions, the public have already been made familiar by writers far better qualified to afford instruction on such matters than I pretend to be.

To a traveller, whose leading objects are connected with the structure of society, there is little in a scantily peopled territory to excite speculation. He that has seen one settler in the backwoods has seen a thousand. Those whom the love of lucre, and consciousness of independence, have induced to seek the recesses of the forest, who gaze daily on the same aspect of nature, who endure the same privations, encounter the same difficulties, and struggle by the same means, for the same ultimate reward, can present but one aspect of human character, and that far from the most interesting. With individuals so situated, indeed, I was necessarily, in different portions of my journey, brought into frequent contact. But I never voluntarily sought them, for I was chiefly anxious to contemplate men in their social and more extended relations, and to observe the influences, moral and political, by which the national character had been formed or modified. My steps, therefore, were directed to the city, not to the solitary *shantee;* to the haunts of large masses of men, rather than to those of isolated adventurers, who have yet to dispute the dominion of the forest with the bear and the panther.

On the second morning after our departure from Louisville, a change in the general character of the river seemed to indicate that we were rapidly approaching the Mississippi. For about fifty miles before the point of union, the surrounding scenery is flat, and the breadth of the Ohio is more than doubled, as if, from a feeling of rivalry, the river god had expanded his waters to the utmost. On the present occasion, the Ohio had the advantage of being very full from the melting of the snows along the whole line of its course, while the Mississippi, descending from higher latitudes, had experienced no such augmentation.

For hours I was on the tiptoe of expectation to catch the first glimpse of "the father of rivers," and with this view, had taken up a station on the highest pinnacle of the forecastle. At length, when yet about five miles distant, the Mississippi, sailing along in dark and solemn grandeur, became distinctly visible. Both rivers were about two miles broad, but the expanse of the Ohio struck me as being somewhat larger than that of its more powerful rival. I do not remember any occasion on which my imagination was more excited. I felt, in parting with the Ohio, as if I had done injustice to its attractions. True, it presents but one phasis of beauty, but that is of the noblest character. For a distance of nine hundred miles I had beheld it roll its clear waters, smoothly and peacefully, and I now, almost with a feeling of regret, bade it farewell.

The *Huntress* kept on her way rejoicing. We passed the small settlement of Cairo, standing on an isthmus between the two rivers, and in a few minutes beheld ourselves borne on the most majestic tribute of waters which Earth pays to Ocean.

It certainly appears strange that the Mississippi, after absorbing the Ohio, presents no visible augmentation of its volume. Below the point of junction, the river is not broader than the Ohio alone. Though flowing in the same channel, the streams are not mingled. For many miles there is a distinct line of demarcation between the waters of the two rivers. Those of the Ohio are clear, while the stream of the Mississippi is ever dark and turbid. When the Mississippi is in flood, it almost dams up the Ohio, and suffers it to occupy but a small portion of the common channel. But in other circumstances the case is different, and the Ohio constitutes, in parliamentary phrase, a very respectable minority.

After quitting *la belle riviere*, as the French first designated the Ohio, one feels as if he had made an exchange for the worse. The scenery of the Mississippi is even less varied than that of the Ohio. It is almost uniformly flat, though in the course of twelve hundred miles a few bluffs and eminences do certainly occur. The wood grows down to the very margin of the river, and the timber, for some hundred miles, is by no means remarkable for size. As the river descends to the southward, however, it is of finer growth; and about latitude 36°, vegetation becomes marked by a degree of rankness and luxuriance which I have never seen equalled anywhere else.

The American forests are generally remarkable for the entire absence of underwood, so that they are easily penetrable by a foot traveller, and generally even by a mounted one. But in the neighbourhood of the Mississippi there is almost uniformly a thick undergrowth of cane, varying in height from four or five to about twenty feet, according to the richness of the soil. Through this thicket of cane I should think it quite impossible to penetrate, yet I have been assured the Indians do so for leagues together, though by what means they contrive to guide their course, where vision is manifestly impossible, it is not easy to understand.

The steam-boats stop twice a-day to take in a supply of wood for the engine. These vessels have become so numerous that a considerable number of settlers make it their business to supply them, and thus turn their labour to better account than would be found in the cultivation of the soil. But the climate is deadly and pestilential; they are worn and sallow; and those with whom I spoke seemed to regard fevers as things of course. Medicine they have none; and when one's eyes rested on the miserable and pallid children, and their haggard mother, it was impossible not to feel compassion for these forlorn outcasts.

Outcasts they literally are. Many have fled for crimes, to a region where the arm of the law cannot reach them. Others are men of broken characters, hopes, and fortunes, who fly not from justice, but contempt. One man told me it was so. He had known better days. Men blamed him when he became poor. He withdrew his poverty from their sight, and came to labour amid the untrodden forests of the Mississippi. The man had been handsome, and still bore about him something of dignity. His manners were remarkably pleasing; but my fellow-passengers assured me that he was one who could stab while he smiled. I certainly should not much have fancied encroaching on the hospitality of his solitary shantee.

These settlers are called Squatters. They *locate* where they please, without troubling themselves about any title to the land they occupy. Should a rival in the business of wood-cutting choose to take up his residence inconveniently near, the rifle settles the dispute. One or other becomes food for the vultures, and the market continues uninjured by competition.

During the whole course of the voyage, we daily passed numbers of large arks or rafts, consisting of rough timbers, nailed together in the shape of a square box, in which the poorer proprietors of the upper country send down the produce of their land to New Orleans. These vessels were often without sails of any kind, and the only skill necessary in the navigation was to keep in the middle of the stream. Time was, and that not far distant, when these rafts constituted almost the only vehicles for conveying produce to the place of embarkation. In those days, a voyage to Louisville and back occupied about nine months, and by means of steam it can now be performed in little more than a fortnight. The application of steam navigation to the purposes of commerce has indeed given a mighty impulse to the prosperity of the central States. In the niches next to Mrs. Trollope, the Cincinnatians should place statues of Fulton and James Watt. To the first they owe celebrity; to the two last, a market for their bacon and flour.

Time passed on board of the steam-boat, if not pleasantly, at least tranquilly. True, there was gambling and drinking, and wrangling and swearing; true, there was an utter disregard of all the decent courtesies of society: but to these things I had gradually become accustomed; for as they hourly and almost minutely "overcame us like a summer's cloud," they were no longer regarded with "special wonder." But there were some things to which I had not become accustomed, and one of these was slavery; and another, eating and drinking and holding communion with a slave-dealer.

Unfortunately, the man generally occupied the place next to me at dinner; and, strange to say, with the soul of a brute, I remarked that he performed all the functions of an ordinary American. He ate, he drank, he voided profusion of tobacco juice, he swallowed brandy every half hour of the day, and passed three-fourths, both of day and night, in gambling. His poor gang of slaves were above stairs, the men loaded with heavy chains, and the women with scarcely rags enough to serve the purposes of decency. I spoke occasionally to both, and the women were certainly the more intelligent. They seemed to take pride in the largeness of the prices they had formerly brought in the market;

and one, with a look of dignity, told me her master had refused three hundred dollars for her. Who, after this, shall presume to say, that vanity is not an inherent attribute of woman?

The men were in a state at once wretched and disgusting. Their chains prevented their performing the ordinary functions of cleanliness, and their skin had become covered with a sort of scaly eruption. But I will not enlarge on a subject so revolting. I remember, however, that no one on board talked about freedom so loudly or so long as this slave-dealer. He at length left us, and the sky seemed brighter, and the earth greener, after his departure.

It has been the fashion with travellers to talk of the scenery of the Mississippi as wanting grandeur and beauty. Most certainly it has neither. But there is no scenery on earth more striking. The dreary and pestilential solitudes, untrodden save by the foot of the Indian; the absence of all living objects, save the huge alligators which float past, apparently asleep, on the drift-wood; and an occasional vulture, attracted by its impure prey on the surface of the waters; the trees, with a long and hideous drapery of pendent moss, fluttering in the wind; and the giant river rolling onward the vast volume of its dark and turbid waters through the wilderness, form the features of one of the most dismal and impressive landscapes on which the eye of man ever rested.

If any man think proper to believe that such objects are not, in themselves, sufficient, I beg only to say that I differ with him in point of taste. Rocks and mountains are fine things undoubtedly, but they could add nothing of sublimity to the Mississippi. Pelion might be piled on Ossa, Alps on Andes, and still, to the heart and perceptions of the spectator, the Mississippi would be *alone*. It can brook no rival, and it finds none. No river in the world drains so large a portion of the earth's surface. It is the traveller of five thousand miles, more than two-thirds of the diameter of the globe. The imagination asks, whence come its waters, and whither tend they? They come from the distant regions of a vast continent, where the foot of civilized man has never yet been planted. They flow into an ocean yet vaster, the whole body of which acknowledges their influence. Through what varieties of climate have they passed? On what scenes of lonely and sublime magnificence have they gazed? Have they penetrated

"The hoary forests, still the Bison's screen,
 Where stalked the *Mammoth* to his shaggy lair,

Through paths and alleys, roof'd with sombre green,
Thousands of years before the silent air
Was pierc'd by whizzing shaft of hunter keen?"

In short, when the traveller has asked and answered these
questions, and a thousand others, it will be time enough to consider how far the scenery of the Mississippi would be improved
by the presence of rocks and mountains. He may then be led to
doubt whether any *great* effect can be produced by a combination
of objects of discordant character, however grand in themselves.
The imagination is perhaps susceptible but of a single powerful
impression at a time. Sublimity is uniformly connected with unity
of object. Beauty may be produced by the happy adaptation of a
multitude of harmonious details; but the highest sublimity of
effect can proceed but from one glorious and paramount object,
which impresses its own character on every thing around.

The prevailing character of the Mississippi is that of solemn
gloom. I have trodden the passes of Alp and Appenine, yet never
felt how awful a thing is nature, till I was borne on its waters,
through regions desolate and uninhabitable. Day after day, and
night after night, we continued driving right downward to the
south; our vessel, like some huge demon of the wilderness, bearing fire in her bosom, and canopying the eternal forest with the
smoke of her nostrils. How looked the hoary river-god I know not;
nor what thought the alligators, when awakened from their slumber by a vision so astounding. But the effect on my own spirits
was such as I have never experienced before or since. Conversation became odious, and I passed my time in a sort of dreamy
contemplation. At night, I ascended to the highest deck, and lay
for hours gazing listlessly on the sky, the forest, and the waters,
amid silence only broken by the clanging of the engine. All this
was very pleasant; yet till I reached New Orleans, I could scarcely
have smiled at the best joke in the world; and as for raising a
laugh—it would have been quite as easy to quadrate the circle.

The navigation of the Mississippi is not unaccompanied by
danger. I do not now speak of the risk of explosion, which is very
considerable, but of a peril arising from what are called *planters*
and *sawyers*. These are trees firmly fixed in the bottom of the
river, by which vessels are in danger of being impaled. The dis-
tinction is, that the former stand upright in the water, the latter

lie with their points directed down the stream. We had the bad luck to sustain some damage from a planter, whose head being submersed was of course invisible.

The bends or flexures of the Mississippi are regular in a degree unknown in any other river; indeed, so much is this the case, that I should conceive it quite practicable for a hydrographer to make a tolerably accurate sketch of its course without actual survey. The action of running water, in a vast alluvial plain like that of the basin of the Mississippi, without obstruction from rock or mountain, may be calculated with the utmost precision. Whenever the course of a river diverges in any degree from a right line, it is evident that the current can no longer act with equal force on both its banks. On one side the impulse is diminished, on the other increased. The tendency in these sinuosities, therefore, is manifestly to increase, and the stream which hollows out a portion of one bank being rejected to the other, the process of curvature is still continued, till its channel presents an almost unvarying succession of salient and retiring angles.

In the Mississippi the flexures are so extremely great, that it often happens that the isthmus which divides different portions of the river gives way. A few months before my visit to the south a remarkable case of this kind had happened, by which forty miles of navigation had been saved. The opening thus formed was called the *new cut;* and it was matter of debate between the Captain and pilot whether we should not pass through it.

Even the annual changes which take place in the bed of the Mississippi are very remarkable. Islands spring up and disappear; shoals suddenly present themselves where pilots have been accustomed to deep water; in many places whole acres are swept away from one bank and added to the other; and the pilot assured me, that in every voyage he could perceive fresh changes.

Many circumstances contribute to render these changes more rapid in the Mississippi than in any other river. Among these, perhaps, the greatest is the vast volume of its waters, acting on alluvial matter, peculiarly penetrable. The river, when in flood, spreads over the neighbouring country, in which it has formed channels, called *bayous.* The banks thus become so saturated with water that they can oppose little resistance to the action of the current, which frequently sweeps off large portions of the forest.

The immense quantity of drift-wood is another cause of change. Floating logs encounter some obstacle in the river, and become stationary. The mass gradually accumulates; the water, saturated with mud, deposits a sediment, and thus an island is formed, which soon becomes covered with vegetation. About ten years ago the Mississippi was surveyed by order of the Government; and its islands, from the confluence of the Missouri to the sea, were numbered. I remember asking the pilot the name of a very beautiful island, and the answer was, five hundred-and-seventy-three, the number assigned to it in the hydrographical survey, and the only name by which it was known. But in the course of these ten years, a vast variety of changes have taken place, and a more accurate chart has become highly desirable.

A traveller on the Mississippi has little to record in the way of incident. For a week we continued our course, stopping only to take in wood, and on one occasion to take in cargo, at an inconsiderable place called Memphis, which stands on one of the few bluffs we encountered in our progress. At length we reached Natchez, a town of some importance in the State of Mississippi. We only halted there for an hour, and the upper town, which stands on a height at some distance, I did not see. But the place was described by the passengers as being the scene of the most open and undisguised profligacy. All I observed in the lower town, certainly gave me no reason to doubt the accuracy of the description. Taverns full of men and women of the most abandoned habits, dancing, drinking, and uttering the most obscene language, were open to the street. I was advised not to walk to any distance from the landing place, for the risk of being robbed was considerable. I did however attempt to reach the upper town, about a mile off, but the bell announcing preparation for departure arrested my progress.

One of the most striking circumstances connected with this river voyage, was the rapid change of climate. Barely ten days had elapsed since I was traversing mountains almost impassable from snow. Even the level country was partially covered with it, and the approach of spring had not been heralded by any symptom of vegetation. Yet, in little more than a week, I found myself in the region of the sugar cane!

The progress of this transition was remarkable. During the first two days of the voyage, nothing like a blossom or a green leaf was to be seen. On the third, slight signs of vegetation were visible on a few of the hardier trees. These gradually became more general as we approached the Mississippi; but then, though our course lay almost due south, little change was apparent for a day or two. But after passing Memphis, in latitude 35°, all nature became alive. The trees which grew on any little eminence, or which did not spring immediately from the swamp, were covered with foliage; and at our wooding times, when I rambled through the woods, there were a thousand shrubs already bursting into flower. On reaching the lower regions of the Mississippi, all was brightness and verdure. Summer had already begun, and the heat was even disagreeably intense.

Shortly after entering Louisiana, the whole wildness of the Mississippi disappears. The banks are all cultivated, and nothing was to be seen but plantations of sugar, cotton, and rice, with the houses of their owners, and the little adjoining hamlets inhabited by the slaves. Here and there were orchards of orange-trees, but these occurred too seldom to have much influence on the landscape.

At Baton Rouge, a fort of some strength, which commands the navigation of the river, we discharged a major and a few private soldiers of the United States army, and on the following evening I found myself at New Orleans.

JOE COWELL RECALLS A VOYAGE
IN THE *HELEN MCGREGOR* IN 1829;

or, Twelve Days Confinement
in a High Pressure Prison

JOSEPH L. COWELL

[*Since Joseph Leathley Cowell was a comic actor as well as
an author and a painter one would not expect him to write
with quite the dignity and restraint of Latrobe or the aloofness of Hamilton. Much of his long experience of life in
America goes to fill his autobiography,* Thirty Years Passed
among the Players in England and America, *first published
in New York in 1844. The following extract is from the
1853 edition, pages 91–95. The reader may be interested
to know that the* Helen McGregor *blew up at Memphis on
her return trip north.*]

The floating palaces which now navigate the Western waters,
bear as little likeness to the style of vessels then in use, as the
manners and characters of the majority of passengers you met
with then, resemble the travellers who now assemble in the magnificent saloons of the present day, where all the etiquette and
decorum is observed of a *table d'hôte* at a well-appointed hotel.

A sketch of *what is* will serve, by contrast, the better to
convey an idea of *what was* considered a first-rate class of boat in
1829. In speaking of the Western steamers of the present day, I
shall only allude to that portion of the vessel appropriated to the
passengers, and that must not be considered as identical, but *an
average description;* the *Missouri*, the *Harry of the West*, and
twenty others, I could name as far exceeding, in many instances,
the portrait I shall draw. The saloon, or principal chamber, extends nearly the whole length of the boat, on the upper deck, over

the machinery and steerage, as it is called—where comfortable accommodations are provided for the deck-hands and deck-passengers—terminating forward with large glazed doors opening on a covered space called the boiler-deck, and aft by the ladies' cabin, with which it communicates by folding doors, which are generally left open in warm weather, in the daytime. The whole is lighted from above by a continuous skylight, round the side of a *long oval*, which looks as if it had been cut out from the ceiling, and lifted some two feet above it perpendicularly, and there supported by framed glass. On either side of this carpeted and splendidly-furnished apartment are ranged the staterooms, the doors ornamented with Venitian or cut-glass windows, and assisting, by their long line of perspective, the general effect. These small chambers usually contain two berths, *never more*, which always look as if you were the first person who had ever slept in them— with curtains, moscheto-bars, toilet stands, drawers, chairs, carpets, and all the elegant necessaries of a cosey bedroom. Another door leads to the guard, or piazza, protected with a railing on the side, and covered overhead; and this forms a promenade all round the boat, and joins the boiler-deck, where you can lounge with your cigar, and view with wonder, perhaps with regret, if your nature is picturesque, the hourly interference of untiring man with the solitude of the long-remembered wilderness.

The ladies are even more carefully provided for; there is usually one, and often two grand pianofortes in their apartment; which I should consider a positive nuisance if obliged to hear them tickled to death by young beginners and nurse-maids amusing themselves by making believe to keep the children quiet; but, Heaven be praised, there is plenty of room to get out of the way, this area being usually from eighty to two hundred feet in length. In many of the larger boats double state-rooms are provided for families, and young married people who are afraid to sleep by themselves, with *four-post* bedsteads, and other *on-shore* arrangements—such as are to be found at the St. Charles's Exchange, or Barnum's Hotel, or, what is better still, *at home*.

Now the *Helen M'Gregor* was a very different affair, but in her day her reputation was as high as anybody's or boat's. It was at night, and in December, raining and making believe to snow, when I arrived on board at Shipping Port, some two miles below Louisville; the boat being very heavily laden, and drawing too much water to get over the falls, and the canal was not then finished—a most beautiful piece of work, by-the-by; the excavation being made in the solid limestone rock, gave it the appearance of an enormous empty marble bath. She was crowded with passengers: perhaps a hundred in the cabin, and at least that number *upon deck;* for at that time the steerage occupied the space now allotted to the saloon, and was filled to overflowing with men, women, and children, chiefly Irish and German labourers, with their families, in dirty dishabille. This *man-pen* was furnished with a stove, for warmth and domestic cooking, and two large, empty shelves, one above the other, all round, boarded up outside about four feet high. These served for sleeping-places for those who had bedding, or those who were obliged to *plank it;* the remaining space above these roosts was only protected from the weather by tattered canvass curtains between the pillars which supported the hurricane-deck, alias the roof, which was spread over with a multitude of cabbages, making sourkrout of themselves as fast as possible, and at least fifty coops of fighting-cocks, each in a separate apartment, with a hole in the front for his head to come through; and their continual notes of defiance, mixed up with the squalling and squeaking of women and children, and the boisterous mirth or vehement quarrelling of the men, in all kinds of languages, altogether kicked up a rumpus that drowned even the noise of the engine, which then was only separated from the cabin by a thin partition. By-the-by, all our old poets speak of "the cock, that is the herald of the morn," as if he did *not* crow in the night! but only at the approach of day, and in the daytime. I know little about rural felicity in my own country; but here, in America, the cocks crow whenever they think proper, *and always all night long*, particularly on board a steamboat, because there you are more likely to take notice of the annoyance.

The cabin was on the lower deck, immediately abaft the boilers, with a small partition at the stern set apart for the females. At the time I speak of, there were very few resident American merchants at New-Orleans at all, and those few generally left their families *at home* in the North and therefore the presence of woman

> "Creature in whom excell'd
> Whatever can to sight or thought be form'd,
> Holy, divine, good, amiable, or sweet!"

was no restraint on naturally barbarous man, and, consequently, "a trip down the river" was then an uncontrolled yearly opportunity for the young merchants and their clerks *to go it with a perfect looseness*, mixed up indiscriminately with "a sort of vagabonds" of all nations, who then made New-Orleans their *"jumping-off place,"* till Texas fortunately offered superior inducements, and there war and disease have bravely thinned the hordes of

> "Rascals, runaways, and base lackey peasants,
> Whom their o'er-cloy'd countries vomit forth
> To desperate venture and assured destruction."

All moral and social restraint was placed in the shade—*there Jack was as good as his master*—and never was Republicanism more practically republicanized than it was during the twelve days of confinement I passed on board this high-pressure prison.

Some such a party I presume it was that Mrs. Trollope met with, which she, *no doubt innocently*, but ignorantly, gives as a specimen of the *"domestic manners of the Americans."* Poor old lady, what a mess she made of it!

There were no *state-rooms*, no *wash-room*, nor even a *social-hall*; and, therefore, on the *guard*—within two inches of the level of the river, and about two feet wide, with nothing to prevent your falling overboard if your foot slipped, or *"was a little swipey"*—you made your toilet, with a good chunk of yellow soap on a stool, to which two tin basins were chained, and alongside a barrel of water. The cabin contained thirty-two berths; and the two next the door Anderson had secured for myself and my dear boy. In the daytime these were piled up with the surplus mattresses and blankets, which, at night, were spread close together on the floor, and under and on the dining-tables, for so many of the remainder of the passengers as were fortunate enough to have precedence even in this luxury, after the berths were disposed of. The remainder of the party sat up, drinking, smoking, playing cards, or grumbling at not being able to find a single horizontal space, under cover, large enough to stretch their weary limbs on; perhaps changing the scene of their discontent by going on shore at a wood-pile, and putting their eyes out by standing in the smoke of the signal-fire, to defend themselves from the bloodthirsty attacks of a million of moschetoes.

Fortunately, the weather was most delightful for the season of the year, and Sam and I passed most of our time on the hurricane-deck, among the cabbages, *leaving their fragrance behind;* and the chicken-cocks, with Sam and the echoes, all imitating one another. Your arrival at the mouth of the Ohio is visibly announced by the sudden and extraordinary discoloration of the water, which gives you notice the moment you pass the threshold of the great Mississippi. From childhood familiar with all the wonders of the ocean, a mental comparison with it and this gigantic river was natural to me, on first making its acquaintance; and I confess it claimed a formidable share of the awe and admiration I had hitherto considered only due, as far as water was concerned, to my old associate. Call it the Missouri—which I wish it had been called—and it measures 4490 miles in length! and if the Mississippi, 2910, and passes through more than twenty degrees of latitude!

What a pity that that microscopic observer of *nature on two legs*, the immense Dickens, should so soon have made up his mind that it wasn't fit either to taste or talk of!

"Oh! think what tales he'd have to tell"

if he, instead of *taking the wrong pig by the ear*, had taken a trip or two up the Missouri with my worthy friend Captain Dennis, of the Thames, or had had the useless experience

"Of wandering youths like me."

The Upper Mississippi, as it is called—God send that every friend I have on earth could behold *for even once* the stupendous wonders through which a portion of the navigable part of the Upper Mississippi rolls along—though *the stream itself* might wander through the world, and be likened to a hundred others, or pass unnoticed; but when it joins the Missouri, or, more fitly speaking, when the Missouri takes possession of its course, its pure and placid character is gone forever. A Bath-brick finely pulverized and stirred up in a pailful of spring water may give a conceived resemblance of its colour and consistency; and this appearance it maintains, with an interminable and never-ceasing rush, for the remainder of its journey, of more than thirteen hundred miles.

Well was it named *"The Father of Waters,"* for even when

the "crystal pavement," for a winter month or two, suspends a
portion of its navigation,

"The whole imprison'd river growls below,"

embracing in its mad career the thousands of miles of waters
emptied into it by the Illinois, the Ohio, the Arkansas, the Red
River, and the innumerable smaller streams, all aiding to increase
its power. And in return, the mighty tyrant overwhelms on the
instant their transparent interference, and carries with it, in its
turgid course, its mountain-stained identity, even for miles, into
the Gulf of Mexico! till, in continuous struggles for the mastery,
it fades away, in oil-like circles, round and round the deep, dark
blue of the old Atlantic.

Who the ladies were on board, I know not: none were ever
seen with the exception of Fanny Wright; and her notorious
anti-matrimonial propensities, at that time, hardly gave her a
claim to come under that denomination. As soon as our breakfast
was over, which occupied an hour and a half or more, the double
row of tables, the extreme length of the cabin, consisting of a
common mahogany one at each end, and the intermediate space
filled up by a pile of shutters laid side by side, and supported by
trestles, had to be three or four times provided with venison, wild
ducks, geese, and turkies, and all the luxuries of this o'erteeming
country, and there called common food. This operation ended, the
original Fanny would take her station at a small table, near the
door of the ladies' cabin, and sit and write or read till late at night,
with the exception of the time for meals, and an hour or two of
exercise upon the guard; and the moment she made her appearance there, without form or show of ceremony, it was respectfully
deserted by the men till her promenade was over. The Americans
are naturally the most unostentatiously gallant people in the
world. An Englishman will make a long apology for not doing
what he should have done, and said nothing about it; and a
Frenchman will upset a glass of *parfait l'amour* in a lady's lap, by
dancing over a tea-stand to hand her a *bon-bon*, in an attitude!

Among the men were some most intelligent and entertaining
companions. A day or two formed us all into little knots or
parties; and I was a member of a most delightful one, among
whom was gladly admitted, for his good-humour and originality,
the proprietor of the fighting cocks. He was a young man, but had

evidently taken so many liberties with Time, that he, in return, had honoured him with many conspicuous marks of early favour, and milk-white hairs began to dispute with his untrimmed auburn locks the shading of his open, manly brow.

He took a great fancy to my dear boy, and, in consequence, I was high in his favour and confidence, and he insisted on telling me a portion of his history. His grandfather was a man of great wealth in the *Old Dominion*, and a distinguished member of her councils. His father, born to inherit his certain share of the property, began to spend it before he actually came in possession of his fortune, married early in life, and lost his wife in giving birth to this only son; and living night and day full gallop, died of literal old age at forty-five.

"The night he died," said my young friend, putting *a deck* of marble-backed cards into his pocket, with which he had just satisfactorily concluded a game at *old sledge*, "the night he died, my father called me to the side of his bed. 'Washington,' said he, taking my hand in his, which felt as cold and clammy as a dead fish, 'Washington, you'll never be able to pay off the mortgage on the property, and you'll be left without a dollar.' I said nothing; it was of no use. 'Here, take my keys,' said he, 'and go to the escritoir, and in the right-hand little drawer you'll find—but no matter, bring the drawer and all.' I did as I was told. 'Now,' said he, picking out the apparatus, 'send the boy to get a chicken, and I'll show you something I paid too dearly for the learning—and that's just it,' said the old man, with a deep sigh; 'if my father had left me nothing else, I should not now leave my boy in poverty.' I couldn't speak, for I saw the old man rub his hand across his eyes, so I kept on waxing the silk as he had directed. The boy had brought the bird—a perfect picture—he didn't touch the feathers; he had learned me all that, and how to hold a chicken, when I wasn't bigger than your boy Sam, but the *heeling* was the grand secret. The old gentleman then trimmed and sawed the spur, and spit upon the buckskin, telling me, all the time, to look on and mind what he was doing; but he was so feeble the little exertion was too much, and he got quite exhausted, and I made the boy take the cock, while I supported father. When he got through, 'There,' said he, triumphantly, with a kind of squeaking chuckle, '*that's the way to gaff a chicken! that will beat the world!*' and fell back upon his pillow. He made the boy jump when he said, *that's the way to gaff a chicken!* and the steel jerked through the nigger's hand—the blood spirted out upon the sheet; and as I turned to sop it up, father's eyes were full upon me, *but yet he didn't look*. 'Father,' I said, softly, and waited, but he didn't speak: 'Father!' I said again, but he didn't answer—the old gentleman was dead. *But he had showed me how to gaff a chicken-cock.*"

Playing at cards was the chief amusement at night, and my skill only extending to a homely game at *whist*, I was more frequently a looker on than a participator. My friend Washington was an adept at all short gambling games; and one that I don't remember to have seen played since, and which he boasted of having been the inventor of, of course he was particularly expert at. It appeared a game of chance, as simple as tossing up a dollar. Two only played at it, and three cards were singly dealt to each, of the same value as at whist, and a trump turned up; and the opponent to the dealer might order it to be turned down, and then make it another suit more agreeable to his hand, or play it as it was. Of course, the great point in favour of the opponent to the dealer was to know if he held *any* trumps, and *how many* he had. For some time luck seemed to be greatly in favour of my chicken friend, and the bets were doubled—trebled, and he gave me a knowing, triumphant look, while glancing at his *pile*. But suddenly there came a sad reverse of fortune.

Sitting by was an apparently uninterested looker-on like myself, peering over my friend's hand, and marking, by his fingers stretched upon the table, the number of trumps he held. The eagle eye of the Virginian soon detected the villany, and taking out his hunting-knife—it was before Bowie christened them—began paring his nails with well-acted indifference, as if entirely absorbed in the game, and laid it quietly on the table without its sheath. The next hand dealt him one trump, and the spy placed his fore-finger on the table, which my friend instantly chopped off!

"Hallo! stranger, what are you about?" shouted the dismembered gentleman. "You have cut off one of my fingers."

"I know it," said old Virginia, coolly; "and if I had had more trumps, you would have had less fingers."

This was considered an excellent practical joke, and we all took a drink together, and I lent the wounded a handkerchief to bind up his hand, which I reminded him last fall, at Gallatin races, that he had forgotten to return.

A lieutenant in the navy, on his way to Pensacola to join his ship, was one of our boatmates, and belonged to the *flooring committee*—so all were called who had to sleep on it. Two ardent devotees at *seven-up*, finding no better place late at night, while he was fast asleep coiled away in his cloak, squatted on either side of him, and made his shoulder their table. The continual *tip, tap,* as the cards were played by each upon his back, rather aided his seamanlike repose; but an energetic *slap* by one of the combatants at being "*High, by thunder!*" awakened him, and looking up, one of the players, slightly urging down his head, said, in a confidential whisper,

"Hold on a minute, stranger; the game's just out—I've only two to go—have twelve for game in my own hand, and *have got the Jack.*"

He, of course, accommodated them, and when the game was out, he found they had been keeping the run of it *with chalk tallied on his stand-up collar.*

One night, while I was getting instructed in the mysteries of *uker*, and Sam was amusing himself by building houses with the surplus cards at the corner of the table, close by us was a party playing *poker.* This was then exclusively a high-gambling Western game, founded on *brag*, invented, as it is said, by Henry Clay when a youth; and if so, very humanely, for either to win or lose, you are much sooner relieved of all anxiety than by the older operation.

For the sake of the uninformed, who had better know no more about it than I shall tell them, I must endeavour to describe the game when played with twenty-five cards only, and by four persons.

The aces are the highest denomination; then the kings, queens, Jacks, and tens; the smaller cards are not used; those I have named are all dealt out, and carefully concealed from one another; old players pack them in their hands, and peep at them as if they were afraid to trust even themselves to look. The four aces, with any other card, *cannot be beat*. Four kings, with an ace, *cannot be beat*, because then no one can have *four aces;* and four queens, or Jacks, or tens, with an ace, are all inferior hands to the kings, when so attended. But holding the cards I have instanced seldom occurs when they are *fairly dealt;* and three aces, for example, or three kings, with any two of the other cards, or four queens, or Jacks, or tens, is called *a full*, and with an ace, though not *invincible*, are considered *very good* bragging hands. The dealer makes the game, or value of the beginning bet, and called *the anti*—in this instance it was a dollar—and then everybody stakes the same amount, and says, "*I'm up.*"

It was a foggy, wretched night. Our bell was kept tolling to warn other boats of our whereabouts or to entreat direction to a landing by a fire on the shore. Suddenly a most tremendous concussion, as if all-powerful Nature had shut his hand upon us, and crushed us all to atoms, upset our cards and calculations, and a general rush was made, over chairs and tables, towards the doors. I found myself, on the flash of returning thought, with my dear boy in my embrace, and Fanny Wright sitting very affectionately close at my side, with her eyes wide open, in silent astonishment, as much as to say, "Have you any idea what they are going to do next?" and her book still in her hand. The cabin was entirely cleared, or, rather, all the passengers were huddled together at the entrances, with the exception of one of the *poker* players; a gentleman in green spectacles, a gold guard-chain, long and thick enough to moor a dog, and a brilliant diamond breastpin: he was, apparently, quietly shuffling and cutting the *poker-deck* for his own amusement. In less time than I am telling it, the swarm came laughing back, with broken sentences of what they *thought* had happened, in which *snags*, *sawyers*, *bolts blown out*, and *boilers burst*, were most conspicuous. But all the harm the *fracas* caused was fright; the boat, in rounding to a wood-pile, had run on the point of an island, and was high and dry among the first year's growth of cotton-wood, which seems to guaranty a never-ending supply of fuel to feed this peculiar navigation, which alone can combat with the unceasing, serpentine, tempestuous current of the *I-will-have-my-own-way*, glorious Mississippi.

The hubbub formed a good excuse to end our game, which my stupidity had made desirable long before, and I took a chair beside the poker-players, who, urged by the gentleman with the diamond pin, again resumed their seats. It was his turn to deal, and when he ended, he did not lift his cards, but sat watching quietly the countenances of the others. The man on his left hand bet ten dollars; a young lawyer, son to the then Mayor of Pittsburgh, who little dreamed of what his boy was about, who had hardly recovered his shock, bet ten more; at that time, fortunately for him, he was unconscious of the real value of his hand, and, consequently, did not betray by his manner, as greenhorns mostly do, his *certainty of winning*. My chicken friend bet that ten dollar and *five hundred dollars better!*

"I must see that," said Green Spectacles, who now took up his hand, with "*I am sure to win*" trembling at his fingers' ends; for you couldn't see his eyes through his glasses: he paused a moment in disappointed astonishment, and sighed "*I pass*," and threw his cards upon the table. The left-hand man bet "*that five hundred dollars and one thousand dollars better!*"

The young lawyer, who had had time to calculate the power of his hand—*four kings and an ace—it could not be beat!* but still he hesitated at the impossibility, as if he thought it could—looked at the money staked, and then his hand again, and, lingeringly, put his wallet on the table, and *called*. The left-hand man had four *queens*, with an ace; and Washington, the four *Jacks*, with an ace.

"Did you ever see the like on't?" said he, good-humouredly, as he pushed the money towards the lawyer, who, very agreeably astonished, pocketed his *two thousand and twenty-three dollars clear!*

The truth was, the cards had been *put up*, or *stocked*, as it is called, by the guard-chain-man while the party were off their guard, or, rather, on the guard of the boat in the fog, inquiring if the boiler had burst; but the excitement of the time had caused him to make a slight mistake in the distribution of the hand; and young "Six-and-eight-pence" got the one he had intended for himself. He was one of many who followed card playing for a living, a very common occupation at that time in that section of the country, but not properly coming under the denomination of the gentleman-sportsman, who alone depends on his superior skill. But in that pursuit, as in all others, *even among the players*, some black-sheep and black-legs will creep in, as in the present instance.

After the actors, there is no class of persons so misrepresented and abused behind their backs as the professional gamblers, as they are called; especially by those who sit down to bet against them every night without their wives and families knowing anything about it, and who would think it most praiseworthy *to cheat them* out of every dollar they had, *if they knew how*. As in my trade, the depraved and dishonourable are selected as the sample of all. But the majority are men too frequently born under similar circumstances with my good-hearted friend Washington, and left without any other resource but the speed of a horse, or the courage of a cock, to obtain wealth, in a world where to be rich is considered of too much importance. My way of life has for years thrown me much in their society, in steamboats and hotels, and as a general body, for kindness of heart, liberality, and sincerity of friendship—*out of their line of business*—they cannot be excelled by any other set of men who make making money their only mental occupation.

And now, wicked reader, go on shore with me at Natchez "under the hill," on a Sunday morning, where our jovial captain, Tyson, *tied up* his boat for the day, for the sake of his passengers' enjoying a *spree*. He was of the race, which miscalled refinement has almost made extinct, who would take the grand mogul or a giant by the nape of his neck and pitch him overboard, to wriggle a minute and then be sucked under the Mississippi, if he did not behave himself; and take a poor woman and her babes as passengers, and nurse, feed, blanket, and physic them all for nothing, and provide them with employment, or put money in their pockets till they found some way of living, all in the same breath. He and Captain Shrieve [Shreve] were selected by the government to combat with the Red River *Raft*, and there they have met with their match. But, now I think of it, you must be tired of this steamboat trip, so we'll pass Natchez by, and land at New-Orleans.

A LADY WRITER REPORTS SOME
INCIDENTS OF STEAMBOAT TRAVEL

MRS. ELIZA STEELE

[*Mrs. Eliza Steele is not to be relied on for some of her historical statements: Kaskaskia, for instance, was not settled by La Salle in 1683 but was established as a Jesuit mission in 1703. Her* riviere au vase *was merely a Muddy River. But she reported details not often set down by male travelers. These pages describing scenes aboard and along the way are from her* A Summer Journey in the West (*New York, 1841, pp. 199–214, 219–20, 220–29). The visit to the West was in 1840.*]

At two o'clock we went on board the steamboat *Monsoon*, in which we were to go to Cincinnati. Every minute we expected to go, but hour after hour passed away and still we did not move. To our questions the captain gave several reasons for the delay which seemed very vexatious to him. We endured the day, as hot as it was, by amusing ourselves with reading, writing, looking at the opposite shores, which we should have visited by means of the steam ferry boats which were crossing continually to Illinois town, had we not imagined we were soon to depart—and in watching the busy crowds upon the wharf, among whom was an old negro before an auction store attracting customers by ringing a bell instead of using a red flag as with us—but when night came, and we were obliged to pass it in our hot narrow berths, among mosquetoes which no net would keep off—listening to the noise and profane converse of the crew of the boats around, and imbibing the perfume of a dock, we became very much vexed and very impatient to be on our way.

July 15th— It was ten o'clock this morning before we started, and then discovered it was the arrival of a large party of St. Louis fashionables which had kept us stationary, and who, instead of coming as expected, chose to remain to attend a party that night.

We, who had been used to the punctuality of our eastern cities, where the captain stands, watch in hand, to give the signal for moving at the appointed moment, were extremely annoyed at such proceedings; but before we grumble too much it may be as well to look upon the other side of the question. The steamers upon these rivers make long voyages, and require much freight, and passengers, to pay their expenses.

From St. Louis to Cincinnati is eight-hundred miles, for which we were to pay twelve dollars each, and finding only a few passengers engaged, the captain waited for this party, hoping in the meanwhile, some of the upper steam-boats would arrive, and bring him some more freight, or passengers. The only thing we could reasonably complain of was his bad faith, if he had openly told us, the state of the case, we should have quietly remained in our hotel, awaiting his summons; instead of placing the delay to the broken machinery, some hands missing, provisions not arrived &c., off at last amidst the shouted adieu from the motley crew of Negro, French, Spaniard, and Yankee, which lined the guards of the long range of steam-boats, lying along the front of the city. There are one hundred and sixty steam-boats plying between this city and other ports. The city and its spires now fades away; and we station ourselves, in a favorable position for beholding this famous country. The Illinois shore is low, covered with forest, and is the rich part of the State, which was called by the Spaniards, American bottom, bottom land being the alluvion which is found upon the river shores between the water and the bluffs, and which is usually overflowed at high water. A feature peculiar to the county is, the land nearest the river is highest owing to the constant deposit, and when the water retires lakes are left along the low land, which gradually dry away. This bottom extends from the Kaskaskiah river to the mouth of the Missouri, two miles from Alton, eighty miles—and from one half to two miles in length to the bluffs which bound it, containing two hundred and eighty-eight thousand square acres. The soil is of inexhaustible fertility, averaging from twenty to twenty-five feet. Coal is abundant in this alluvion, and in the bluffs. This is carried to St. Louis in great quantities, over the railroad, to Illinois town. The Missouri side rises into high limestone bluffs, upon which is

built near the city, Jefferson barracks, a fine quadrangular building, containing fifteen hundred United States troops, and a few
miles farther Herculaneum, having at the edge of the cliff a high
shot tower. Near this tower is a bowlder of vermiculae limestone
fifty feet by three hundred. Through a cleft in the rocks comes
rushing down the clear bright Maramec. It takes rise among hills
covered with pine trees, so valuable in this region. Its banks are
rich with lead, iron and salt, and has formerly been a favorite
haunt of the Indian tribes from the quantity of pottery, bones, and
arrow heads found there. Behind these cliffs commences the celebrated lead region, where such quantities are exported. The min-
eral region of Missouri, Iowa, and Wisconsin, are stated by Dr.
Owen, the State geologist, to be capable of producing more of
this article than the whole of Europe. Missouri sends some to
China, and has exported this year, to that country, five hundred
pigs of lead, to be used for lining tea chests. The rocks appear
broken up in odd fantastic shapes, taking the name of devil's tea
table, backbone, oven, grand tower, etc. This last in a tall solitary
rock, about one hundred feet high, covered by a tuft of cedars, its
stratification as distinct as if it was a stone tower. The cornice
rocks are a ledge which runs along the top of the bluffs for nearly
ten miles. These rocks are said by geologists, to have been once
the barrier of a large lake or inland sea, over them poured another
niagara, which, wearing through them, caused their jagged appearance. When it burst through, it carried with it and deposited
that enormous mass of alluvion which extends an hundred miles
into the gulf of Mexico. The rock along this shore is mostly a blue
compact limestone, thought by Schoolcraft to be the muscle kalck
of the Germans; sometimes it occurs foetid. Near the city of St.
Louis, in this limestone, were found the impressions of two
human feet, as if the person had stood upon it while soft. The
impressions were perfect, and were not sculptured in the rock.
This slab was cut out and taken to New Harmony, upon the
Wabash.

    The scenery I am attempting to describe is very beautiful
and varied. The broad river, about a mile wide carries us rapidly
along from promontory to point, crowned by a village, ever showing us new beauties. The high wall at our right hand is not a mere
line of rocks, but supports the land which commences from their
summits, as if the river once flowing at that height had gradually

worn its way down. This, however is not the case, the deep bed having been scooped out by diluvial torrents. An amateur of geology at Alton, has another theory, and attributes the location and course of their rivers to fissures in the coal measures. One side of the fractured strata is raised and the other depressed, so that perpendicular rocks do not appear upon both sides of the rivers. Whether this be the cause of their direction I know not; but that the cliffs occur upon but one side of the stream, I observed upon the Illinois and Mississippi. St. Genevieve, which we passed this afternoon, is one of those old French towns, which were built during the sway of France over these fertile regions. We stopped at the landing where are a few houses, while the village is a short distance up the Gabouri creek, upon which it is built. We could see the steep slate roofed French houses, neatly white-washed; the court house and catholic church, whose cross glittered in the afternoon sun. Beside the river is a fertile portion of land which was allowed to the town by the Spaniards as *common land* upon which was raised the produce for town consumption. The town once stood here beside the Mississippi, but as the bank began to crumble away they removed farther inland. About thirty miles in the interior are the celebrated iron mountains, formed of micaceous iron ore. The pilot knob is three hundred and one feet high, with a base of a mile in circumference. The iron occurs here in masses of several tons weight. The other hill is three hundred and fifty feet high, both ores yeilding eighty per cent. Near the town is a quarry of fine white marble, and a deposite of dazzling white sand which is sent to Pittsburgh and sold to the glass factories. This is one of the ports from which the iron and lead is shipped.

Kaskaskia is another French town nearly opposite this place, but being built four miles up the Kaskaskia river, we could only see its landing. It was settled by La Salle in 1683, and was supported by the Indian fur trade, and afterwards by flour, exporting in 1746, eight hundred weight to New Orleans. There is here a catholic nunnery. The Kaskaskia river is a fine stream which runs into the Mississippi, a short distance above St. Genevieve upon the Illinois shore. It is four hundred miles long, but navigable not quite a hundred, owing to obstructions which could, with small expense, be cleared away. Some of the best land in the State is upon its banks.

Chester is a small town a few miles beyond it, seated at the foot of a high range of cliffs. Although small in appearance it carries on a brisk trade, its exports by steamboat being, in 1836, one hundred and fifty thousand dollars. Among other manufactories is one for making castor oil. Near this is fort Chartres, built by the French in 1720, to defend themselves against the Spaniards. It was a fine specimen of the style of Vaubon, and built in the most solid manner, but now lies in ruins, having large trees growing upon its prostrate walls.

At the mouth of Big Muddy river, forty miles below Kaskaskia, we stopped to take in wood, and we went on shore to take an evening stroll. The French named this stream *riviere au vase*, from a vase of earthen ware discoverd upon its banks. There is much good coal upon its shores. We wandered through the 'the forest's leafy labyrinth,' wondering at the great size, and luxuriant foliage of the trees. The locust here grows to the height of eighty or ninety feet; the beeches, oaks, and sycamores, are enormous. The parsimon grows larger here than with us. We also observed the Chickasaw plum, the pawpaw, and cotton tree. We seated ourselves upon the bank of the river, and looked upon it with wonder as it came rushing wildly past, much like a stream which has just plunged over some high ledge of rocks. Upon its bosom it bears a forest of trees, some old and water-worn, shorn of their honors, and some torn away in all the glory and beauty of their youth. The water comes with such velocity that it tears away the earth from one side of the river carrying it to the other, thus constantly changing the shape of the shores, and varies its channel so that the navigator is often puzzled to find his course.

I am glad I have looked upon the Mississippi. To read of it and to see it are two different things. All these wondrous works of the Creator give us clearer ideas of his power and his goodness. It is indeed an extraordinary sight—a river over three thousand miles long, and from a mile to one and a half miles wide, traversing eighteen degrees of latitude through various climates, from the arctic to the equator, over 'more degrees of latitude than any other river in the world.' Some writers call this river the Miss Sipi, 'father of waters,' while others tell us its name is Namaesi Sipu, Tish river. It flows from Itasca lake, a transparent cool reservoir of water, fifteen hundred feet above the gulf of Mexico, a clear beautiful stream; plunges over the falls of St. Anthony, and then, a broad river one mile and a half wide, it sweeps in long regular bends through a wide valley adorned with varied scenery, until it enters the gulf of Mexico. Sometimes it is lined with bluffs from one hundred to four hundred feet high, or a soft green prairie, sloping banks, impenetrable marshes, large cities, and pretty villages. The clay which the Missouri brings with it is heaped upon the shores, or in a pile at the bottom of the river, upon which a snag, a long trunk of a tree is flung, which, standing upright, pierces the bottoms of vessels; or as a sawyer, rises and falls, to strike the unfortunate bark which happens to pass over it. The danger from these is, however, much diminished by the ingenuity of Captain Henry M. Shreve, who has contrived a machine worked by steam, by means of which, when the water is low, he raises the snags and sawyers from the river. We were told he this year extracted fifteen hundred, besides tearing away from the banks many thousands which were 'topling to a fall.' It seems a hopeless task to pull away the hanging trees from the wooded shores of a river three thousand one hundred and sixty miles long, whose banks are constantly undermined by the waters; besides the Ohio which runs twelve hundred miles; and when these are cleared the mad Missouri coming down over three thousand miles through a forest clad country, continually sends down fresh victims which it has wrenched from their homes, to consign in all the 'pride of life' to destruction. As if not content with the mischief, the Mississippi sometimes takes a fancy to make a *cut off;* instead of following the curve or bend which it has made into the country for perhaps twenty miles, it dashes with fury against the earth in front until it cuts its way through and reaches its former channel, tearing away with it houses, lands, and whatever had stood in its path. This malicious conduct the Indians impute to its enmity to the white man, and fills up its channel, plants snags and sawyers to vex and to wreck him. The earthquake in the year 1811, the year in which Fulton launched the first boat upon the western waters, they say was caused by their Manitou, to frighten the white man away from his country. The earthquake was felt in many places slightly, but at New Madrid, upon the Mississippi, it was very severe. Houses and chimneys were thrown down; land raised for some distance down the river, and in many places it cracked apart vomiting up fire and red hot sand. Lakes were formed of miles in length which still remain. The introduction of steam is fast conquering all obstacles. Before its introduction three or four months were employed in voyages where now it is done in so many weeks. The flat-boat floated upon the tide, or pushed along with poles; and when a point was to be cleared the crew landed, and fastening ropes to the trees drew their bark along; this process was called *cordelling*. There are now upon these waters four hundred and thirty-seven steamboats, from thirty to seven hundred and eighty-five tons, besides flat and keel boats, but no sloops or sail boats, except an occasional sail put up by the keel boats. These boats are very different from those used upon our eastern waters. Our cabins and saloon you know are upon the same deck with the machinery, and dining rooms below, while above is a fine long promenade deck. When you enter one of these boats you step upon the lowest deck, having the machinery in the centre, while the ends are covered with freight, or deck passengers who cannot pay the cabin fare. Ascending a stair-way you find yourself upon the guards, a walk extending all around the boat like a narrow piazza, from which several doors open into the rooms. The whole deck here is thrown into three apartments; the ladies cabin at the stern having staterooms around it, opening upon the deck or into the cabin; from this folding doors lead into the dining-room surrounded with gentlemen's berths; beyond is the bar-room, from which you pass into an open space where, around two smoke pipes, the male passengers assemble to smoke and chat. The ladies cabin is handsomely furnished with every convenience, and in some instances with a piano. Above this is yet another deck called the hurricane deck. This is the best situation for viewing the scenery, were it not for the steam-pipe which, as these are high pressure boats, sends out the steam with a loud burst, like a person short of breath.

July 16th — I arose with the dawn, to obtain a peep at the junction of the Ohio with the Mississippi. We turned from the wide Mississippi and its turbid waters, into the glassy Ohio, around a point of land upon which is built the town of Cairo. The land is low here, and subject to inundations, but it is expected the art of man will overcome this, and Cairo, at the junction of these two great rivers, will become a large city. The central railroad is to commence here, which will cross Illinois to Galena, from thence to the Mississippi river, a distance of four hundred and fifty-seven and a half miles. There are several other towns upon, and near this point, as America, Unity, Trinity, and Fulton, where a statue to the great steamboat projector will be erected. A little farther on is another village, called Caledonia.

Our passengers consist of a party of fashionables, on a jaunt of pleasure to the Suphur Springs, of Virginia; some travelling merchants, and several persons visiting the towns upon the river. A state room was observed to be constantly closed, and a young man about twenty, who occasionally came from it, squeezed himself in, as if afraid his companion would be seen from without. The curiosity of the young ladies was soon excited, and by means of the chambermaid they ascertained it was the young man's wife, a young girl, apparently about fourteen, who was thus carefully secluded. A run-away match was immediately whispered about; the young people became quite in a fever to obtain a glimpse of the fair heroine. It was a long time ere their wish was gratified, as she never left her room, taking even her meals there. Our mornings on board are generally very social, the ladies sitting with the gentlemen of their party upon the guards, or gathering in groups with their work, while the male passengers are smoking, talking politics, or gambling. The negro banjo, and merry laugh, or joke, of some son of Erin, echoes up from the lower deck; but in the afternoon the siesta is the fashion, and every one turns in his berth to take a nap. I did not follow this custom, as I was unwilling to lose any of the scenery, so that I usually stole out of my state room, like a mouse from its hole, and after a long look up and down the river, stole in again, the heat being too great to allow of a long stay. Yesterday afternoon, oppressed with thirst and with heat, for the thermometer on board stood at ninety-six, I went into the ladies' cabin in search of water, a jar of which filled with lumps of ice, was placed upon a marble table in one corner of the cabin. The ladies were all in their berths except two, who were using every 'means and appliance,' to keep themselves cool. They were each in a rocking chair kept in motion, their feet upon an ottoman, [which] made a table for their books, while a large feather fan in one hand, and a lump of ice in another, were tolerable arms against the fire king. Miss Martineau expatiates upon the indifference of our females to the scenery of nature, and I dare say, she would place these two upon her list of nil admirari ladies, but travellers are very apt to look upon the surface of things; these ladies, and indeed almost all we meet in steamboats, have been so often over the scene, that they know it by heart, and need not brave heat and storms to see it, as a stranger would. Our people are a restless body, and men, women and children are always upon the move. As thirsty as I was, I hesitated to drink the thick muddy water, for while standing in our tumblers, a sediment is precipitated of half an inch. Oh how I longed for a draught of cool spring water, or a lump of Rockland lake ice! While drinking, one of the ladies advanced for the same purpose. 'Dear me! what insipid water!' she said, 'it has been standing too long. I like it right thick.' I looked at her in surprise. 'Do you prefer it muddy, to clear?' I asked. 'Certainly I do,' she replied, 'I like the sweet clayey taste, and when it settles it is insipid. Here Juno!' calling to the black chambermaid who was busy ironing, get me some water fresh out of the river, with the true Mississippi relish.' Every one's back is indeed fitted to his burden. This person had lived upon the banks of the Mississippi, had drank its waters all her days, and now it required to be muddy ere it was palateable. The chambermaid descended to the lower deck, where a gallant black beau drew a bucket from the river, and after satisfying the lady, she resumed her ironing. Against this practice of ironing in the ladies cabin I must uplift my voice. I suffered from this annoyance upon the Illinois, Mississippi and Ohio. Constantly there was a woman washing upon the lower deck, where the water thrown from the wheel, falls upon the deck in a pretty cascade, and another is ironing above. All the ironing of the boat, and crew, and often of the passengers, is done in the ladies small sitting room, the steam and perfume of the wet clothes, charcoal furnace and of the ironer is extremely disagreeable. In one instance I knew this to be the case all night, the girls taking it by turns; and I never travelled one day without this addition to the heat and other discomforts of a steamboat. In such long voyages it may be necessary to wash for the captain and crew, but surely bed and table linen enough might be provided to reach Cincinnati, where they stop long enough to have them washed. If not, why may there not be a room in some other part of the deck. The captain in some instances reaps the profits, as the chambermaids are his by hire or purchase, and if they charge all as they did us, one dollar and fifty cents a dozen, the profit must be considerable. It is sometimes, as in our case, a great convenience to travellers, but another place should be provided. But to go on with my afternoon adventures. I left the cabin and walked out upon the shady side of the guards. All was still except the booming steampipe; every one was asleep or reading. I leaned over the railing and found the banjo player and his audience all in slumbering attitudes, or swinging in their hammocks, and every thing denoted silence and repose. Suddenly a terrific and astounding bang, clang and clatter, as if the boat had been cracked to atoms, the wheel house was broken in pieces, the boards flew over me, and a torrent of water flowing from it nearly washed me from the deck. In a moment every one tumbled out and rushed upon the deck exclaiming, 'what's the matter?' 'are we snagged'—'had the boiler burst'—'is it a sawyer.' The old Kentucky lady who had stepped out first, took her pipe from her mouth and said quietly, 'It's only a log;' 'Oh, only a log;' 'nothing but a log,' echoed from every mouth, and returning to their cabins they all stepped into their berths again. I looked around me in amazement. 'Only a log!' said I to myself and what is a log. The steamboat is broken and stops, all is confusion and crash, and I am told it is nothing but a log. 'Madam,' said I, turning to the Kentucky woman, 'will you have the goodness to tell me what a log is.' 'There they are,' she said, pointing with her pipe to the river. Floating along like so many alligators, were long branchless trunks, which had been wafted along thousands of miles from the Rocky Mountains perhaps. 'But, pardon me madam, how are these logs able to create such a disturbance?' 'You seem a *stranger* child,' she replied; 'as these are floating along, and we are riding among them, what more natural than that they should get in the water wheel, break it, and stop the boat. But see, the carpenters are already at work, and I dare say they will have it repaired in the course of two or three hours.' So saying she knocked the ashes out of her pipe, took off her cap, and passed into her state room, to sleep away the hours we were doomed to pass under a July southern sun inactive. The most remarkable event connected with this accident, was the discovery of the fair unknown of the closed state-room. When the noise was first heard, the young man rushed out, bearing a plump rosy young girl in his arms who, as soon as he put her down, began to tell the beads of a long rosary which hung from her neck. One glance sufficed to tell him the nature of the accident, and he left her to walk towards the wheel house just as the

Kentucky lady disappeared. Seeing the poor thing's agitation, I turned towards her and endeavored to sooth her. 'I thank the Virgin Mary it is no worse,' she said kissing her cross, 'but something dreadful will come to punish my wickedness. Oh how could I leave my dear mother Abbess and the sisters!' Stopping suddenly she gazed around her in affright, for she had unconsciously said more than she intended. 'Oh dear, what am I saying!' she exclaimed 'where is Edward, why did he leave me!' I soon succeeded in soothing her, and when I related my conversation with the old woman, she laughed merrily at my ignorance. Her young husband returned, and was so delighted to see her cheerful, that he immediately drew chairs, we all sat down and were soon as social as old friends. I was much amused with the surprise of my companion who had come in search of me, when he saw me upon such familiar terms with this mysterious couple. The little creature seemed delighted to escape from her confined quarters, and relished a little chat so much that she this morning came to my room, and sat some time with me. . . .

At sun down we stopped to take in wood and to procure milk. As it was rather damp I did not land, but was much amused with the antics of men and boys, who delighted to have space, frolicked and jumped about the woods. The southerners in their thin pink and purple or blue striped coats, added to the gaiety of the scene. Our steward with his tin kettle entered a small cottage, or rather log cabin, near, and procured a supply of fresh milk, which we saw a young country lass draw from their cow she had just driven home. While our husbands strolled together, my little catholic confided to me her history, after the fashion of travelling heorines you know. She was the daughter of a wealthy planter in Kentucky, who, although of the presbyterian faith, had sent his child to a catholic nunnery to be educated. She had, as is very common in such cases, become a convert to the catholic faith, and when her parents came to carry her home, declared it her intention to take the veil and never leave her convent. Her parents intreaties and despair were of no use; stay she would, and did. A convent, however, was not to be her destiny, for she fell in love with a young gentleman, brother of a friend of her's at the same convent, who often came there to see his sister. The attachment being mutual, they had, with the assistance of the sister, contrived to elope. They were now on their way to New York, and she was so fearful of being recognized and brought back, that she would not at first leave her state-room. 'Were you not sorry to leave your mother?' I asked her. 'Oh dear yes, she and the sisters were always so kind to me.' 'I mean your mother and your father, not the mother abbess.' 'Alas! my parents are such sad heretics that I ought not to love them. I shall never see them in the next world, and it is better to be seperated here.' I wish to say nothing against the catholic religion, but if parents are unwilling their children should imbibe its tenets, they certainly do wrong to place them where they are taught. It is a custom too common in the west and south, and this is not the first instance I have known of division between parents and children in consequence. . . .

The heat drove me into the ladies' cabin, which being empty, I sat down to put down a few notes. I had scarcely seated myself, when the young catholic runaway, I mentioned before, rushed in, and throwing herself beside me, hid her head in my lap exclaiming, 'Oh, they are here, my mother, my father! they will separate me from Edward forever!' I looked towards the door with much anxiety, for I had heard the southern planters were a gouging, raw head and bloody bones sort of people, who whipped a slave to death once a week, and I feared for the fate of the poor young wife. My information however, had been taken from foreign tourists, and I found this idea like many others I had imbibed from them, was far from truth. Imagine my surprise, when a pleasant, good humored looking man entered the room, and seating himself in a chair, gave way to a hearty fit of laughter. His wife, a tall, slender, lady-like looking personage, walked directly up to her daughter, and folded her in her arms, while gentle tears flowed over her cheeks. I looked at the father in perplexity, wondering at this extraordinary merriment, and at Edward who stood beside him, having, I thought, a most unbecoming smirk upon his countenance. The lady looked up to her husband reproachfully, but said nothing. 'My dear madam,' he said at last to me, 'I understand you have taken a kind interest in my little girl's concerns, and I owe it to you to explain the circumstances of the case. Anxious to give my daughter the best of education, I sent her to a convent not far from my estate, where there were some very accomplished ladies from Europe, who could teach her all I wished her to know. But when I went to take her home, my lady fancied herself a catholic, and renounced her home and friends forever. I returned home in despair, and while revolving my future proceedings in this disagreeable affair, Edward, the son of a dear friend, who several years since had removed to New York came to make us a visit. In telling him my difficulties, I added how glad I should have been, had this not occurred, to give her and my plantation to him. 'I will scale the convent and carry her off,' he said, in a jest. The idea struck me as a good one, I pressed it upon him, and you see here they are, and have my hearty blessing.' The bride, as her father spoke, had gradually dried her tears, and raised her head a little. When she began to understand the denouement, she first blushed deeply with mortification, then pouted, and at last burst suddenly into a merry laugh, and ran like a fawn into her father's outspread arms, exclaiming, 'Oh, you naughty papa! you good for nothing papa!' The party soon after departed, and I received kind expressions and adieus from all, and a few tears from the bride.

DECK PASSAGE TO NATCHEZ, 1838

HENRY B. MILLER

[*Henry B. Miller from York County, Pennsylvania began keeping a journal in St. Louis on January 1, 1838. Described by his editor as having been at various times "a school teacher, plasterer, and builder of cemetery vaults," he was also an observant diarist. In October of that year he left St. Louis for Natchez as a deck passenger on the steamboat Alton. His journal was published in the* Missouri Historical Society Collections, *VI (1931), 213–87. The brief omissions are those of his editor, Thomas Maitland Marshall.*]

Sunday (October 14th) — Spent the week in making preparations for going down the river to the southern country to spend the winter there; this is very customary in the upper country; many of the mechanics emigrate from the Southern country in the spring & return again in the fall of the year. The distance is but 12 or 1500 miles which is brought near home by our steam boats; so much so that many of the young men here take the notion one day and are off the next and think no more of going to Vicksburg, Natchez, or New Orleans than we formerly did of going but 10 or 15 miles; so much difference do the present facilities of traveling have on us to what the former had. We prepared ourselves for travelling & made choice of the Steam Boat *Alton*, Capt Holland.

Sunday (October 21st) — Took our things aboard the boat in the morning; went back to the house and bade Farewell to my friends. After getting aboard and bidding Adieu to our Friends that accompanied us down to the river, we pushed off & soon lost sight of St. Louis. We took a deck passage. After making some of the necessary arraingments before hand, we fixed ourselves as well as we could. The boat was very much crowded & some contention amongst the passengers for the rights of the Bunks;

we, however, got ours. I travelled & messed with one young man (Mr. Pitman). We had laid up a good store of provision, Bread, Crakers, boiled Ham, Pies, Coffee, Tea, & Sugar, all in order & a Coffee Pot to make our Coffee & tea, & tin Cups to drink. Mr. Pitman was cook and had the dishes to wash, which by the way was easily done; we had each one of us a good Buffaloe Skin to lie on, which made a very comfortable bed. We had considerable sport in our new lodgings and would have passed along tolerable well had the boat not been so much crowded. Here, indeed, there was variety; the Deck passengers of the New Orleans Steamboats are generally the hardest kind of people, mostly of the lower or labouring class of people; in this respect they differ much from the Pittsburg Steam Boats; the deck passengers on them are generally emigrant families & sometimes very respectable, but on the Orleans boats things differ; much Dutch & Irish, & those too of the lowest kind, take passage down the river to the Southern country to spend the winter, and when the Germans have Tobacco & large Pipes (which they are always sure to have) and the Irish have whiskey (which they will alwas have as long as it lasts, which, however, is not very long). There are some of the greatest kind of times; the Germans sit and smoke their hugh pipes (rolling it out of their mouths like a house on fire) with the greatest gravity and apparent composure; give a German a Pipe about the size of a Teapot with a stem about three feet long, let him have his pipe well filled with tobacco & handsomely light up, and he will then appear to notice nothing more around him; of all smokers these appear to me to enjoy it the best. The Irish, when they get the whiskey in motion & themselves in order, are the very reverse; all is noise & agitation, tumult & disorder; nothing of composure and gravity, but the very reverse. We had several noisy times on the boat; there were several times that we had quarrels with some of them. It may be thought that this way of travelling is very disagreeable and that no respectable man would go into such a crowd unless compelled by necessity; this is not always the case; many of the mechanics travelling to the Southern country travel this way; there are generally several travel together, & as acquaintances are soon made aboard Steam Boats, they generally unite themselves to keep from being imposed on, and get along very well, with many amusing sights occasionally. Before we reached the mouth of the Ohio river, we came up with the Steam Boat

Romeo (for Orleans); she had been snagged and her hold filled with water; there were a great many passengers on her & some of the lowest kind. We took her passengers aboard & some little Freight by which time our boat was very much crowded.

At New Madrid we took on a number of Horses & Mules, which still crowded us more & which finally became rather disagreeable from the stench that they caused, which made our Irishmen make long complaints but to no purpose.

Sunday (*October 28th*) — We were still driving along as usual; had reached the mouth of Arkansas river. This river is very low at present, as well as White river, which is some distance above. The scenery is becoming more beautiful. Cotton Plantations are numerous on both sides of the river, many of which are very beautiful; they are mostly on the river bank; there is often a very fine house for the owner of the Plantation, surrounded with rows of China trees & a beautiful garden; the out houses are often of frame, weatherboarded, & well whitewashed, which gives the Plantations a very neat appearance. At a distance nothing can look more beautiful than a handsome Plant[ation] in the rays of the setting sun.

The Highlands are scarce after leaving the mouth of the Ohio. The rock bound shore whic[h] is very common from St. Louis down to near the mouth of the Ohio one side of the river, sometimes on the Eastern side but mostly on the Western or Missouri side, has entirely disappeared below the mouth of the Ohio. The only highlands or bluffs now seen are hills composed of sand or soil; some are midling high; about Randolph there are a number of these bluffs or sand hills which come up to the river which shows very bold banks here; we occasionally see such on down to Nat[c]hez. The country on the opposite side of the river is generally a level plain that frequently extends for miles back covered with timber; the timber land on the plains sometimes deceive the eye and make you immagine that there is a considerable rise back. The Alluvial deposits of the river are carried on in such a way by the shifting of its bed that there is a deposite made & covered with trees for a certain extent, which may remain so for some time untill the river makes farther depredations on the opposite shore and moves the bed over farther, when there is another deposite made & allowed to remain which is soon covered with trees of a smaller growth, by which means the larger trees will be so much higher that it will have the appearance of Highlands. These views are very common on the lower Mississippi and is sometimes the only change of surface we have & contributes much to the beauty of the scenery.

Another feature of the river (and one too that adds much to the beauty of the scenery) is its bends, of which there are many; the regularity of the curves is very beautiful; oftimes, after turning a point of land, we get a full view of them, or sometimes to better advantage when in the middle or concave part of the bend; we can see the shore gracefully sweeping round for miles, with all the regularity of being swept with a pair of Compasses, the concave side being high banks, while the opposite is generally a sand bar that keeps pace with the encroachments of the river on the opposite shore. These curves are sometimes more than half a circle in some places; where it would not be more than 2 miles the curve is from 8 to 10 miles round. The land has fell in more along the river this season than for the few last years; all along the river we see more or less; in some places there are Acres tumbling down; parts of Cotton fields, Negro houses on some of the Plantations, & some of the towns have not escaped. Vicksburg is materially injured, & Rodney has fared worse still; Natchez & New Orleans have even not escaped. The lowness of the river is assigned as the cause of these calamities; this Calamity will ever attend these places as they are all built on the concave side of the banks of the river where the ground is ever liable to be washed away. They are built on these sides of the river to have deep water; if they were built on the opposite side, there would be no danger of their washing away, as they would be more likely to be removed out into the country, as it would appear by the sand bar forming before them. True it may be many years before they are materially injured, but old Father Mississippi will do as he pleases.

We reached Natchez on Wensday; the day fine; took our things ashore, & put them in a place of safety, and then travelled round the city. Found things rather dull, but were fortunate enough to get into employment. Took a ride on the rail road out to Washington, a small village about 6 miles from Natchez in the latter part of the week; found it quite pleasant and agreeable.

THE LITTLE STEAMBOATS
OF THE MISSISSIPPI

T. B. THORPE

[*In this brief sketch Thomas Bangs Thorpe has preserved a glimpse of the little steamboats that served the backwaters of the Mississippi in the days "before the war," a glimpse that we do not get from other sources. It is from that rich mine of western materials,* The New York *Spirit of the* Times, *March 9, 1844, XIV, 19.*]

The steamboats of the Mississippi are as remarkable for size and form as is the river itself. Gigantic specimens of art, that go bellowing over the swift and muddy current like restless monsters, breathing like the whisperings of the hurricane, clanking and groaning as if an earthquake was preparing to astonish the world, obscuring in clouds of smoke the sun in the day time, or rolling over the darkness of night a volume of flame, as if the volcano had burst from the bosom of the deep. Who sees them for the first time, without wondering, as they rush along, filled with the ever busy throng of travellers, and loaded with boundless wealth, that teems from the rich soil, as the reward of the slight labor of the American husbandman. The Mississippi is also remarkable for little steamboats, small specimens of water craft, that are famous for their ambitious puffings, noisy Captains, gigantic placards, boats that "run up" little streams that empty into bayous, that empty into rivers, that empty into the Mississippi— boats that go beyond places ever dreamed of in geography, ever visited by travellers, or even marked down in the scrutinizing book of the tax collector. The first time I found myself on one of these boats I looked about me as did Gulliver when he got in Lilliput. It seemed as if I had got larger, and more magnificent than an animated colossal. When I walked on board of the boat, I found my feet on the lower deck and my head upstairs; the "after" cabin was so disposed of, that you could set inside of it and yet be near the "bows." The ladies' cabin had but one berth in it, and that was only as wide as a shelf. The machinery was tremendous, two large kettles firmly set in brick, attached to a complicated looking coffee mill, two little steam pipes, and one big one. And then, the way the big steam pipe would smoke, and the little ones let off steam was singular. Then the puffing of the little coffee mill! why, it worked spiteful as a tom cat with his tail caught in the crack of a door. Then the engineer, to see him open "the furnace" doors and pitch in wood; and open the little stop cocks to see if the steam was not too high, all so much like a big boat. Then the name of the boat, THE U. S. MAIL, *Emperor*, the letters covering over the whole side of the boat, so that it looked like a locomotive advertisement. Then the U. S. MAIL deposited in one corner of the cabin, and two rifles standing near it, as if to guard it, said mail being in a bag that looked like a gigantic shot pouch, fastened to a padlock, and said pouch filled with three political speeches, franked by M.C.'s, one letter to a man that did not live at the place of its destination, and a bundle of post-office documents put in by mistake.

The bell that rung for this boat's departure, was a tremendous bell; it swung to and fro awfully; it was big enough for a Cathedral, and as it rung for the twentieth last time, one passenger came on board weighing about three hundred, and the boat got under weigh. "Let go that hawser," shouted the Captain, in a voice of thunder. Pe, wee, wee, pish-h-h, went the little steam pipe, and we were off. Our track lay for a time down the Mississippi, and we went ahead furiously, overhauled two rafts and a flat-boat within two hours, and resented the appearance of a real big steamer most valiantly, by nearly shaking to pieces in its waves. Being light myself I got along very well, but whenever the fat passenger got off of a line with the centre of the cabin, the pilot would give the bell *one tap*, and the Captain would bawl out "trim the boat." Dinner came on, and the table was covered with the biggest roast beef, the biggest potatoes, and the biggest carving knife and fork that ever floated, and the steward rung the biggest bell for dinner, and longer than any other steward, and the Captain talked about the immense extent of the Mississippi, the contemplated canal through the isthmus of Darien, and the ability of steam war ships; he said that in the contemplation of the subject "his feelings were propelled by five hundred horse power, that the bows of his imagination cut through the muddy waters of reality, that the practicability of his notions were as certain as a rudder in giving the proper direction, that his judgment, like a safety valve to his mind, would always keep him from advocating any thing that would ever burst up, and and that it was unfortunate that Robert Fulton had not lived to be president of the United States." With such enlarged ideas he wiled away the hour of dinner; arrived at the mouth of "dry outlet," (a little gutter, that draws off some of the water of the Mississippi when very high) turned the bows of the *Emperor* into its mouth, and shot down it along with an empty flour barrel, with an alacrity that sent the bows of the boat high and dry on the land, the first bend it came to. A great deal of hard work "got us off," and away we went again, at one time sideways, at another every way, hitting against the soft alluvial banks, or brushing our pipes among the branches of overhanging trees. Finally the current got too strong, and carried us ahead with alarming velocity; the bows of the boat was turned in the opposite direction from what we were going, and thus managed to keep an onward progress compatible with our safety. The banks of the "dry outlet," were very low, very swampy, and were disfigured occasionally with wretched cabins, in which lived human beings, who, the captain of the *Emperor* informed me, lived, as far as he could judge, by sitting on the heads of barrels and looking out on the landscape, and at his boat as it passed; from the fact that they had no cultivatable land, and looked like creatures fed on unhealthy air, we presume that was their only occupation.

In time we arrived at the "small village," the destination of the "mail pouch," and landing, visited the town. It was one of the ruins of a great city, conceived of by land speculators in "glory times." Several splendid mansions were decaying about, in the half finished frames that were strewn upon the ground. A barrel of whiskey was rolled ashore, the mail delivered, the fat man got out, and we departed. The "dry outlet" merged itself into a broad inland lake, that itself, as a peculiarity of the tributaries of the Mississippi emptied into that river. Our little boat plunged on, keeping up with untiring consistency all its original pretension and puffing, and the same clanking of tiny machinery, scaring the wild ducks and geese, and scattering the white cranes over our heads, and making the cormorant screech with astonishment in hoarser tones than the engine itself. Occasionally we would land at "a squatter's settlement," turn round and come up to the banks with grandeur, astonishing the squatter's children and two very invalid hens that lived in the front yard. The captain would pay up the bill for wood, and off he would go again as "big as all outdoors," and a great deal more natural. Thus we struggled on, until sailing up a stream with incessant labor such as we went down when we commenced our sketch, we merged into the world of water that flows in the Mississippi. Down the rapid current we gracefully went, the very astonishment of the regular inhabitants on its banks.

Again for the "innumerable time," the "furnaces" consumed the wood, and as it had to be replenished, we ran alongside one of those immense woodyards, so peculiar to the Mississippi, where lay in one continuous pile thousands of cords of wood. The captain of the "Emperor," as he stopped his boat before it, hallowed out from his "upper deck," in a voice of the loudest kind—

"Got any wood here?"

Now the owner, who was a very rich man, and a very surly one, looked on the "heap," and said "he thought it possible."

"Then," said the captain, "how do you sell it a cord?"

The wood-man eyed the boat, and its crew, and its passengers, and then said "he would not sell *the boat* any wood, but that the crew might come ashore, and get their hats full of chips for nothing."

Hereupon the five hundred horse power of the captain's feelings, the rudder and the safety-valves of his well-regulated mind became surcharged with wrath, and he vented forth abuse on the wood-yard and its owner, that were expressive of "thoughts that breathe, and words that burn." A distant large boat, breasting the current like a thing of life, gave me a hint, and rushing ashore amid the shot, we bid the "Emperor" and its enlarged captain a hearty and great good-bye, and in a few moments we dwindled into mere insects on board of the magnificent ———— the pride and wonder of the western waters.

Concordia, La., Feb., 1844.   **T.B.T.**

CONCERNING THE CONDUCT
OF THE CAPTAIN OF THE *Casket*

―――――――

[*Some of the tribulations of steamboat travel are summed up
in the following account of the voyage of the* Casket *from
Louisville to St. Louis in October, 1837, as related in the
"Table Talk" section of the* North American Quarterly Re-
view *for March, 1838, IX, 187–92. The author was almost
certainly Sumner Lincoln Fairchild, a minor poet and editor
of that periodical. The original charges against the captain
were published in the St. Louis* Missouri Republican *on October 24, 1837; a "true" statement of facts, made in re-
joinder by friends of Captain Hamilton, appeared in the next
day's issue of that paper and was repeated on the following
day.*]

The waters of the beautiful Ohio had subsided when we left
Louisville for St. Louis; therefore, the steamboat groaned and
jarred on the sandbars day after day, while the numerous passengers, half famished through the tedious delay, *amused* themselves
by turning the everlasting windlass, or playing games in which
they felt no interest, or scolding one another for being discontent,
or sleeping away the hours, or darting in skiffs and canoes over
the transparent waters of La Belle Riviere. It was a picturesque
though a vexatious scene; eighteen steamboats, at one time,
jammed and interlocked, were struggling over the bar. Thousands of bales of cotton, attached by cords, were floating hither
and thither, or lay, half buried, among the falling masses of the
bluff. The captain looked on with exemplary resignation, while
the mate looked around with the eye of a tyrant, and the sailors
shouted and cheered, and some cried, 'she moves,' and others said
'No.' But, after all their struggles and toils, there the steamboat
lay.

At last, after many honest and exhausting endeavours, we
effected our liberation, and floated again on the blue waters. But

still another day was consumed in the restoration of the soaked
and trampled cotton bags. Soiled, torn and filthy, they resembled
a loafer after a night's debauch, or a midnight thief creeping forth
from a sewer. But, after many an hour's severe toil, and many a
perilous leap by the mate from one fluctuating mass to another—
the ejected cargo was at last recovered; and on we went, with a
puff, roar and quiver, down the beautiful tributary of the terrific
Mississippi. All things will have an end; we arrived at Paducah, a
little, unfinished, backwoods village, about sixty miles from the
mouth of the Ohio. Here we passed a miserable night on planks
fresh from the sawmill, and battled heroically for national right,
with musquetoes, bugs and vermin of all names. At daylight, we
were awakened by a forester's outcry, that a boat was departing
for St. Louis: he said it was the *Spectre*, and our nerves quivered
at the announcement of its omenous name—but it was the *Casket*, though few were the gems it ever contained. Clambering over
the obstructions of two or three other boats, at last we reached the
deck of this illfated steamer, and for the first time, beheld its
profligate and evilhearted commander. Scarcely had we arrived in
the cabin, impatient and irritable from our comfortless lodgings,
ere a gentleman, who had been on board from Cincinnati, inquired anxiously whether we had not taken passage on the wrong
boat. "It will go to St. Louis?" we asked. "Yes, Sir, certainly, but"
—"That is all we require," was the quick reply; and we passed on
to watch the arrangement of our luggage. That being adjusted,
we walked into the gentlemen's cabin, and, finding the person
who had volunteered his services to instruct us, inquired what he
meant to imply by the significant warning he had given. "Why,
Sir," said he, "the captain of the *Casket* is a bad man—a gambler, a desperate braggart, who respects no laws but his own will,
and swindles his passengers, after abusing their best feelings, as
it may suit the humour of a moment." "In a word," subjoined a
grave personage sitting by the side of the speaker, (it afterwards
appeared that he was the Rev. Mr. Selleck, leaving Connecticut to
settle at Alton in Illinois,) "in a word, Sir, this Captain Hamilton
is no better than a *pirate*!" Struck by the force of his expression,
we deeply regretted the necessity of travelling, with such a man,
up the rapid, eddying, dismal and dangerous waters of the Mississippi. But, at this moment, the boat began to move, and we
resigned ourselves to the trials that might occur. These speedily
commenced. Our child, seven years old, was charged the full

price of an adult; and to all remonstrances, whether of man or woman, Hamilton refused to listen. The money was paid, a receipt demanded, and the imposture threatened to be exposed. From that time forth we travelled prepared for any rencontre which the villainy of Hamilton might produce. No conflict, however, occurred; the piratical captain knew and felt that his own life would be sacrificed to the general indignation, if he assailed one passenger on board; and, therefore, though with infinite flourishes and cowardly threats among his crew and clique of gamblers, he forebore to implicate his own life, or attempt to take that of another, except in the particular instance mentioned below, under the sixth charge against him. But, meanwhile, our situation, and that of all on board of the *Casket*, was most painful. Nothing, we believe, would have prevented this desperado from destroying both steamboat and passengers, except the dread of liability to the owners of the vessel; and even with this fear hanging over him, he might have disabled his engineer, as he had injured his mate, if some of the passengers had not been ever vigilant, and thereby possessed the power to impute the destruction of the boat to accident, not design—a nefarious stratagem often practised on the western waters.

Under circumstances of excitement and apprehension, we continued our ascent of the tumultuous and terrible Mississippi; and, at last, beheld the lofty domes of St. Louis with a high degree of pleasure and delight. Our design to expose the infamous mismanagement and outrage of Hamilton, was known to him during two days before we left the boat; and it was thought probable by some of the passengers, that he might attempt to maltreat and maim, if not to kill, us on landing at the city of our destination. Many persons, however, were around us, and as bravoes are always cowards, Hamilton was invisible when we departed from the *Casket*—never to see it again.

On the morning following our arrival in St. Louis, the subsequent article was published in the Republican newspaper of that beautiful and prosperous city:

To the Public

We, passengers on board of the steamboat *Casket*, from Cincinnati to St. Louis, being justly aggrieved by the conduct of **THOMAS S. HAMILTON**, captain of said boat, and the allowed insolence and neglect of his crew, do hereby adopt and sign the following resolutions, with feelings of deep disgust and indignation, viz:

1. That Capt. Hamilton not only permits, but authorizes games of hazard, (in which he himself joins to the neglect of his duty as commander,) that continue until very late at night—contrary, not only to the rules and regulations of all western boats, but, also, to good manners and morality.

2. That, in respect to some unprotected and unprovided passengers, he has manifested a wanton and cruel disposition—having, arbitrarily, fined several persons who did not *instantly* attend his summons, when on shore, (the passengers being, at the moment, in the immediate vicinity of the boat,) and having, after inhuman abuse of an unprotected lady, landed her on the river shore—contrary, both to his duty as a public carrier, and to her rights as a passenger.

3. That, in his price of passage, he varies as he finds occasion—— the fixed rates of transportation being subject to his own will and pleasure—which are frequently expressed in the most insolent and unmannerly language.

4. That the provisions, which have been furnished on board the boat, have been of the most insufficient and disgusting nature —(such as even the captain himself would seldom partake) though an abundance of the best quality could have been readily procured at many places on the river. The best provision would have been but a fair compensation for the exorbitant charges of the voyage.

5. That we believe our lives to have been in peril through the misconduct of said Hamilton, who has frequently violated the sacredness of female feeling and flagrantly insulted the honour of men.

6. That, on the night of the 21st instant, the second steward of the *Casket* (whether actuated or not, by others in authority on board of the boat, we shall not determine,) did place himself on a pallet in front of a lady's stateroom, with a musket or rifle by his bedside—and that when many passengers had been alarmed by such unprecedented conduct, the said Hamilton severely flogged the said second steward, and discharged him in the night—which act, we believe, was intended to disguise his own evil designs and intentions.

Believing, therefore, that the rapacity and recklessness, and profanity of Capt. Hamilton, demand the expression of our extreme displeasure, disgust and reprobation, we, individually, subscribe our names.

Mrs. Ellender Gressman, Mrs. Harriet Gage,
Mrs. Anna Holmes, Mrs. Melinda L. Mills,
Mrs. Elizabeth Camdel, Mrs. S. Lincoln Fairfield,
Mrs. Ann M. Hallett, Mrs. Selleck, James Hallett, late
of Philadelphia; Sumner Lincoln Fairfield,
Baltimore, Md.; Wm. P. Richards, Macomb, Ill.;
Rev. C. G. Selleck, Ridgefield, Ct; Wm. H. Bradley,
New Haven, Ct; B. Smith, Ridgefield, Ct; C. Pitcher,
St. Louis; J. E. Douglass, Peoria; C. Comstock,
Quincy, Ill.; D. Comstock, St. Louis; D. Robinson,
Wisconsin; M. Robinson, Wisconsin; W. C. French,
Chester, Ill.; John Corcoran, Samuel Smith, St. Louis;
George Barry, Boston, Mass.; A. Gressman,
H. T. Burrill; D. Hardon, O. A. Gage, C. C. Bibbee,
Chancey Ehler, James Campbell, Jacob P. Perby,
William Allen, New Richmond, Ohio; James S. Bradley,
Ridgefield, Ct.

Mr and Mrs Smith, of Nashville, Tenn.; Mr and Mrs Sargeant, of Mississippi, and Mr and Mrs Dunbar, of Evansville, Indiana, having left the *Casket* at an early period, authorized the insertion of their names to a statement similar to the above.

This statement produced discussion, displeasure and excitement, which Hamilton in vain attempted to allay by publishing, on the next day, a reply that was everywhere received with contempt.

Under these circumstances, the vindictive passions of Hamilton broke forth. From the condition of a common steamboat workman he had become a steward, and from that station he leapt, at once, into the berth of a captain. What but impudence and profligacy could be imagined to exist in such a character? What but gross despotism, vulgar assumption, the bravado of a fool, and the recklessness of a villain? Such persons abound on the western waters. Born in the lowest condition, without education or manners, principle or humanity—many there command when they should obey, and peril limb and life, when they should be woodcutters amid the marshes of the Mississippi. We shall declare our sentiments on this subject, more at length, hereafter. We hope the bill before Congress, however, will supercede the necessity, henceforth, for any such remarks as it is our duty to utter.

The consequence of our advertisement was a prosecution for libel. At about nine o'clock in the evening, we sat reading in the private parlour of the National Hotel—a most excellent house, conducted by *gentlemen*—wife and child had retired, and we were absorbed in a novel of interest, when Mr Brotherton, the Sheriff of St Louis, was announced. Like many other meddling people, he began, in a maudlin mood, to talk about the weather, etc., when we interrupted his preliminary by requiring to know his business. It was an indictment demanding $1000 security, and $3000 damages. After examining the voluminous enumeration of offences, we requested Brotherton to remain until a counsellor could arrive; and, he having assented, a servant was despatched for a lawyer. Briefly, after the absence of the domestic, the drunken sheriff exhibited symptoms of impatience, and said he would wait no longer. We asked him to take wine, but he wanted brandy; and, in defiance of our quiet remonstrances, began to pull us by the arm and require us to go with him. "With you?" we said, "without counsel, for whom you consented to wait." "Yes," he hoarsely cried, staggering as he arose, "you shall go now." "Mr Brotherton," we replied, "why will you not wait for our counsel—he will be here soon." "No, I won't wait—come along— come!" "What, without boots or hat—bareheaded, and in slippers? Is this the way you conduct business?" Still, in his stupid mood, he continued to reply to everything said. "Come, come along," at the same time pulling us by the arm. Wearied, at last, and indignant, we said, "allow us to get our boots and hat, and we will go with you." "No, no," he would not. "Well, then," we replied, "since you are resolved to depart from everything accordant with common judgment and public decency, we are determined to abide by our own conviction of what is just and right; we are resolved to maintain our integrity as an American citizen, and vindicate ourself against all kinds of oppression." "Hush, now," drawled the sheriff; "do not let us excite remarks or attention."

"Whatever be the remarks, we care not, since they will be

just, and on justice we rely." "Stop, now—come along," was the
answer, as again he exercised a constable's dominion. "No!" we
replied, "that we shall never do. We stand upon our right as an
American Citizen, and will not be treated like a defaulter or a
felon; and we ask every citizen of the United States, within the
sound of our voice, to reply to our appeal." Fifty gentlemen,
chiefly merchants of St Louis, rushed into the room. Great confusion ensued. We were strangers, and, of course, little acquainted
with the disposition or character of the persons with whom it was
our destiny to deal. But, amid the distraction of a sudden occurrence, we endeavoured to explain why and wherefore we were
held in durance. Half an hour was wasted, amidst multitudinous
discussion—noise—uproar, and all possible disturbance, ere an
explanation was given. But, when the gentlemen comprehended,
as we endeavoured to develope the causes of the present affair,
they were quickly convinced that wrong had been perpetrated,
and that we were sufferers from injuries inflicted by those who
should have been the first to abstain from outrage. Ten of them,
therefore, came forward to offer their bond for our appearance, on
the next morning, at the court house; but Brotherton refused the
proposition. We rejoice that he did; we are glad to know that
great hearts and high feelings abound even while vulgar passions
and lowminded despotism pervade the land. In our estimation,
humanity is exalted and ennobled by such manifestations of mind
and feeling, as we witnessed in St Louis. A stranger, who had
fulfilled his duty to the utmost, was exposed to great charge and
peril because a villain was his antagonist. This villainy was defeated, and truth is triumphant.

When Brotherton refused the bond of ten opulent merchants, the indignation was universal. "The gentleman is
wronged!" was the cry, "or *our* pledge would be sufficient. We
and our city are dishonoured by the iniquitous conduct both of
this captain and the sheriff. We will not permit it to continue: if
law is lawless, or administered by those unqualified to fulfil its
offices, the time has arrived when we should create a law unto
ourselves. Come, gentlemen," said Mr. Dalzell Smith, one of the
first merchants in Missouri, "let our duty be discharged; appoint
a teller; I am certain that not a gentleman here will retire until
this business is finished. We will pay the money required; neither
female affection, nor the emotion of a child, nor the honour of a

man, shall be insulted and outraged by such behaviour as this."
Every gentleman present accorded in opinion and a thousand
dollars, as the security of a stranger, were delivered to the sheriff.
The names of the gentlemen, with the sums attached, appear.

Henry Root, ...	$ 100 00
O. H. Wright, ...	90 00
Mr Fairfield, ...	140 00
John Banchor, ...	100 00
E. H. Watson, ...	70 00
Thomas W. Gibson, ...	100 00
John J. Anderson, ...	100 00
Dalzel Smith, ...	100 00
Stickney & Knight, ...	50 00
E. W. Bronson, ...	100 00
J. W. Davis, ...	50 00
	$1000 00

Speedily after this unprecedented manifestation of true
greatness and liberality, the sheriff departed, not without feeling
the effects of excited opinion. On his departure, the gentlemen
resolved that what had been done was insufficient; that the affair
should be investigated, and all its bearings well understood. Accordingly, about fifty persons assembled again in the parlour,
appointed a chairman, secretary and committee of examination,
and proceeded, at once, to business. It was, now, past midnight,
but the late hour did not deter the high-hearted people of the
West from the inquisition which was demanded. After a deliberate and strict examination of the witnesses who had been fellow-
passengers on board of the *Casket*, but who, as the reader will
perceive, had not signed the alleged libel, the committee reported
the following opinion, which was ordered to be printed and posted
on the corners of the streets of St Louis before 8 o'clock in the
morning. It was nearly 2 o'clock, A. M. before the assembly
dissolved, but the subsequent placard appeared as directed, both
in time and place, and awakened universal excitement.

Meeting.

At a meeting of the boarders of the National Hotel, Tuesday evening, Oct. 24th, Dr. Van Zandt was called to the Chair, and John Banchor appointed Secretary.

Resolved, That a committee of five be appointed, to make inquiries relative to the publication which appeared in the Missouri Republican of this morning, concerning the conduct of the Captain of the *Casket*.

The committee consisted of Messrs Walton, Burnett, Bronson, Wright and Knight.

The committee report that they have full confidence in the statement made by the passengers on board the steamboat *Casket*, and that Mr Fairfield, one of the passengers, has been arrested for a libel, by the Captain; we feel satisfied that he has been deeply injured, and call upon the citizens of St Louis to protect a stranger who has been most infamously abused.

An investigation will be held to-morrow, Wednesday, Oct. 25th, at 10 o'clock, A. M., at the Court House. All passengers on board the said steamboat, and those who feel an interest therein, are requested to give their attendance.

Resolved, That the proceedings of this meeting be signed by the Chairman and Secretary.

Wm Van Zandt, *Chairman.*

John Banchor, *Secretary.*

Tuesday evening, Oct. 24th.

All who desire to know and feel the intensely excitable and hightoned character of our western citizens, should have beheld the procession which accompanied us to the Court House, and have heard the indignant thoughts declared. There the money was redelivered to the contributors, and again we were a prisoner; but Brotherton, knowing he had already gone too far, dared not to appear. The Court was not in session, therefore, it was necessary to determine the case at the office of the Judge, distant half a mile, on the most busy and public street in St Louis. Again the procession moved on—the Sheriff's deputy being among the crowd, but not daring to approach us who walked with our counsel. The office of the judge was speedily filled, and overflowed—not even standing-room being allowed. The quietness of deep feeling pervaded the assemblage, while our legal adviser briefly stated the defects of the indictment, and the injustice of our accuser. The plaintiff, neither by person or attorney, was present, although he had secured the services of two lawyers at great expense.

The quick result of Mr Gamble's argument, was our acquittal and discharge. Then the hurried departure of the multitude, and the cry "now for the boat!" speedily acquainted us with what was intended. We returned to the hotel, and heard Mr Banchor's report in the evening. Four or five hundred citizens descended the bluff, and, through a committee, ordered Hamilton to leave the port of St. Louis within three hours, or to await the consequences of a refusal. In consistency with his character, he distributed anathemas and blasphemies abundantly—protesting that he would not go; but, notwithstanding, cast off his lines, and departed ere the hour that was limited. Fear was wisdom in this instance, for hundreds of resolute people were awaiting his resolve. The owner of the boat anticipated the consequences of such iniquitous conduct, and ordered Hamilton to leave without passengers or cargo. Before his departure, however, he procured a second indictment against us, which was despatched as speedily as the first, and, our business being concluded, on we went to Illinois.

We have told our story, Reader, and hope it may amuse *you*, though the action of it was no amusement to us. It displays the character of a liberal, proud and magnanimous people; it exhibits the paramount dominance of Public Opinion, which is superior to all legislative enactments—especially in our western confederacies; and it exalts the idea of our common humanity. We *should* live to aid each other—to be a succour in the hour of trial, and a refuge in disaster and peril. Yet how often we desert or are deserted! Had not St Louis arisen, as one man, to espouse our cause, ruin would have been the reward of our public duty. Under any circumstances, the conviction that what was just and right, had been fulfilled, might have solaced our dreary solitude, as it has done that of many a martyr and patriot in old times. But, not the less, are we bound ever to remember and honour the inhabitants of that far distant city, which, destined to become one of the greatest on this continent, already is one of the most enterprising, opulent, and magnanimous.

[*Missouri Republican*, October 25, 1837]

To the Public.

Having seen a publication in to-days paper, in which Captain Hamilton of the steam boat *Casket*, is unjustly accused of several heinous offences which I know he is entirely innocent of, I have taken the trouble of laying the true statements of facts before the public.

1ˢᵗ   That Captain Hamilton permitted games of cards on his boat. This is true, and so do all the boats running the river, providing they do not play in the cabin after the passengers have retired to rest, this was not the case, there was no playing in the cabin for money from the time she left Cincinnati till she arrived in St. Louis.

2ⁿᵈ   That in respect to some unprovided and unprotected passengers, he has manifested a wanton and cruel disposition, having arbitrarily fined several persons who did not instan[t]ly attend his summons, he did fine one I believe, having warned him that he could not stop for him every time the boat landed, longer than it would take to complete her wooding, but he paid no attention whatever to the advices, but gave him the trouble of stopping his boat for him twice, once at Evansville, and once at French Island, also, that after having inhumanly abused an unprotected lady, that he put her ashore; as for captain H. having any lady put on shore, that is altogether incorrect. The statement of the case is as follows: One Mrs.—— came on board of the boat and took passage for Louisville, perhaps she would go to St. Louis, but after the starting of the boat, it was found, all the berths were taken, the lady was perfectly satisfied to take a berth on the floor, but in the night, some man who pretended to be a gentleman, asked the captain if he could not procure a state room for two Missouri ladies of his acquanitance, the captain told him he could if they or he would settle the fare and secure the room, he said he would do so, but we saw nothing of him or lady until just before he got off the boat at Madison Indiana; and when capt. H. made inquiry about the state room, Mrs.—— said she knew nothing about the gentleman that got her the state room. Captain H. then told her she could go no farther than Louisville on his boat, and this is the only case of any lady leaving the boat.

3ʳᵈ "That in his price of passage, he varies as he finds occasion." This is untrue—there was but one instance of this kind on board. Mr. Fairfield and Lady came on board at Paduca, and asked the price to St. Louis—they were told ten dollars, they then asked how much it would be for their servant—the Captain told them it would be full price, if she occupied a seat at the first table. The servant proved to be the daughter of the Gentleman and Lady, and they were charged full price.

4ᵗʰ "That the provisions which have been furnished on board the boat have been of the most insufficient and disgusting nature, such as even the Captain would not partake of," is untrue. Having about a hundred passengers on board and getting aground at French Island, it was found no easy matter to procure provisions but the best that could be got was furnished. And the reason the Captain did not always attend the table, was, he was trying to get the boat off the bar.

Henry D. Johnson,	Wm. C. Stevenson,
James Gabien,	Ruben Keyes, St. Louis;
Charles King,	C. R. McFall,
James C. MacDonald,	W. W. Andrews,
Wm. K. Taylor,	F. M. Gleim.

STATE OF MISSOURI, *County of St. Louis.*

THIS day personally appeared before me, Elihu H. Shepard, a Justice of the Peace, within and for the county of St. Louis, Henry Johnson, F. M. Gleim, Charles McFall, Robert Keyes, who being duly sworn on their oaths, say, that the foregoing statement, to which they have subscribed their names, is true.

Sworn to before me this 24th day of October, A.D. 1837.

Elihu H. Shepard, Justice.

STEAMBOAT MANNERS

M. DE GRANDFORT

[*Madame de Grandfort did not have a higher opinion of
manners aboard a Mississippi steamboat than many other
travelers. The extracts here are drawn from her little book*
The New World *as translated from the French by Edward C. Wharton* (New Orleans, 1855), *pp. 77–78,
79–81.*]

There were about three hundred passengers on board. Some
passed the day asleep in their state-rooms; others conversing, that
is, talking very loudly, in the cabin; the majority seated in a circle
on the front guard of the boat, smoked in silence, or cut up pieces
of wood, assuming the while the most singular attitudes. It is a
mania with the Americans, when they talk or walk or are waiting
for some one or some thing, to "whittle." Provided with a large or
a small knife, they lay hands on the first bit of stray wood that
falls in their way, or the branch of a tree, or a cane, or an
umbrella left in a corner. If they are deprived of these, they attack
the furniture; they pitilessly cut into counters, window sills,
doors, chairs, sofas, billiard tables, church pews; in fact, nothing
nothing is sacred against their knife-blades. The railings of the
guards on certain boats on the Mississippi have been transformed
into gigantic saws by this Yankee process. I have often seen, on
steamboats on the Ohio, gentlemen vigorously whittling away the
arms of the chairs they were seated on, beneath the eyes of the
Captain himself. This fashion is so general in the United States,
that the desks of almost all the State Legis[la]tures, and even of
Congress itself, are, during the sessions, provided each morning
by the pages or clerks, with small pieces of "whittling" wood for
the use of the members. The occupation is a sensible one, and
must greatly develop the intellectual faculties of the Senators and
Representatives. Were I a French ministerial journalist I would

strongly advocate the adoption by the two Chambers of this
method of amusement. The independent as well as the satisfied
members would whittle wood during the entire session, and the
opposition would thus be entirely suppressed.

But it is the attitudes of the Americans that merit special
study. I have rarely seen one whose position, when he was seated,
was not a miracle of equilibrium and imagination. Generally they
place their feet on a mantle-piece, or against a stove-pipe, or a
wall, or a post, but always so that the feet are more elevated than
the head. On the steamboat I was travelling on, I one day heard
the sounds of a piano. They came from the ladies' cabin. Some of
the passengers walked thither; I followed their example. They
took seats in the cabin, and with loud discordant voices, joined in
the national air that an *adorable* young lady of thirty-two years,
was playing. Four of these gentlemen seated themselves around a
slender pillar, in the middle of the cabin, supporting the ceiling.
Their feet were gathered in a bunch around this pillar at so great
a height, that the only portions of their bodies resting in the
chairs were their heads and their backs. A fifth, seated in front of
the musician, majestically displayed his legs on the piano itself,
appearing thus to make the lady an offer of his boots; a sixth had
taken possession of a sofa, whilst several ladies, not finding seats,
were standing, grouped around the player; a seventh had climbed
upon his chair, and was seated on the back of it, tilted against the
partition; and to conclude, an eighth, having sought in vain for a
place for his feet, ended by putting them on the shoulders of the
gentlemen seated near the piano. That person received the compliment gracefully and smilingly. When the song was over, these
amateurs applauded, by *whistling* and giving utterance to loud
cries. The one perched on the chair, carried away by enthusiasm,
and forgetting that his position did not allow him much freedom
of movement, applauded by clapping his hands. He lost his equilibrium, and falling on the corner of another chair, came near
putting out an eye. Notwithstanding, ten minutes after, I saw him
seated in a position more dangerous and incredible than before.

We stopped at Memphis, and a crowd of the inhabitants
came on board and took possession of our "bar," while, on the
other hand, almost all my fellow passengers went ashore to visit
the "bars" there. On shore, as on "board," a new drinking place
possesses irresistible attractions for the Americans who, never fail

to gather there and pay each other the usual courtesies. Fortunate are the "bars" that happen to be in the neighborhood of these followers of Tantalus, with throats as deep as they are fiery! . . .

We resumed our trip up the river. Hardly had we lost sight of Memphis, when we saw, about two miles ahead, a steamboat that had just finished taking in a supply of wood, and was bound, like us, for St. Louis. It was five o'clock in the afternoon; the Captain had reached at least his eighth "drink" for the day. He threw out a signal and determined on having a race. The boat ahead answered by another signal, which meant that our challenge was accepted. Immediately our Captain called up the engineers, and ordered them to "fire up" as much and as speedily as possible. Our steamer, like most of those on the Mississippi, was a high-pressure boat. The furnaces were crammed full of combustibles, in order to raise the hottest fire; oil, turpentine and even barrels of tar were thrown in. Far from being alarmed, the passengers were running below every moment and calling out to the crew: "Fire up! fire up! that *rascal* must not show his stern any longer!" One of the passengers however, frightened at the jerks of the boat and loud hissing of the steam, went to the Captain, saying:

"Sir, I have on board with me five young men from different schools in New Orleans. I have undertaken to bring them back in safety to their homes; I am responsible for their lives. In the name of Heaven! give up a struggle that nothing obliged you to commence, and which may end, for us, in a terrible catastrophe!"

"You are a fool!" replied the Captain. "In five minutes, we will pass that 'shoe' ahead of us, or else we'll be blown a hundred and fifty feet in the air!"

The poor Mentor said nothing in reply, but his countenance spoke for him. Like a certain character in an old comedy, he looked as if he were saying to himself: "I wish I could get out of this."

Little by little it was evident we were gaining on our opponent. But our boat creaked and labored all over; she rushed through the water like a dolphin; the howling of the piston was loud and continuous; the wheels seemed to be whirled round by an invisible but tremendous hurricane. At length, after several anxious moments, we caught up with the "rascal." A frightful outburst of exclamation and cries took place on our boat. Then when we had got somewhat ahead of our rival, our Captain wheeled the stern of his boat directly in front of the other's bow, and ironically called out to him that he might throw a rope to us, as we would tow him gratis. The cries and noise with us then became indescribable—Captain, officers, crew, servants, passengers, firemen—all were gathered on our guards, insulting by voice and gestures, the few persons who ventured to appear on the other boat. If all the Indians in the new world had assembled on our decks, they could not have uttered such strange cries or made such a frightful noise.

This event was for our Captain a complete triumph, and the passengers noticed it appropriately. Like all rejoicings in the United States, this ended in a series of libations that lasted all night.

"NEVER SUCH A COLLECTION OF UNBLUSHING, DEGRADED SCOUNDRELS"

G. W. FEATHERSTONHAUGH

[*George William Featherstonhaugh, English geologist in the service of the United States, saw much of the Mississippi Valley in the 1830's and later published two works relating his experiences and observations. From his* Excursion through the Slave States . . . with Sketches of Popular Manners and Geological Notes (2 *volumes, London, 1844*), II, 237–45, *come the following pages describing his impressions of the public manners of fellow passengers on a Mississippi boat late in December, 1834.*]

Upon embarking on board of this steamer I was certainly pleased with the prospect that presented itself of enjoying some repose and comfort after the privations and fatigues I had endured; but never was traveller more mistaken in his anticipations! The vexatious conduct of the drunken youth had made a serious innovation upon the slight degree of personal comfort to be obtained in such a place, but I had not the slightest conception that that incident would be entirely thrown into the shade by others a thousand times more offensive, and that, from the moment of our departure from the post of Arkansas until our arrival at New Orleans, I was destined to a series of brutal annoyances that extinguished every hope of repose, or a chance of preserving even the decencies of existence.

I had been told at the post of Arkansas that ten passengers were waiting to come on board, and that several of them were notorious swindlers and gamblers, who, whilst in Arkansas, lived by the most desperate cheating and bullying, and who skulked about alternately betwixt Little Rock, Natchez, and New Orleans, in search of any plunder that violent and base means could bring into their hands. Some of their names were familiar to me, having heard them frequently spoken of at Little Rock as scoundrels of the worst class. From the moment I heard they were coming on board as passengers I predicted to Mr. T—— that every hope of comfort was at an end. But I had also been told that two American officers, a Captain D—— and a Lieut. C——, the latter a gentleman entrusted with the construction of the military road in Arkansas, were also coming on board; and I counted upon them as persons who would be, by the force of education and a consciousness of what was due to their rank as officers, on the side of decency at least, if not of correct manners; and if those persons had passed through the national military academy at West Point, or had served under the respectable chief of the Topographical Bureau at Washington, I should not have been as grievously disappointed as it was my fate to be. It was true I had heard that these officers had been passing ten days with these scoundrels at a low tavern at this place, in the unrestrained indulgence of every vicious extravagance, night and day, and that they were the familiar intimates of these notorious swindlers. Nevertheless, believing that there must be some exaggeration in this, I continued to look forward with satisfaction to having them for fellow passengers, confident that they would be our allies against any gross encroachments of the others.

Very soon after I had retired to the steamer at sun-set, the whole clique came on board, and the effect produced on us was something like that which would be made upon passengers in a peaceful vessel forcibly boarded by pirates of the most desperate character, whose manners seemed to be what they aspired to imitate. Rushing into the cabin, all but red-hot with whiskey, they crowded round the stove and excluded all the old passengers from it as much as if they had no right whatever to be in the cabin. Putting on a determined bullying air of doing what they pleased because they were the majority, and armed with pistols and knives, expressly made for cutting and stabbing, eight inches long and an inch and a half broad; noise, confusion, spitting, smoking, cursing and swearing, drawn from the most remorseless pages of blasphemy, commenced and prevailed from the moment of this invasion. I was satisfied at once that all resistance would be vain, and that even remonstrance might lead to murder; for a sickly old man in the cabin happening to say to one of them that there was so much smoke he could hardly breathe, the fellow immediately said, "If any man tells me he don't like my smoking I'll put a knife into him."

As soon as supper was over they all went to gambling, during which, at every turn of the cards, imprecations and blasphemies of the most revolting kind were loudly vociferated. Observing them from a distance where Mr. T—— and myself were seated, I perceived that one of them was the wretched looking fellow I had seen at Hignite's, on my way to Texas, who went by the name of Smith, and that his keeper Mr. Tunstall was with him. The most blasphemous fellows amongst them were two men of the names of Rector and Wilson. This Rector at that time held a commission under the national government as Marshal for the territory of Arkansas, was a man of mean stature, low and sottish in his manners, and as corrupt and reckless as it was possible for a human being to be. The man named Wilson was a suttler from cantonment Gibson, a military post about 250 miles up the Arkansas: he had a remarkable depression at the bottom of his forehead; and from this sinus his nose rising with a sudden spring, gave a fural expression to his face that exactly resembled the portrait of the wicked apprentice in Hogarth. The rubric on his countenance too was a faithful register of the numerous journeys the whiskey bottle had made to his proboscis.

If the Marshal, Mr. Rector, was the most constant blasphemer, the suttler was the most emphatic one. It was Mr. Rector's invariable custom, when the cards did not turn up to please him, to express a fervent wish that "his soul might be sent to ——," whilst Mr. Wilson never neglected a favourable opportunity of hoping that his own might be kept there to a thousand eternities. This was the language we were compelled to listen to morning, noon, and night, without remission, whenever we were in the cabin. In the morning, as soon as day broke, they began by drinking brandy and gin with sugar in it, without any water, and after breakfast they immediately went to gambling, smoking, spitting, blaspheming, and drinking for the rest of the day. Dinner interrupted their orgies for a while, but only for a short time, and after supper these wretches, maddened with the inflaming and impure liquors they swallowed, filled the cabin with an infernal vociferation of curses, and a perfect pestilence of smoking and spitting in every direction. Lieut. C—— occasionally exchanged a few words with me, and appeared to be restrained by my presence; he never sat down to play, but was upon the most intimate terms with the worst of these blackguards, and drank very freely with them. Capt. D——, with whom I never exchanged a word, was a gentlemanly-looking youth, and was not vulgar and coarse like the others, but I never saw a young man so infatuated with play, being always the first to go to the gambling table and the last to quit it. Such was his passion for gambling that it overcame everything like decent respect for the feelings and comfort of the other passengers; and one night, after the others had become too drunk and tired to sit up, I was kept awake by his sitting up with Rector and continuing to play at high, low, jack, and the game, until a very late hour in the morning. Perhaps, however, the most remarkable character amongst them was Smith, the New Englander, with his pale dough face, every feature of which was a proclamation of bully, sneak, and scoundrel. I never before saw in the countenance of any man such incontrovertible evidences of a fallen nature. It was this fellow that had charge of the materials for gambling, and who spread the faro table out the first evening of their coming on board, in hopes to lure some of the passengers; none of whom however approached the table except the drunken youth who had behaved so ill on a previous occasion, and they never asked him to play, probably knowing that he had no money.

Having found no birds to pluck on board, they were compelled to play against each other, always quarrelling in the most violent manner, and using the most atrocious menaces: it was always known when these quarrels were not made up, by the parties appearing the next time at the gambling-table with their Bowie-knives near them. In various travels in almost every part of the world I never saw such a collection of unblushing, low, degraded scoundrels, and I became at length so unhappy as often to think of being set on shore and taking a chance fate in the wild cane-brakes, rather than have my senses continually polluted with scenes that had every appearance of lasting until the end of the voyage: but for the comfort I derived from the society of Mr. T——, who was as miserable as myself, and who relied altogether upon me to set a good countenance upon the whole matter, I certainly should have excuted my intention.

Above the cabin where these scenes were enacted, was a smaller one called the Ladies' Cabin, and when I found what sort of a set we had got, I applied to the steward to give Mr. T——

and myself berths there; but he informed us this could not be done, because Capt. D——'s sister was there, having come on board with him at the post. She might be his sister for aught I ever learnt to the contrary, but whatever she was she kept very close, for she never appeared either below or upon deck. My remonstrances with the captain produced no effect whatever; when I talked to him about his printed rules, he plainly told me that he did not pretend to execute them; that what I complained of were the customs and manners of the country, and that if he pretended to enforce the rules, he should never get another passenger, adding, that one of the rules left it to a majority of the passengers to form their own by-laws for the government of the cabin.

On recurring to them I found it was so, the terms being that by-laws were to be so made, "provided they were in conformity with the police of the boat." As there was no police in the boat, it was evident the printed rules were nothing but a bait to catch passengers with, and I never spoke to him on the subject again. I had heard many stories of gangs of scoundrels who wandered about from New Orleans to Natchez, Vicksburg, and Little Rock, with no baggage but broad, sharp butcher knives, loaded pistols, and gambling apparatus, and I was now compelled to witness the proceedings of such ruffians. These would have been less intolerable if the two U. S. officers had kept aloof from these fellows and formed a little society with us, as I reasonably expected they would do when I first heard they were coming on board; but Capt. D—— never once offered either Mr. T—— or myself the least civility, or exchanged a word with us; and although that was not the case with Lieut. C——, yet an incident took place very early in the voyage which convinced me we had nothing to expect from him. Wilson, the man with the nose, was standing with his back to the stove before breakfast, unrestrainedly indulging in incoherent curses about some one he had quarrelled with, when Mr. C—— in the most amiable manner put his hand inside of the ruffian's waistcoat, drew forth his stabbing knife, unsheathed it, felt the edge as if with a connoisseur's finger and thumb, and was lavish in its praise. Such were the unvarying scenes which were re-enacted for the many days we were shut up in the steamer with these villains, and with this statement of them I return to the topographical details of the voyage.

ADVENTURES OF THE ARTIST

JOHN BANVARD

[*John Banvard, first to paint a moving panorama of the Mississippi (it opened at Louisville in 1846), was no slouch as his own press agent. Several early publicity stories about the origin of "by far the largest picture ever executed by man" he blended in 1849 into the account of the "Adventures of the Artist" with which he thereafter opened the program pamphlet describing his "Three-Mile Painting." For the history of his production see John Francis McDermott,* The Lost Panoramas of the Mississippi *(Chicago, 1958). For the variations in the descriptive pamphlets see McDermott, "Banvard's Mississippi Panorama Pamphlets,"* Bibliographical Society of America Papers, *XLIII, 48–62 (First Quarter, 1949).*]

[NOTE. As many inquiries respecting the past history of the artist have been made by those who have viewed his painting, at the suggestion of a number of his friends the following sketch of his adventures is compiled from Howitt's Journal, London; Chambers' Edinburgh Journal; and Morris & Willis' Home Journal, New York.]

The day was bright, and the setting sun was casting its mellow light over the ever beautiful autumnal foliage of an American landscape, bordering on the noble Mississippi. A tiny skiff was floating upon the mirror'd surface of the stream, unguided by its solitary occupant, a boy, of scarce sixteen, who sat, with folded arms, contemplating with wonder and delight, the glowing scenes around him. That boy was JOHN BANVARD. He had heard, and now realized, that America could boast the most picturesque and magnificent scenery in the world; and as he glided along by the beautiful shores, the boy resolved within himself to be an Artist, that he might paint the beauties and sublimities of his native land.

Some years passed away, and still this fatherless, moneyless youth, dreamed of being a painter. What he was in his waking, working moments, we do not know; but, at all events, he found time to turn over and over again the great thought that haunted him, till at length, ere he had attained the age of manhood, it assumed a distinct and tangible shape in his mind, and he devoted himself to its realization. There mingled no idea of profit with his ambition, and indeed, strange to say, we can learn nothing of any aspirations he may have felt after artistical excellence. His grand object, as he himself informs us, was to produce *the largest painting in the world*. He determined to paint a picture of the beautiful scenery of the Mississippi, which should be as superior to all others, in point of *size*, as that prodigious river is superior to the streamlets of Europe—a gigantic idea! which seems truly kindred to the illimitable forests and vast extent of his native land.

We will now say something of his eventful and romantic life, which, with its hardships, disappointments, and privations, had fitted him for the accomplishment of his herculean undertaking. He was born in the city of New York, where he received a good education, and is descended from an old French family. His grandfather was driven out of France by the bloody sword of persecution during one of the revolutions of the country, and fled to Amsterdam, in Holland. From thence he sailed to America, bringing with him little else but the heraldic honors of his family, for the Bon Verds (corrupted by the *patois* of the country to Banvard) were of highly respectable lineage. The coat of arms patented the family by the government, with the large antique silver seal, is now in possession of the Rev. Joseph Banvard, brother to John, pastor of the Harvard Street Church, Boston. Our hero showed the bent of his genius at a very early age. Being of delicate health in childhood, he was unable to enjoy the active, out-door sports of other boys, and, accordingly, he amused himself by drawing and painting, for which he exhibited decided talents, by becoming quite an accomplished draughtsman while yet a mere lad.

While his more favoured brothers were in the open air at play, he sometimes would be in his room projecting some instrument of natural science, a camera obscura, or solar microscope. He once came very near losing his eye-sight, by the explosion of a glass receiver, in which he was collecting hydrogen gas. His room was quite a laboratory and museum. He constructed a respectable diorama of the sea, having moving boats, fish, and a naval engagement. He saved the pennies that were given him, not spending them in toys or sweetmeats, as most youths would, and bought some types for a wooden printing press, of his own construction, and printed some handbills for his juvenile exhibitions. We have one of them now in our possession, and it is quite a genteel specimen of typography. The child was truly the father of the man in this, as in so many other cases, but he had much to pass through before the promise of the boy could be developed in the accomplishments of the man, as the sequel will show.

Young Banvard was intimate with Woodworth, the poet, the author of the "Old Oaken Bucket," whose family were neighbours to his father. He evinced a great taste for poetry, at which he early began to try his versatile genius. He wrote some very pretty verses when he was about nine years of age. He has continued occasionally to amuse his leisure hours in this way, up to the present time, and several of his poetical productions have recently appeared in the city papers. His poem of the White Fawn, which he recites to his audiences, in illustration of a scene in his beautiful picture, certainly stamps him a poet of no ordinary abilities.

When Banvard was about fifteen years of age, his family met with a severe reverse of fortune. His father lived just long enough to see his property, collected by frugal industry and perseverance, swept away from him by the mismanagement of an indiscreet partner, and his family turned houseless upon a pitiless world. John then went to the West, poor and friendless, and far away from his mother, brother and sisters, and those he held dear. He arrived at Louisville, Kentucky, sought employment, and procured a situation in a drug store; but this did not suit his taste. Instead of making pills, his employer would often find him with a piece of chalk, or coal, sketching the likenesses of his fellow clerks upon the walls of the rooms, where they were putting up medicines. His employer told him he thought he could make better likenesses than he could pills. John thought so too, and so "threw physic to the dogs," and left the druggist.

We next find him engaged in his favourite employment of painting—he having made an engagement to ornament and decorate a public garden. But this concern soon failed, and left him without money or employment. At this time he was about sixteen years old. Our hero, nothing daunted, by persevering labour obtained a little money, engaged a room, and pursued the business of painting for himself. The day had not arrived for success in his chosen pursuit; so being fond of adventure, he started down the river with some young men of his acquaintance, to seek anew his fortune.

When they had reached the mouth of the Saline river, they met with a disaster which had well nigh proved fatal to the young artist. The river was lashed by a terrific storm; the night was dark; the boat broke loose from its moorings. By great exertions of all hands on board, in pumping and bailing all night, they succeeded in keeping the craft afloat, and made a safe landing. During this perilous night, our young adventurer, at the hazard of his own life, saved the life of one of his comrades who fell overboard. When day broke they discovered a stock-boat but a few yards below them, whose proximity they had not observed during the night, from the noise of the storm. It was an ill-fated night for the stockboat. It was sunk, all the stock was drowned, and the men were found sitting on the bank, nearly frozen, whom the more fortunate party generously relieved. A large number of boats met with a similar fate with the stock-boat, on that fatal night.

The next we find of Banvard, is in the village of New Harmony, on the Wabash river, where, in company with three or four other young men, he "got up" some dioramic paintings, fitted them up for public exhibition, in a flat boat, which they built for the purpose, and started off down the Wabash, with the intention of "coasting" that river into the Ohio, and so down the Mississippi to New Orleans; thus exhibiting to the sparse population of the wilderness, specimens of the fine arts, at the same time replenishing their exhausted funds. This proved to be a very unfortunate speculation. The capital of the company gave out before they were able to complete their plans, and they left port with their boat in an unfinished condition, calculating to finish it with their first proceeds, they having invested their last few dimes in a supply of bacon, corn, meal, and potatoes; but fate conspired against them. The river was low, and none of them had ever descended the Wabash; consequently they were ignorant of the channel, lodged on the sand bars, and hung on the snags, until they exhausted their scanty supply of provisions. They, at length, found themselves fast on a sand bar, and down to their last peck of potatoes at the same time. They laboured hard all day to get

out of this predicament, but without success; and having roasted
their last potatoes, they went to bed, or rather to bench, for their
money gave out before they had procured bedding, and they had
to content themselves with the softest plank of their seats for their
slumbers. Next morning they were up before the sun, with their
spirits refreshed by a night's repose; but without any breakfast,
they jumped into the water, and with their rails went stoutly to
work again, to force their boat over the bar. Over exertion, together with being in the water too long without food, brought a
severe fit of ague upon Banvard. The bar upon which they were
fast, was called the "Bone Bank" bar, as, immediately opposite,
on the shore, the bank of the river was full of organic remains.
Some of the large bones were then protruding out of the side of
the bank in full view. As Banvard lay on the soft sand of the bar,
it being more comfortable than the hard plank of the boat, his
head burning with the fever and his limbs racked with pain, he
looked at these gloomy relics of an antediluvian race, and felt as
though his bones would soon be laid with them. But at sunset the
rest of the company got the boat over the bar, took Banvard
aboard, and landed in the woods, all nearly exhausted. Food was
as scarce here as it was upon the bar, and all hands went supper-
less to bed. Next morning they started early, not intent on exhibiting specimens of the fine arts, but on obtaining something to eat,
as by this time they were nearly half starved. But the contrary
winds landed their luckless craft on Wabash Island, which was
uninhabited. Here, fortunately, they found some pawpaws, and
they all feasted voraciously on them, except Banvard, who was
too sick to eat anything, and who lay upon one of the benches,
burning with a violent fever. Next day they sent their handbills
down to the village of Shawneetown, which was in sight, about
seven miles ahead, informing the inhabitants that something
would be "exhibited" in the dioramic line that evening, at their
wharf; and so there was; for as the company approached the
wharf with their boat, no doubt with high expectations of a good
supper, they observed a large audience awaiting their arrival. But
the exhibition turned out different from what was expected. The
boat lodged on a ledge of rocks about half a cable's length from
the shore. The men from the boat got out a line to the people on
the wharf, who pulled with the same eagerness that the half-
starved company on board pushed and pried with their poles. But

fate, regardless of the philosophy of action and reaction, as well as of the interests of the fine arts at Shawneetown, held the boat fast, and the audience went away without a sight of the paintings, and the artists to sleep again without a supper. That night the swells from a passing steamer lifted the boat from the rocks, and set it afloat down the river; and when those on board awoke in the morning, they found themselves hard aground again on the Cincinnati bar, about eight miles below Shawneetown. The boat was got off with but little trouble, and they landed in a settlement. Here they were very liberal in their terms, as money was scarce, and they wanted to make sure of something to eat. A bushel of potatoes, a fowl, or a dozen of eggs, were good for an admission to their interesting exhibition. That night, after they got through exhibiting their paintings, they had a luxurious supper. Fasting so long, appeared to have done Banvard some good, for it starved the fever out of him; he found, as we often do, that adversity has its blessings, and in a few days he was entirely well.

The adventurers continued on with their boat, stopping at the settlements along the shore, and "astonishing the natives" with their dioramas. The boat was not very large, and if the audience collected too much on one side, the water would intrude over their low gunwales into the exhibition room. This kept the company, by turns, in the un-artist-like employment of pumping, to keep the boat from sinking. Sometimes the swells from a passing steamer would cause the water to rush through the cracks of the weather-boarding, and give the audience a bathing. Banvard says they made no extra charge for this part of the exhibition, although it was not mentioned in the programme.

Money being scarce, they were compelled to receive "truck and trade" for admissions, such as onions, potatoes, eggs, et cetera. It was no unusual thing to see a family coming to witness the "show boat," the father with a bushel of potatoes, the mother with a fowl, and the children with a pumpkin a-piece, for their admission fees. On a certain night, while they were exhibiting, some rogue let the boat loose, and it drifted off several miles down the stream with the unconscious spectators, who were landed in a thick cane brake, about two miles below. They were obliged to make their way home as best they could.

At Plumb point the boat was attacked by a party of the Murell robbers, a large organized banditti, who infested the country for miles around; and here our hero came near losing his life. Several pistol shots were fired at him, but being in the dark, none of them took effect, although several lodged in the deck of the boat, within a few inches of him. After a desperate resistance, during which one of the robbers was shot, the boat was rescued. During the encounter, one of the company received a severe wound in the arm from a bowie knife, but the rest escaped unhurt. Mr. Banvard continued with the boat until it arrived at the Grand Gulf, where he obtained a commission to paint some views. He had found the receipts of the floating expedition to be more potatoes than dimes, more eggs than dollars, so he sold out his interest, and left. We know nothing further of this expedition, but Banvard seems to have been satisfied with floating dioramas.

After this, he engaged in painting at New Orleans, Natchez, and subsequently at Cincinnati and Louisville, and was liberally rewarded. Not content, however, he executed a very fine panorama of the city of Venice, and exhibited it in the West with considerable success. He finally lost this painting by the sinking of a steamer, upon which it was being transported to the city of Nashville. Having accumulated, by his art, a little capital, we next find him at St. Louis, as the proprietor of the St. Louis museum, which he had purchased. But here fate frowned again upon his efforts. He remained in St. Louis just long enough to lose all he had previously earned, and then left for Cincinnati, where he fared little better. He then procured a small boat, and started down the Ohio river without a dime, and living several days upon nuts, which he collected from the woods. His next stopping place was a small town, where he did some painting, and sold a revolving pistol, for which he had given twelve dollars in St. Louis, for twenty-five dollars. With this capital he bought a larger boat, got some produce aboard, which he retailed out along shore; then sold his concern for fifty dollars. Having now a little capital, the young artist made several very successful speculations, and managed to make, during this Quixotic expedition, several thousand dollars. With the capital thus accumulated, he commenced his grand project of painting the Panorama of the Mississippi.

For this purpose, he procured a small skiff, and descended the river to make the necessary drawings, in the spring of 1840, and the first sketch was made just before he became of age. Had he been aware, when he commenced the undertaking, of the vast amount of labour it required, he would have shrunk from the task in dismay; but having commenced the work, he was determined to proceed, being spurred on to its completion, perhaps, by the doubts of some of his friends, to whom he communicated his project, as to its practicability. The idea of gain never entered his mind when he commenced the undertaking, but he was actuated by a patriotic and honourable ambition, that he should produce the *largest painting* in the world.

One of the greatest difficulties he encountered, was the preparatory labour he had to undergo in making the necessary drawings. For this purpose he had to travel thousands of miles alone in an open skiff, crossing and recrossing the rapid stream, in many places over two miles in breadth, to select proper points of sight, from which to take his sketch; his hands became hardened with constantly plying the oar, and his skin as tawny as an Indian's, from exposure to the rays of the sun and the vicissitudes of the weather. He would be weeks together without speaking to a human being, having no other company than his rifle, which furnished him with his meat from the game of the woods or the fowls of the river. When the sun began to sink behind the lofty bluffs, and evening to approach, he would select some secluded sandy cove, overshadowed by the lofty cotton wood, draw out his skiff from the water, and repair to the woods to hunt his supper. Having killed his game, he would return, dress, cook, and from some fallen log would eat it with his biscuit, with no other beverage than the wholesome water of the noble river that glided by him. Having finished his lonely meal, he would roll himself in his blanket, creep under his frail skiff, which he turned over, to shield him from the night dews, and with his portfolio of drawings for his pillow, and the sand of the bar for his bed, would sleep soundly till the morning; when he would arise from his lowly couch, eat his breakfast before the rays of the rising sun had dispersed the humid mist from the surface of the river, then would start fresh to his task again. In this way he spent over four hundred days, making the preparatory drawings. Several nights during the time, he was compelled to creep from under his skiff, where he slept, and sit all night on a log, and breast the pelting storm, through fear that the banks of the river would cave upon him, and to escape the falling trees. During this time, he pulled his little skiff more than two thousand miles. In the latter part of the summer he reached New Orleans. The yellow fever was raging in the city, but, unmindful of that, he made his drawing of the place. The sun the while was so intensely hot, that his skin became so burned, that it peeled from off the back of his hands, and from his face. His eyes became inflamed, by such constant and extraordinary efforts, from which unhappy effects he has not recovered to this day. His drawings completed, he erected a building at Louisville, Kentucky, to transfer them to the canvas. His object in painting his picture in the West was to exhibit it to, and procure testimonials from, those who were best calculated to judge of its fidelity, the practical river men; and he has procured the names of nearly all the principal captains and pilots navigating the Mississippi, freely testifying to the correctness of the scenery.

The following interesting letter from S. Woodworth, an officer of the United States navy, who passed through Louisville, bearer of despatches to Oregon and California, to his friend, General Morris, at New York, and published in the "Home Journal" of that city, gives a graphic description of the artist, as he appeared at work upon his great painting.

St. Louis, April 13, 1846.

"MY DEAR GENERAL:

Here I am, in this beautiful city of St. Louis, and thus far 'on my winding way' to Oregon and California. In coming down the Ohio, our boat being of the larger class, and the river at a 'low stage,' we were detained several hours at Louisville, and I took advantage of the detention to pay a visit to an old school-mate of mine, one of the master spirits of the age. I mean Banvard, the artist, who is engaged in the herculean task of painting a panorama of the Mississippi river, upon more than *three miles of canvas*—truthfully depicting a range of scenery of upwards of two thousand miles in extent. In company with a travelling acquaintance, an Englishman gentleman, I called at the artist's studio, an immense wooden building, constructed expressly for the purpose, at the extreme outskirts of the city. After knocking several times, I at length succeeded in making myself heard, when the artist himself, in his working cap and blouse, palette and pencil in hand, came to the door to admit us. He did not at first recognise me, but when I mentioned my name, he dropped both palette and pencil, and clasped me in his arms, so delighted was he to see me, after a separation of sixteen years.

"My fellow-traveller was quite astonished at this sudden manifestation, for I had not informed him of our previous intimacy, but had merely invited him to accompany me to see in progress this wonder of the world, that is to be, this leviathan panorama. Banvard immediately conducted us into the interior of the building. He said he had selected the site for his building, far removed from the noise and bustle of the town, that he might apply himself more closely and uninterruptedly to his labour, and be free from the intrusion of visitors. Within the studio, all seemed chaos and confusion, but the life-like and natural appearance of a portion of his great picture, displayed on one of the walls in a yet unfinished state. Here and there were scattered about the floor, piles of his original sketches, bales of canvas, and heaps of boxes. Paint-pots, brushes, jars and kegs were strewed about, without order or arrangement, while along one of the walls several large cases were piled, containing rolls of finished sections of the painting. On the opposite wall was spread a canvas, extending its whole length, upon which the artist was then at work. A portion of this canvas was wound upon an upright roller, or drum, standing at one end of the building, and as the artist completed his painting he thus disposed of it. Not having the time to spare, I could not stay to have all the immense cylinders unrolled for our inspection, for we were sufficiently occupied in examining that portion on which the artist is now engaged, and which is nearly completed, being from the mouth of the Red river to Grand Gulf. Any description of this gigantic undertaking that I should attempt in a letter, would convey but a faint idea of what it will be when completed. The remarkable truthfulness of the minutest objects upon the shores of the rivers, independent of the masterly style and artistical execution of the work, will make it the most valuable historical painting in the world, and unequalled, for magnitude and variety of interest, by any work that has ever been heard of since the art of painting was discovered. As a medium for the study of geography of this portion of our country, it will be of inestimable value. The manners and customs of the aborigines and settlers—the modes of cultivating and harvesting the peculiar crops—cotton, sugar, tobacco, &c.—the shipping of the produce, in all the variety of novel and curious conveyances employed on these rivers for transportation, are here so vividly portrayed, that but a slight stretch of the imagination would bring the noise of the puffing steamboats from the river and the songs of the negroes in the fields, in music to the ear, and one seems to inhale the very atmosphere before him. Such were the impressions produced by our slight and unfavourable view of a portion of this great picture, which Banvard expects to finish this summer. It will be exhibited in New York in the autumn—after which, it will be sent to London, for the same purpose.

The mode of exhibiting it is ingenious, and will require considerable machinery. It will be placed upon upright revolving cylinders, and the canvas will pass gradually before the spectator, thus affording the artist an opportunity of explaining the whole work. After examining many other beautiful specimens of the artist's skill, which adorned his studio, we dined together in the city. As our boat was now ready to start, I shook hands with Banvard, who parted from me with feelings as sad as they had been before joyful. His life has been one of curious interest, replete with stirring incidents, and I was greatly amused in listening to anecdotes of his adventures on these western rivers, where, for many years past, he has been a constant sojourner, indefatigably employed in preparing his great work.

WOODWORTH."

Banvard was a self-taught artist—no—he had a teacher. He went not to Rome indeed, to study the works of hands long since passed away; but he studied the omnipresent works of the One Great Living Master! Nature was his teacher. Many a time, at the close of a lovely summer's day, after finishing his solitary evening meal, would he sit upon some lonely rock, near the margin of the noble river, where all was still, save the sweet chaunt of the feathered songsters of the adjacent forest, or the musical ripple of the eddying waters at his feet, and watch the majestic bluff as it gradually faded through the gray twilight from the face of day into the darker shades of night. Then would he turn and study the rising moon, as it peered above the opposite shore, ascending the deep blue ether, high in the heavens above, casting its mellow light over the surrounding landscape, and gilding the smooth surface of the river with its silvery hue. It was then and there he studied nature in its lonely grandeur, and seized those glowing moonlight scenes which now adorn his canvas, so vividly too, as if painted with a pencil dipped in the silvery beams of the living moon itself.

During the time this undaunted young man was transferring his drawings to the canvas, he had to practice the most rigid economy, lest his money should give out before the picture was completed. He could not afford to hire a menial assistant to do the ordinary labour about his paint-room; and when the light of the day would recede from the canvas, upon which he was at work, instead of taking relaxation when the night came, he would be found grinding his colours, or splitting his wood for the ensuing day. Still, with all these self-denials and privations, his last cent was expended long before his last sketch was transferred to his last piece of canvas. He then endeavoured to get credit for a few pieces of this material, from a merchant of whom he had purchased the principal part for his painting, and with whom he had expended hundreds of dollars while speculating on the river, but in vain. Still, not discouraged, he laid his favourite project aside for a time, and sought other work. Fortunately, he obtained a small job to decorate regalia for a lodge of Odd Fellows, and with a light heart went cheerfully to work, to earn the money which would purchase the material to complete his picture. With the avails, he procured the needed canvas.

At last, his great project is finished! the Mississippi is painted! and his country now boasts the largest painting in the world! But the trials of our persevering artist were not all passed. The history of the first exhibition of this wonderful production is curious, and furnishes another illustration of the necessity there is, never to despair. The gas company of Louisville, before they would put up fixtures for him, compelled him to deposit *double* the price of such fixtures in their bank. To raise this amount, he *gave* a piece of philosophical apparatus to a society in the city, provided they bought fifty tickets in advance. They agreed to this, as they desired the apparatus very much, it being worth twice the amount they gave for the tickets. The city authorities also ordered him to pay a tax for exhibiting his work, a work of which they ought to have been proud, and which would not only reflect honour upon the city, but make it noted throughout the civilised world.

The first night he opened his great picture for exhibition, in Louisville, not a single person thought it worth while to visit it. He received not a cent—the night was rainy. The artist returned to his room with a sorrowful heart, he sat down upon a box, and looked upon the blank wall, where, but a few days before, with high spirits and cheerful heart, he had put the finishing touch to his task of long years of toil and hope. His heart almost sank within him; but he did not despair. The next day he sallied out among the boatmen, by the river, and gave them tickets; telling them they must see it; that it was their river he had painted. At night the boatmen came, and with them a few of their friends. When they saw the accuracy of the painting, they were delighted, and their wild enthusiasm was raised as one well known object after another passed by them. The boatmen told the citizens it was a grand affair; that it was correctly delineated, and its accuracy could be relied upon. Finally, the public became convinced that the picture was really worth looking at, and then they rushed to see it by crowds.

The great artist left the city and went to New York and Boston, where his beautiful painting was duly appreciated. Admiring thousands upon thousands visited it, many coming hundreds of miles, from the remotest parts of the States, to view this wonderful production. Indeed, so great was the desire to see it, that the railroad companies ran express trains from adjacent towns into the cities for the accommodation of the eager throngs who wished to view the greatest achievement of individual enterprise upon record. And in these cities our persevering young artist reaped the reward for his years of toil, for the public fully appreciated his great work. The fame of the artist is his country's property. "His genius and enterprise will be honoured," as Governor Briggs beautifully remarked, "so long as the great Father of Waters, and its numerous tributaries, continue to pour their flowing tides into the great ocean."

DESCRIPTION

OF

BANVARD'S PANORAMA

OF THE

MISSISSIPPI & MISSOURI RIVERS,

EXTENSIVELY KNOWN AS THE

"THREE-MILE PAINTING,"

EXHIBITING A VIEW OF COUNTRY OVER

3000 MILES IN LENGTH,

EXTENDING FROM THE

MOUTH OF THE YELLOW STONE TO THE CITY OF NEW ORLEANS,

BEING BY FAR

The Largest Picture

EVER EXECUTED BY MAN.

———◦✶◦———

LONDON:

PRINTED BY W. J. GOLBOURN,

6, PRINCES STREET, LEICESTER SQUARE.

——

1849.

DESCRIPTION OF BANVARD'S PANORAMA

JOHN BANVARD

———

[The following description of views in his panorama Banvard issued after he had added the Missouri River section in order to outdo his closest competitor, John Rowson Smith. Two sections of the pamphlet (as published in London in 1849), describing "The Rivers" and "Life on the Mississippi," have been omitted here because they were lifted without credit from Timothy Flint. In a later English printing some testimonials from Charles Dickens and other noted persons were added to the American endorsements.]

The Panorama.

As the Painting alternately ascends on one representation, and descends the next, it will be necessary for the reader, when ascending, to commence at the end of this description, and follow it back to the beginning.

YELLOW STONE BLUFFS

Of the Missouri—View looking several miles up the river. The Missouri river, although it is called a tributary to the Mississippi, is considered by many to be the main stream, and strictly speaking it is. The upper Mississippi should have been called the Missouri, for it is much shorter, and brings down less water in the main channel than the latter stream.

ASSINNABOIN'S BAR

Dividing the river at the base of a lofty precipice.

THE DOMES

Here we have some of the most unique scenery probably in the world. Large clay bluffs, of different coloured clays, rear their heads towards the heavens, the tops are washed away by the rains into circular forms, so that at a distance they resemble immense domes of some gigantic city.

GRAND DÉTOUR

Here the river makes a very large circuit, and the spectator, instead of following the river round, is carried across the Isthmus.

INDIAN ENCAMPMENT

And the Sioux, dancing their war dance upon the

GRASSY PLAINS

Which stretch far away in the distance.

INDIANS HUNTING BUFFALOES

Large numbers of these animals are taken yearly, merely for their hides, which the Indians sell to the white traders.

VILLAGE OF THE DEAD

Or an aboriginal cemetery. Here will be seen the curious manner the Indians dispose of their dead.

GRAND PRAIRIE

With its tall waving grass, and myriads of wild flowers—one of the most beautiful sights in nature.

PRAIRIE ON FIRE

Burning away in the distance, as far as the eye can reach.

INDIAN VILLAGE (by Moonlight)

And the return of the Grand Détour.

KNIFE RIVER

And the Square Hills. In the fore-ground is Mr. Banvard, seated upon a log, with his rifle by him, and his little skiff moored by the bank of the stream. Upon the gum tree, near him, will be seen one of the gorgeous tints of American foliage.

INDIAN RUINS

A deserted village of the Mandans, an extinct tribe.

TETON ISLANDS

And the steamer General Taylor.

BRICK KILNS

These are some very peculiar cliffs, of different coloured clays, but principally red, which give them the name. The rains are washing them down in many fanciful shapes, not unlike the stalactites of a subterranean cavern.

MISSOURI RIVER

This is the largest tributary of the Mississippi river, discharging more water into the channel than the Upper Mississippi itself: in fact, it is the longer river of the two. At its confluence, it is about half a mile wide; the united stream, from this point to the mouth of the Ohio, has a medial breadth of about a mile. This mighty tributary appears rather to diminish, than to increase the width, but it materially alters the depth of the channel.

A short distance above the mouth of the Missouri stands the town of Alton, situated at the base of a beautiful bluff, which rolls in on the river in a graceful outline, clearly defined against the bright sky beyond.

Immediately in the foreground, under the shade of some stately elms, is an encampment of Shawnee Indians, the warriors reclining lazily upon the green sward, while their squaws are preparing their rude repast.

Below the junction of the Missouri stands out, in fine relief, some very beautiful islands, clad in the brightest verdure.

BLOODY ISLAND

The name being given to it from the number of duels that have been fought within its shades.

ST. LOUIS

St. Louis is one of the oldest, and first settled towns in the Mississippi Valley. It was settled and occupied by the French, until the country was purchased by the American government. A great number of steamboats, and river craft of all descriptions, bound to all points of the boatable waters of the Mississippi, are seen at all seasons of the year lying in the harbour. Miners, trappers, hunters, adventurers, emigrants, and people of all character and languages, meet here, and disperse, in pursuit of their various objects, in every direction, some even beyond the remotest points of civilization. Population about 60,000.

UNITED STATES ARSENAL

It is beautifully situated on a gentle declivity, immediately below the city, at the foot of "the bar." A short distance below the arsenal commence some rocky bluffs, upon which are situated, very prominently, several lofty shot towers; they have a very striking appearance when viewed from the river.

VIDE POUCHE (or, in English, Empty Pocket)

And a log cabin in the foreground. Here may be noticed the rich and varied hues of the American foliage. I have seen several different colours upon the same tree. During the end of the summer months and the beginning of autumn the leafing is gorgeous. The trees are clothed in the deepest crimson, contrasted with the brightest yellow, or orange, and strongly relieved by the undying green of the terebenthines. A certain writer terms it *rainbow* foliage.

JEFFERSON BARRACKS

Pleasantly situated on a low hill, which rises gradually from the river, presenting a very fine view to the spectator passing on a boat, and calling up patriotic emotions, as he beholds the noble star-spangled banner waving, with graceful folds, in the loyal western air.

PLATEEN ROCKS

Extending ten or twelve miles along the banks of the river; they have a wild, romantic appearance, some of them shooting up into towers and spires, and, as Jefferson remarks, not unlike those of cities.

HERCULANEUM

Standing as it were in an immense natural amphitheatre. The high rock below the town has a very peculiar, castle-like appearance. Further up the river, we have the "Cornice Rocks," and the Cornice Island.

BLUFFS OF SELMA

These bluffs have a very striking and majestic appearance, varying from two to four hundred feet in height; some of them are beautifully variegated, and resemble the façades of mighty temples—the face of them having uniform arches and carved niches, almost as regular and order-like as if they were chiselled out by the hands of man.

RUSH ISLAND

And bar, with the wreck of the steamer "West Wind," which was snagged here in June 1846, at the time the artist was painting this portion of the river. This was a very unfortunate boat, having been previously blown up, at the same time killing a large number of persons.

N.B., *The views of the painting above the mouth of the Ohio, are all on the western shore; below the Ohio, they are all on the eastern shore.*

MOUTH OF THE OHIO

This is a very beautiful stream, called by the French, "La Belle Rivère." Its banks are thickly settled, and contain many fine cities.

The spectator has, at the Mouth of the Ohio, a view of *three States at one time*. To his right, he will see the State of Kentucky; in the centre, between the two rivers, the State of Illinois; to his left, the State of Missouri. On the delta of the two rivers stands the city of

CAIRO

Which, like New Orleans, is protected by levees, raised above the highest known floods; from thence, to the Gulf of Mexico, the navigation is always open for steamers of the largest class. Above this point, the Ohio and Mississippi, in winter, are often closed by ice, and in summer, impeded by low water. Hence the importance of the Central Railroad, commenced from this place by the State, to connect with the Illinois and Michigan Canal, Galena and Chicago, upon which was expended a million of dollars; and, whenever completed, will form the most direct, speedy, and certain route, at all seasons, between the South-western and Northern States. Cairo, from its geographical position, and the immense range of navigable rivers, all centering at this point, is destined to become one of the largest inland cities in the United States.

IRON BANKS

And the town of Columbus, are the first objects that strike the eye of the voyager after passing the Ohio. They are introduced into the picture by moonlight, with the magnificent steamer "Peytona" wooding; one of the largest and fastest boats on the river, commanded by Captain John Shallcross, a well known and gentlemanly commander of the West. In the distance, can be seen the

CHALK BANKS

A high bluff of white clay, falling nearly perpendicularly to the river, which washes its base.

MILLS POINT

This is not a point of the river, but a point, or spur, of high lands that strike into the river, and affords an excellent location for a town. In the foreground of the view is a diving bell at work on the wreck of a steamer.

INDIAN MOUNDS

And Island Number Twenty-Five. The islands on the Mississippi, below the Mouth of the Ohio, have all been numbered; but at present the numbers are very irregular, owing to the circumstance of many being washed away by the force of the moving waters; the "chutes" of others "growing up," as it is termed, and new ones continually forming.

This "growing up" of the islands of the Mississippi, is one of the most striking characteristics of this mighty river, and one that would not present itself to the eye of the voyager in passing along the stream, unless the islands that were growing up were pointed out, and the philosophy explained to him. This singular peculiarity even escaped the observation of Mr. Flint, as he makes no allusion to it in his excellent description of the Mississippi, contained in his geography of the Western States.

The cause of this "growing up" of the islands is this: where the current strikes diagonally off, from a point above the head of an island, the eddying waters produce a sand bar under the point at the mouth of the "chute," or channel, round the island. Upon this bar collects the alluvial soil of the river, from which spring the young cotton woods, and, being of very rapid growth, soon shoot up into tall trees, and completely shut out the channel from the view of the river. The "chutes" behind the islands then form lakes. Upon the waters of these lakes congregate all kind of aquatic fowls—swans, geese, ducks, pelicans, and the like. These lakes are likewise the resort of alligators.

PLUMB POINT

This is one of the most difficult places to boatmen on the Mississippi, from the frequency of the change of channel, the snags, bars, and sawyers. A large number of steam and other boats have been lost here. It was a short distance from this place where Murell, the notorious land pirate and robber, had his encampment.

When the artist first descended the river, the small flat boat on which he was travelling laid by here; and in the night the boat was attacked by these robbers, and it was only by a desperate resistance, during which one of the robbers was shot, that the boat was rescued, after cutting the lines, and leaving them on the shore. During the conflict, Mr. Banvard had a volley of shot fired at him, the balls whistling past, and splashing in the river by him; but, fortunately, none of them took effect, although several struck in the planking of the boat, only a few inches from him.

FULTON

On the First Chickasaw Bluffs, an unimportant town, with the town of

RANDOLPH

On the Second Chickasaw Bluffs, seen in the distance; the view looking down the chute of Number Thirty-Four.

MEMPHIS

This city is beautifully situated on the Fourth Chickasaw Bluffs, presenting a very fine appearance as you descend the river.

FORT PICKERING

A new place laid off by speculators. It is very handsomely situated opposite the head of

PRESIDENT'S ISLAND

A large and beautiful island, which divides the river just below. Here the voyager will begin to see fine cotton plantations, with the slaves working in the cotton fields; he will also see the beautiful mansions of the planters, rows of "negro quarters," and lofty cypress trees, the pride of the Southern forests. A little farther down, he passes the town of

COMMERCE

Situated at the head of a deep bend of the river.

STACK ISLAND

By moonlight. Here we have a beautiful view of about ten miles up the river, the island in the centre reposing quietly upon the surface of the river, which is broken by the ripples of a passing steamer; the moon, observed aloft, shedding its mellow light, and gilding the surrounding landscape with its silvery hues.

Here we have the first view of the Spanish Moss, hanging in gloomy grandeur from the bough of the cypress trees; likewise the Palmetto, with its broad, fan-like leaf, the lofty Cotton Wood, the sea grass, the impenetrable canebrake, and all the concomitants of a Southern forest.

VICKSBURG

Situated on the Walnut Hills. These hills come in and extend along the river for about two miles. They rise boldly, though gradually, with alternate swells and gullies, to the height of nearly 500 feet; and present one of the most beautiful prospects to be met with on the Lower Mississippi. At the lower end, the city of Vicksburg is situated, on the shelving declivities of the hills, and the houses are scattered in groups on the terraces, and present a very striking view as the spectator descends the river. A few miles farther down will be seen the small town of

WARRENTON

The seat of justice for Warren County, Mississippi.

PALMYRA ISLAND

With the steamer "Uncle Sam." This is one of the finest boats on the river, commanded by clever officers, and makes very regular trips from Louisville to New Orleans. All the steamboats introduced into the Panorama of the Mississippi, are correct likenesses of boats that are now plying on those waters.

In the foreground of this view we have a wood yard, and the Pecan tree tresselled with the Muscadine vine. After passing these, we come to the city of

GRAND GULF

Situated at the base of a bold and solitary bluff. A few miles below this, is the

PETITE GULF

And the town of Rodney. A few miles below Rodney, near the point, stands a very fine cotton plantation, belonging to General Zachary Taylor.

NATCHEZ

This city is romantically situated on a very high bluff of the east bank of the river, and is much the largest town in the State of Mississippi. The river business is transacted in that part of the city which is called "under the hill." Great numbers of boats are always lying here. Some very respectable merchants reside in this part of the city. The upper town is elevated on the summit of the bluff, 300 feet above the level of the river, and commands a fine prospect of the surrounding landscape. It is, at present, supposed to contain 5000 inhabitants. It is 300 miles above New Orleans.

ELLIS'S CLIFFS

These cliffs have a very peculiar and majestic appearance; being of sand, the rains are washing them off into a variety of fanciful shapes, some of them resembling towers and battlements. After passing these, the traveller will see the little town of

FORT ADAMS

Romantically situated on the side of a beautiful hill, with a noble bluff just below the village, called Loftus's Heights. Here are the remains of an old fort, erected during the administration of John Adams, in honor of whom it was named.

BAYOU SARA

By moonlight. A short distance above this town stands an old dead tree scathed by the fire, where three negroes were burnt alive. Each of them had committed murder: one of them murdered his mistress and her two daughters. After passing Bayou Sara, the traveller will see some very beautiful cliffs, called the

WHITE CLIFFS

On which are situated the small towns of Port Hudson and Port Hickey; and immediately below these is the very picturesque and romantic looking

PROPHET'S ISLAND

Here formerly lived and died Wontongo, an Indian prophet, the last of his tribe.

BATON ROUGE

This is now the capital of the state of Louisiana. This place is handsomely situated on the last bluff that is seen in descending the river.

From Baton Rouge, the river below, to New Orleans, is lined with splendid sugar plantations, and what is generally termed the "Coast," a strip of land on either side of the river, extending back to the cypress swamps, about two miles. It is the richest soil in the world, and will raise nearly all the tropical fruits—oranges, figs, olives, and the like. This coast is protected from inundations by an embankment of earth of six or eight feet in height, called a levee. Behind the levee, we see extensive sugar fields, noble mansions, beautiful gardens, large sugar houses, groupes of negro quarters, lofty churches, splendid villas, presenting, in all, one of the finest views of country to be met with in the United States. The inhabitants are chiefly native French, or Creoles.

Just before arriving at New Orleans, will be seen a beautifully situated town, in the bend above, called

CARROLTON

From this point there is a railroad extending to the centre of New Orleans. After passing a left-hand point, the traveller will be off the city of

LA FAYETTE

This is attached to New Orleans, but under a separate corporation. It is where all the flat boats land that descend the river.

NEW ORLEANS

This is the great commercial emporium of the South, situated on the *eastern* shore of the river, in a bend so deep and sinuous, that the sun rises to the inhabitants of the city over the *opposite* shore. It stands in latitude north, 29° 57' and 13° 9' west from Washington, about one thousand miles from the mouth of the Ohio river, and a little more than one thousand two hundred miles from the mouth of the Missouri.

Viewed from the harbour on a sunny day, no city offers a more striking panoramic view. It envelopes the beholder something in the form of a crescent. An area of many acres, covered with all the grotesque variety of flat boats, keel boats, and water craft of every description, that have floated from all points of the valley above, line the upper part of the shore. Steamboats rounding to, or sweeping away, cast their long horizontal streams of smoke behind them. Sloops, schooners, brigs, and ships occupy the wharfs, arranged below each other in the order of their size, showing a forest of masts. The foreign aspect of the stuccoed houses in the city proper, the massive buildings of the Fauxbourg St. Mary, the bustle and movement on every side, all seen at one view, in the bright colouring of the brilliant sun and sky of the climate, present a splendid spectacle.

TESTIMONIALS.
Copy of Resolutions offered by the Hon. Mr. CALHOUN, *and which were* UNANIMOUSLY *adopted by the Senate and House of Representatives at the city of Boston, United States of America.*

Resolved, That we regard the Panorama of the Mississippi river, painted by Mr. John Banvard, as a truly wonderful and magnificent production; and we deem it but a just appreciation of its extraordinary merit, to express our high admiration of the boldness and originality of the conception, and of the industry and indefatigable perseverance of the young and talented artist, in the execution of his herculean work.

Resolved, That the immense extent of this picture, its truthfulness to nature, as certified by those who are familiar with the river; its minuteness of detail; the wonderful illusion of its perspective, and the great variety of its scenery and objects, render it a useful medium for imparting correct information respecting an interesting portion of our beautiful country.

Resolved, That it is with emotions of pride and pleasure we commend this splendid painting, and its talented artist, who, by its production, has reflected so much honour upon himself, and upon the country of his birth, to the favourable consideration of the admirers of the fine arts, and of all others, who cherish a disposition to encourage genius and enterprise.

Geo. N. Briggs,
Governor of the Commonwealth.

Letter from the Hon. EDWARD EVERETT, *late American Minister to the Court of St. James, to* Sir RODERIC J. MURCHISON, *of the Royal Geographical Society.*

Cambridge, Sept. 11, 1848.

DEAR SIR,

I have thought that the Royal Geographical Society might take some interest in a PANORAMA OF THE MISSISSIPPI. Strange as it may sound, Mr. Banvard has executed a painting of the whole course of that river, from original drawings, most laboriously executed upon the spot. He is the first projector of the enormous paintings of this clasa, which are now rapidly multiplying, and which, if executed with fidelity, like his, will have a scientific interest for the geographer. It is spoken of in terms of the highest commendation by good judges, and it has been most favourably received by the public. Mr. Banvard, I regret to hear, has been anticipated in Europe, by a party of speculators, who have tried to make a surreptitious copy of his painting; but I should hope that the superior merit of the original work will be readily perceived by all persons of intelligence in London,

I remain, dear Sir R.,
With the kindest regards,
Very faithfully yours,
(Signed)   *Edward Everett.*

Sir Roderic J. Murchison,
    &c. &c. &c.

This is to certify that I have examined Mr. Banvard's Painting of the Mississippi river, and having been engaged for a number of years in the employ of government, raising snags, and removing other obstructions, am well acquainted with the river, and unhesitatingly pronounce Mr. Banvard's Painting remarkably correct, and faithful to nature.

        U. S. Engineer.
        J. Morehead,

Louisville, Nov. 8, 1846.

We, the undersigned, being officers of steamboats continually plying on the Mississippi river, have examined Mr. Banvard's great Painting, and take much pleasure in recommending it for its fidelity and truthfulness to nature, and giving a correct delineation of the scenery and peculiar characteristics of this mighty river.

J. Joiner,	CAPTAIN.	*B. Smith,*	PILOT.
Daniel Dashiel,	"	*Henry E. Lee,*	"
C. S. Castleman,	"	*N. Ostrander,*	"
T. Coleman,	"	*Alex. Badger,*	"
Jac. Dillon,	"	*John Crawford,*	"
Sam. Pennington,	"	*Jas. D. Hamilton,*	"
Eli T. Dustin,	"	*D. S. Haley,*	"
Robert Brown,	"	*James O'Neal,*	"
Thomas Northup,	"	*Eli Vansickle,*	"
R. De Hart,	"	*Allen Peel,*	"

Over one hundred more names omitted for want of room.

STATE OF KENTUCKY,⎱
  City of Louisville. ⎰ ss.

I, F. A. KAYE, Mayor of the city of Louisville, do hereby certify that I am personally acquainted with nearly all of the gentlemen who have certified to the correctness of the great Panorama of the Mississippi river, painted by Mr. John Banvard; and certify further, that they are all practical navigators of the Mississippi river, are gentlemen of veracity, and entitled to full credit as such.

Fred. A. Kaye, Mayor.

{L. S.}

Mr. Banvard is the sole author of the great Panorama of the Mississippi River, which I have seen in common with tens of thousands of our citizens, and it is universally deemed a perfect representation of that wonderful river and its banks. I take great pleasure in commending this exhibition of skill and industry to the public.

Abbot Lawrence.

Boston, Sept. 19, 1848.

The undersigned has been navigating the Mississippi river for thirty years, and am as well acquainted with it as I am with the deck of the boat I command; and having twice examined Mr. Banvard's great Painting of the Mississippi river, take great pleasure in testifying to its truthfulness, and correctness to nature.

John Shallcross,
Master of Steamer "Peytona."

New Orleans, Nov. 20, 1846.

Banvard's Panorama is one of the most stupendous, grand, and wonderful creations of man: it is impossible to convey by words even a faint conception of this great work of genius and art. One must *see* it, and then he has all that is grand, noble, beautiful, and sublime, impressed, in vivid colours upon the tablet of his mind, but what language can never describe to others. — *New York Mirror.*

PANORAMA OF WESTERN TRAVEL

(*Designed for Exhibition in England*)

[*The panorama fever continued to flourish for decades—
Mark Twain was to find humorous capital in a traveling
panoramist as late as the 1800's* (Life on the Mississippi, *Chapter 59*). *Certainly, the vogue for such moving pictures was still strong a decade after the production of the five great panoramas of the Mississippi
(1847–49), if we are to judge from these sketches
made by a cartoonist named Arrowsmith for the December, 1858 issue of* Harper's Magazine (*XVIII, 141–
42*).]

Western Steamboat, with full cargo.

Pittsburgh on a clear morning.

Engineer on duty : two feet water on lower deck.

A Hot Boat.—Ten 56lbs. weights on safety-valve.

Running on a Bank.

View of Cincinnati.—[Perfectly accurate.]

Going over Falls of Ohio.—[Not exaggerated.]

Crossing Flint Island Bar at low water.

Curious effect produced on Steamer by running
aground.—[A frequent occurrence.]

Striking a Sawyer.

Sketch of Baggage belonging to Southern Gent. who occupied Stateroom with Arrowsmith.

Scene at Dinner-table.—Every man for himself.—
[This sketch is very correct.]

View of Steamer's Bar.—[Have we a Bourbon
among us?]

Portraits of several Colonels, Majors, Members of Congress, etc.—Found on board Steamer.

Panoramic view of Scenery of the Mississippi, from Cairo to New Orleans.

ON BOARD A KEELBOAT
DURING AN EARTHQUAKE

JOHN BRADBURY

———

[*John Bradbury, English botanist returning from his collecting trip up the Missouri River with the Astorians, left St. Louis for New Orleans on his way back to Liverpool in December 1811. At about ten o'clock on the night of the 15th his keelboat was tied up at the Chenal du Diable when the great New Madrid earthquake tore the country apart and set the river raging. The following account is from the second edition of his* Travels in the Interior of America in the Years 1809, 1810, and 1811 (*London, 1819*) *as reprinted in Reuben Gold Thwaites, editor,* Early Western Travels (*Cleveland, Arthur H. Clark Company, 1904*), IV, 201–11.]

In the evening of the 14th, we arrived at New Madrid, and having occasion for some necessaries, I bought them in the morning. I was much disappointed in this place, as I found only a few straggling houses, situated round a plain of from two to three hundred acres in extent. There are only two stores, which are very indifferently furnished. We set off about nine o'clock, and passed the Upper Chickasaw Bluffs; these bluffs are of soft sand-stone rock, of a yellow colour, but some parts being highly charged with oxyd of iron, the whole has a clouded appearance, and is considered as a curiosity by the boatmen. At the lower end of the bluffs we saw a smoke, and on a nearer approach, observed five or six Indians, and on the opposite side of the river, but lower down, we heard a dog howling. When the Indians perceived us, they held up some venison, to show us that they wished to dispose of it. Being desirous of adding to our stock of fresh meat, I hastily got into the canoe, and took with me one of the men, named La France, who spoke the Chickasaw language, as I supposed the

Indians to be of that nation. We very imprudently went without arms an omission that gave me some uneasiness before we reached them; especially as the boat, by my direction, proceeded leisurely on.

We found that the Indians had plenty of deer's flesh, and some turkies. I began to bargain for them, when the people in the boat fired a shot, and the dog on the other side of the river instantly ceased howling. The Indians immediately flew to their arms, speaking all together, with much earnestness. La France appeared much terrified, and told me that they said our people in the boat had shot their dog. I desired him to tell them that we did not believe that our people had done so, but if they had, I would pay them any price for him. They seemed too much infuriated to hearken to him, and surrounded us with their weapons in their hands. They were very clamorous amongst themselves, and, as I was afterwards told by La France, could not agree whether they should immediately put us to death, or keep us prisoners until we could procure goods from the boat to pay for the dog, on which it appeared they set high value. Most fortunately for us, the dog, at this instant began to bark opposite to us, having run a considerable distance up the river after the shot was fired. The tomahawks were immediately laid aside, and I bargained for half a deer, for which I gave them a quarter dollar and some gunpowder. I was not very exact in measuring the last, being rather anxious to get away, and could perceive that La France had no desire to stay any longer.

On reaching our canoe we seized our paddles, and being told by La France that we were not yet out of danger, we made every exertion to get out of their reach. When we conceived ourselves safe, we relaxed, and he told me that even when we were leaving them, they were deliberating whether they should detain us or not; some of them having remarked that the dog might be wounded. We had been so long delayed by this adventure, that it was more than an hour before we overtook the boat. I blamed the boatmen much for firing, and charged them with having fired at the dog: this, however, oppeared not to have been the case, as they fired at a loon, (*mergus merganser.*) In the course of this day, we passed no fewer than thirteen arks, or Kentucky boats, going with produce to Orleans; all these we left a considerable distance behind, as they only float with the stream, and we made considerable head-way with our oars. In the evening we came in view of the dangerous part of the river, called by the Americans the *Devil's Channel*, and by the French *Chenal du Diable*. It appears to be caused by a bank that crosses the river in this place, which renders it shallow. On this bank, a great number of trees have lodged; and, on account of the shallowness of the river, a considerable portion of the branches are raised above the surface; through these the water rushes with such impetuosity as to be heard at the distance of some miles.

As it would require every effort of skill and exertion to pass through this channel in safety, and as the sun had set, I resolved to wait until the morning, and caused the boat to be moored to a small island, about five hundred yards above the entrance into the channel. After supper we went to sleep as usual; and in the night, about ten o'clock, I was awakened by a most tremendous noise, accompanied by so violent an agitation of the boat that it appeared in danger of upsetting. Before I could quit the bed, or rather the skin, upon which I lay, the four men who slept in the other cabin rushed in, and cried out in the greatest terror, "*O mon Dieu! Monsieur Bradbury, qu'est ce qu'il y a?*" I passed them with some difficulty, and ran to the door of the cabin, where I could distinctly see the river agitated as if by a storm; and although the noise was inconceivably loud and terrific, I could distinctly hear the crash of falling trees, and the screaming of the wild fowl on the river, but found that the boat was still safe at her moorings. I was followed by the men and the *patron*, who, in accents of terror, were still enquiring what it was: I tried to calm them by saying, "*Restez vous tranquil, c'est un tremblement de terre,*" which term they did not seem to understand.

By the time we could get to our fire, which was on a large flag, in the stern of the boat, the shock had ceased; but immediately the perpendicular banks, both above and below us, began to fall into the river in such vast masses, as nearly to sink our boat by the swell they occasioned; and our *patron*, who seemed more terrified even than the men, began to cry out, "*O mon Dieu! nous perirons!*" I wished to consult with him as to what we could do to preserve ourselves and the boat, but could get no answer except "*O mon Dieu! nous perirons!*" and "*Allons à terre! Allons à terre!*" As I found Mr. Bridge the only one who seemed to retain any presence of mind, we consulted together, and agreed to send two of the men with a candle up the bank, in order to examine if it had separated from the island, a circumstance that we suspected, from hearing the snapping of the limbs of some drift trees, which were deposited between the margin of the river and the summit of the bank. The men, on arriving at the edge of the river, cried out, "*Venez à terre! Venez à terre!*" and told us there was a fire, and desired Mr. Bridge and the *patron* to follow them; and as it now occurred to me that the preservation of the boat in a great measure depended on the depth of the river, I tried with a sounding pole, and to my great joy, found it did not exceed eight or ten feet.

Immediately after the shock we observed the time, and found it was near two o'clock. At about nearly half-past two, I resolved to go ashore myself, but whilst I was securing some papers and money, by taking them out of my trunks, another shock came on, terrible indeed, but not equal to the first. Morin, our *patron*, called out from the island, "*Monsieur Bradbury! sauvez vous, sauvez vous!*" I went ashore, and found the chasm really frightful, being not less than four feet in width, and the bank had sunk at least two feet. I took the candle to examine its length, and concluded that it could not be less than eighty yards; and at each end, the banks had fallen into the river. I now saw clearly that our lives had been saved by our boat being moored to a sloping bank. Before we completed our fire, we had two more shocks, and others occurred during the whole night, at intervals of from six to ten minutes, but they were slight in comparison with the first and second. At four o'clock I took a candle, and again examined the bank, and perceived to my great satisfaction that no material alteration had taken place; I also found the boat safe, and secured my pocket compass. I had already noticed that the sound which was heard at the time of every shock, always preceded it at least a second, and that it uniformly came from the same point, and went off in an opposite direction. I now found that the shock came from a little northward of east, and proceeded to the westward. At day-light we had counted twenty-seven shocks during our stay on the island, but still found the chasm so that it might be passed. The river was covered with foam and drift timber, and had risen considerably, but our boat was safe. Whilst we were waiting till the light became sufficient for us to embark, two canoes floated down the river, in one of which we saw some Indian corn and some clothes. We considered this as a melancholy proof that some of the boats we passed the preceding day had perished. Our conjectures were afterwards confirmed, as we learned that three had been overwhelmed, and that all on board had perished. When the daylight appeared to be sufficient for us, I gave orders to embark, and we all went on board. Two men were in the act of loosening the fastenings, when a shock occurred nearly equal to the first in violence. The men ran up the bank, to save themselves on the island, but before they could get over the chasm, a tree fell close by them and stopped their progress. As the bank appeared to me to be moving rapidly into the river, I called out to the men in the boat, "*Coupez les cordes!*" on hearing which, the two men ran down the bank, loosed the cords, and jumped into the boat. We were again on the river: the *Chenal du Diable* was in sight, but it appeared absolutely impassable, from the quantity of trees and drift wood that had lodged during the night against the planters fixed in the bottom of the river; and in addition to our difficulties, the *patron* and the men appeared to be so terrified and confused, as to be almost incapable of action. Previous to passing the channel, I stopped that the men might have time to become more composed. I had the good fortune to discover a bank, rising with a gentle slope, where we again moored, and prepared to breakfast on the island. Whilst that was preparing, I walked out in company with Morin, our *patron*, to view the channel, to ascertain the safest part, which we soon agreed upon. Whilst we were thus employed, we experienced a very severe shock, and found some difficulty in preserving ourselves from being thrown down; another occurred during the time we were at breakfast, and a third as we were preparing to re-embark. In the last, Mr. Bridge, who was standing within the declivity of the bank, narrowly escaped being thrown into the river, as the sand continued to give way under his feet. Observing that the men were still very much under the influence of terror I desired Morin to give to each of them a glass of spirits, and reminding them that their safety depended on their exertions, we pushed out into the river. The danger we had now to encounter was of a nature which they understood: the nearer we approached it, the more confidence they appeared to gain; and indeed, all their strength, and all the skill of Morin, was necessary; for there being no direct channel through the trees, we were several times under the necessity of changing our course in the space of a few seconds, and that so instantaneously, as not to leave a moment for deliberation. Immediately after we had cleared all danger, the men dropped their oars, crossed themselves, then gave a shout, which was followed mutual congratulations on their safety.

We continued on the river till eleven o'clock, when there was another violent shock, which seemed to affect us as sensibly as if we had been on land. The trees on both sides of the river were most violently agitated, and the banks in several places fell in, within our view, carrying with them innumerable trees, the crash of which falling into the river, mixed with the terrible sound attending the shock, and the screaming of the geese and other wild fowl, produced an idea that all nature was in a state of dissolution. During the shock, the river had been much agitated, and the men became anxious to go ashore: my opinion was, that we were much safer on the river; but finding that they laid down their oars, and that they seemed determined to quit the boat for the present, we looked out for a part of the river where we might moor in security, and having found one, we stopped during the remainder of the day.

At three o'clock, another canoe passed us adrift on the river. We did not experience any more shocks until the morning of the 17th, when two occurred; one about five and the other about seven o'clock. We continued our voyage, and about twelve this day, had a severe shock, of very long duration. About four o'clock we came in sight of a log-house, a little above the Lower Chickasaw bluffs. More than twenty people came out as soon as they discovered us, and when within hearing earnestly entreated us to come ashore. I found them almost distracted with fear, and that they were composed of several families, who had collected to pray together. On entering the house, I saw a bible lying open on the table. They informed me that the greatest part of the inhabitants in the neighbourhood had fled to the hills, on the opposite side of the river, for safety; and that during the shock, about sun-rise on the 16th, a chasm had opened on the sand bar opposite the bluffs below, and on closing again, had thrown the water to the height of a tall tree. They also affirmed that the earth opened in several places back from the river. One of the men, who appeared to be considered as possessing more knowledge than the rest, entered into an explanation of the cause, and attributed it to the comet that had appeared a few months before, which he described as having two horns,

over one of which the earth had rolled, and was now lodged
betwixt them: that the shocks were occasioned by the attempts
made by the earth to surmount the other horn. If this should be
accomplished, all would be well, if otherwise, inevitable destruction to the world would follow. Finding him confident in his
hypothesis, and myself unable to refute it, I did not dispute the
point, and we went on about a mile further. Only one shock
occurred this night, at half past seven o'clock. On the morning of
the 18th, we had two shocks, one betwixt three and four o'clock,
and the other at six. At noon, there was a violent one of very long
duration, which threw a great number of trees into the river
within our view, and in the evening, two slight shocks more, one
at six, the other at nine o'clock.

*19*ᵗʰ— We arrived at the mouth of the river St. Francis, and had
only one shock, which happened at eleven at night.

*20*ᵗʰ— Detained by fog, and experienced only two shocks, one at
five, the other at seven in the evening.

21″— Awakened by a shock at half past four o'clock: this was
the last, it was not very violent, but it lasted for nearly a minute.

On the 24ᵗʰ in the evening, we saw a smoke, and knowing
that there were no habitations on this part of the river, we made
towards it, and found it to be the camp of a few Choctaw Indians,
from whom I purchased a swan, for five balls and five loads of
powder.

*25*ᵗʰ— Monsieur Longpre overtook us, and we encamped together in the evening. He was about two hundred miles from us
on the night of the 15th, by the course of the river, where the
earthquakes had also been very terrible. It appeared from his
account, that at New Madrid the shock had been extremely violent: the greatest part of the houses had been rendered uninhabitable, although, being constructed of timber, and framed together, they were better calculated to withstand the shocks than
buildings of brick or stone. The greatest part of the plain on
which the town was situated was become a lake, and the houses
were deserted.

A LITTLE DIFFICULTY WITH ICE

CHARLES AUGUSTUS MURRAY

———

[Charles Augustus Murray, after a pleasant visit in St. Louis following his summer excursion to the Pawnee Country, found some difficulty in getting away to New Orleans because of ice in the river. The description of this experience is from his Travels in North America during the Years 1834, 1835, & 1836 *(2nd edition, 2 volumes, London, 1839), II, 166–72. The time was November 1835. The cousin referred to was the well known Scottish sportsman, Captain William Drummond Stewart, who had returned from a hunting trip to the Wind River Mountains with the intention of wintering in New Orleans.]*

I now prepared to leave the town with much regret. The frost had set in with considerable severity; and large floating masses of ice were scattered so thickly on the bosom of the water, that the navigation of the river became every day more difficult and dangerous. I was anxious to get as soon as possible to New Orleans, because I had desired all my European and other letters to be sent thither to wait my arrival.

I was fortunate enough to be able to collect a very pleasant little party, and we agreed to embark and keep together: it consisted of Captain S——, a cousin and old acquaintance of mine in Scotland, who had been above two years among the Indians, in and beyond the rocky mountains; my friend V——, and a Dr. W——, also from Scotland, a lively and well-informed companion. We took our passage on board of *The Far West*, Captain Fox; her machinery had been newly put in, and, although several parts of it were rather loose and out of order, the boilers were strong, and the cabin-berths, &c. remarkably neat and cleanly.

We embarked on the 29th of November, and were obliged to cross the river to the Illinois side, in order to take in some freight. On the following day the ice ran so heavy and thick, that the captain dared not attempt to descend the river, and with much difficulty regained the landing at St. Louis. Here we were obliged to lie two days. The committee of insurance came down and warned the captain, that, if he started while the ice was so dangerous, he must do it at his own risk; and we began to entertain serious apprehensions that the river would close up, and we should be shut in for the season. However, the weather changed; and on the afternoon of the 2nd of December, we got off, and went down as far as Vuides-poches, about six miles. It was a bright moon, and fine frosty night, so V—— and I determined to gallop off to the arsenal, and spend one pleasant hour more with Captain S—— and his agreeable lady. The landlord of the tavern, a good-natured Irishman, lent us a couple of horses, and we set off at full speed over the snowy slippery road. As it was only four miles, we were soon at our journey's end; and the astonishment of our friends at our appearance was not small, as they thought us half-way to New Orleans. They received us with their usual kind hospitality; my ears got another Cramer feast, and our amiable hostess prepared a bowl of egg-nogg, which was to serve as a "*diachin dhorrish,*" and to fortify us against the night air.

Bidding them another adieu, we returned to Vuides-poches, and went on board about midnight. Our landlord gave me a bottle of Irish whisky, and would not accept of a farthing either for that or for the use of his horses. How grieved I am, that the Irish people should tarnish the generous and noble qualities which they really do possess, by the violence and lawlessness of their habits! In explanation of this well-known fact, we are always told that it is owing entirely to the oppression and misgovernment of the English. It may be *partly* so, but no more. The Irish in America —in every State from Maine to Louisiana, where they are certainly not oppressed, and are free from tithes, from heavy taxes, from ecclesiastical burthens, from want, in short, from every subject of complaint and grievance in Ireland, are still the most improvident, quarrelsome, turbulent population on this continent.

Nature has been liberal to Ireland in her soil and climate; she has endowed its inhabitants with humour, readiness both of conception and language, bravery and generosity; but she seems to have been less liberal in providing them with judgment and a just moral sense, the absence of which qualities, impairs or perverts the above endowments.

On the following day, December 3rd, we met with no accident; but were obliged to go very slowly, in consequence of the thick and heavy masses of ice which covered the river. On the 4th, however, our misfortunes began. We ran on a sand-bar at nine o'clock, A.M., but got off again, in an hour; at eleven we ran aground again and stuck fast till three P.M. We grounded again soon after dusk, and floated off about nine, without having any wood on board; and we had to drop down with the stream at considerable risk, for two or three miles, when we reached a wood-yard.

5ᵗʰ— We soon found that the pilot either knew nothing of his business, or that he ran us aground on purpose; or else that the heavy descent of ice had altered the channel, and created new banks of mud or sand. We ran on a bar at nine A.M., and remained there all day. Several boats passed us: I went on board one with our captain, to request her assistance in hauling us off; her captain, however, was deaf to entreaties, and even to liberal offers of payment. To complete our ill-luck, the yawl in which we had boarded this boat (*The G. Clark*,) was knocked under by her wheel and swamped, not half a minute after we had jumped out of her. She was held on by the painter; but we lost all our oars and two or three of the men's jackets. We had to bale her out with buckets, and with much labour towed her, half full of water, behind *The G. Clark*'s yawl back to *The Far West*. *The G. Clark* and her obliging captain then went off, leaving us in what might be called down-east, a "particular considerable unhandsome fix."

We contrived in a few hours to rig a couple of clumsy sweeps, baled out the yawl, and kedged our anchor, with the aid of which we hauled off the bar; and once more afloat, went down two or three miles to a wood-yard, where we lay-to for the night. We now thought that our troubles were over, as we had got through the worst of the ice; but, on the following day (the 6th), at half-past eight, we ran on a bar near a place called Devil's Island. Here, I almost believed that the gentleman in black had possessed our pilot; for he ran our boat right on a sand-bank, which a schoolboy might have seen and avoided, inasmuch as there was a great log of wood and a quantity of drifted ice lying upon it. We were going ten or twelve miles an hour, and the boat bounded, jumped, and made every exertion to get over, but in vain; her plunging only lodged her the deeper, and we, drawing five and a half feet, lay comfortably imbedded in mud and sand, with only three feet and a half of water.

We remained here several hours; it was impossible to drag her off by her anchor, and I began to fear that her fate was sealed, and that we (the passengers) must leave her by the first boat that passed. I was really grieved at this; for our captain was a most good-natured obliging man: it was his first trip since the complete refitting of his boat; and if she lay here long with her broadside exposed to the huge masses of ice that come down the river at this season, she must have gone to pieces in a few weeks.

After a few hours, a small steamer, named *The Indian*, hove in sight: we hailed her, and she came alongside. Our captain agreed to give four hundred dollars if she would take some of our freight and tow us off the bar: after much time and trouble, she did so: and as soon as we floated, she went off down the channel, expecting us to follow immediately: we endeavoured to do so, but something went wrong in the machinery, and we could not make the right course; consequently we dropped down again upon the bank and became imbedded as fast or faster than ever.

The little *Indian*, though out of sight, soon missed us and returned; and, in order to obtain her further assistance to get us off, our poor captain was obliged to give a thousand instead of four hundred dollars. Notwithstanding the united efforts of the passengers and both crews, we lay there all the next day; but about eight o'clock on the 8th instant, having put all our freight on board *The Indian*, which was fortunately empty, we got off and made good our passage through this difficult channel. In the course of the day we found *The Indian* anchored in the middle of the river, having broken her paddles and otherwise injured her machinery: we took her in tow and brought her ashore; for which I trust our captain obtained some diminution of the enormous sum which she had exacted from him. We reached the mouth of the Ohio without further accident or difficulty; but the machinery was not in perfect order, owing to the illness of the engineer, who could not leave his bed.

SKETCHES OF THE MISSISSIPPI

JACOB A. DALLAS

Though Jacob A. Dallas was born in Philadelphia, he knew the western country at first hand, for as a boy he was taken by his family to Missouri and lived there for at least ten years. Later he made one or more trips to the Mississippi Valley. In 1854, he exhibited at the National Academy of Design three paintings of western subjects: An Encampment of Negroes at Memphis; Scene in French Market, New Orleans; *and* Waiting for the Ferry: An Incident in Arkansas. *He died in September 1857. With one exception the woodcuts reproduced here were made after original drawings by Dallas to illustrate two articles: "Up the Mississippi" in* Emerson's Magazine and Putnam's Monthly, *v, 433–56 [October, 1857] and "The Upper Mississippi" in* Harper's New Monthly Magazine, *xvi, 433–54 [March, 1858]. Neither text was by Dallas. The remaining sketch first appeared as an illustration for T. B. Thorpe's "Remembrances of the Mississippi" in* Harper's Magazine, *xii, 35–41 [December, 1855].*

ENTRANCE TO THE MISSISSIPPI
(*From* Emerson's Magazine and Putnam's Monthly, v [*October, 1857*], *433*)

Here the tug bears down on "the white-winged ship. Her wings are closed and she is borne away with irresistible power over the bars, and through the slimy mud, till she enters between long, low mud lines, which here border the 'Father of Waters' "

FORT SNELLING
(*From* Harpers New Monthly Magazine, xvi [*March, 1858*], *444*)

ST. PAUL, MINNESOTA
(*From* Harper's New Monthly Magazine, xvi [*March, 1858*], *445*)

PRAIRIE DU CHIEN, WISCONSIN
(*From* Harper's New Monthly Magazine, xvi [*March, 1858*], *448*)

THE LEAD REGION—GALENA IN THE DISTANCE
(*From* Harper's New Monthly Magazine, xvi [*March, 1858*], *448*)

INDIAN LODGE IN MINNESOTA
(*From* Harper's New Monthly Magazine, xvi [*March, 1858*], *435*)

INDIAN BURIAL-PLACE, MINNESOTA
(*From* Harper's New Monthly Magazine, xvi [*March, 1858*], *435*)

THE DEVIL'S TOWER
(*From* Harper's New Monthly Magazine, xvi [*March, 1858*], 434)

DEVIL'S BAKE OVEN
(*From* Harper's New Monthly Magazine, xvi [*March, 1858*], *434*)

TIMBER RAFT ON THE MISSISSIPPI
(*From* Harper's New Monthly Magazine, XVI [*March, 1858*], 452)

VIRGINIA HOE-DOWN—INTERIOR OF A FLATBOAT
(*From* Harper's New Monthly Magazine, XII [*December, 1855*], 38)

WOODYARD ON THE MISSISSIPPI
(*From* Emerson's Magazine and Putnam's Monthly, v [*October, 1857*], *452, 456*)

The wood-cutter's "shanty stands on some elevated bank, above the reach of ordinary floods, surrounded with ranks of firewood. . . . Boats coming down the river are obliged to round-to and tie up, while taking wood aboard."

STEAMBOAT LANDING ON THE LOWER MISSISSIPPI
(*From* Emerson's Magazine and Putnam's Monthly, v [*October, 1857*], *435*)

HORSEMAN WAITING FOR THE FERRY
(*From* Emerson's Magazine and Putnam's Monthly, v [*October, 1857*], 450)

A CREVASSE ON THE LOWER MISSISSIPPI
(*From* Harper's New Monthly Magazine, xvi [*March, 1858*], 451)

FLATBOAT IN DANGER OF BEING RUN DOWN AT NIGHT
(*From* Emerson's Magazine and Putnam's Monthly, v [*October, 1857*], *448, 455*)

"No little risk is run by the flat-boats, which come drifting down the river, of being run down in a dark night, or in the fog, by a steamer coming up with full head of steam. . . . as the sound of the steamer is the signal of her coming, and as the flat-boat can give no signal, it wakes the flat-boatmen to great activity, and her long sweeps are worked as though they were reeds until she is past the danger; and then all settle again to a lazy repose."

STEAMBOAT WOODING AT NIGHT
(*From* Emerson's Magazine and Putnam's Monthly, v [*October, 1857*], *453*)

STEAMBOAT APPROACHING A WHARF-BOAT

(*From* Emerson's Magazine and Putnam's Monthly, v [*October, 1857*], *453, 456*)

"The rise and fall of the river being so great, permanent wharves are impossible; their place is supplied, at all stopping-places of any business, with a floating dock, called a wharf-boat. This being tied to the bank, rises and falls with the floods, and is thus safe and convenient. It is the center of activity, and is usually thronged upon the arrival or departure of boats."

INTERIOR OF A WHARF-BOAT
(*From* Emerson's Magazine and Putnam's Monthly, v [*October, 1857*], *454, 456*)

"About these wharf-boats congregate all the idle and good-for-nothing fellows of the town, who having no steady occupation, hope to pick up some
job which will keep them supplied with the two things needful—whisky and
tobacco. In the sheltered interior of the boat, it is not uncommon for the
master and his friends to while away the tedious hours of waiting (and they
are many) with a social game of cards or a rousing song."

HIGH WATER ON THE LOWER MISSISSIPPI
(*From* Emerson's Magazine and Putnam's Monthly, v [*October, 1857*], *451*)

NEGRO CAMP, WITH STEAMBOAT LOADING COTTON

(*From* Emerson's Magazine and Putnam's Monthly, v [*October, 1857*], *442, 456*)

"In this mild climate much of the life is out-of-doors, and one constantly comes upon negro-camps, where existence is enjoyed in its simplest forms."

STORE BOAT INTERIOR

(*From* Emerson's Magazine and Putnam's Monthly, v [*October, 1857*], *452*)

SUGAR WORKS IN LOUISIANA
(*From* Emerson's Magazine and Putnam's Monthly, v [*October, 1857*], *447*)

NEGRO WOMEN AND A PEDLAR NEAR A SUGAR PLANTATION
(*From* Emerson's Magazine and Putnam's Monthly, v [*October, 1857*], *444, 445*)

The traveler "need not be surprised if he should meet with singular groups, such as he meets nowhere else; but always the negroes, carrying their fruits or loads on their heads, are the most interesting."

THE LEVEE AT NEW ORLEANS
(*From* Emerson's Magazine and Putnam's Monthly, v [*October, 1857*], *435, 437*)

" 'Tis a busy, driving, dreadful place, piled with bales and boxes, with hogsheads and casks, and cattle and bureaus, and bedsteads, and horse-carts, and pulpits, and all the other multitude of things which come pouring out of that wonderful cornucopia, the Valley of the Mississippi."

GERMAN IMMIGRANTS AT NEW ORLEANS
(*From* Emerson's Magazine and Putnam's Monthly, v [*October, 1857*], *436, 439*)

"One would have pity, if one had time, for those poor strangers who, plunged into this chaos [on the Levee], raw and ignorant, speak no language but an unknown one, know not where to go, have no friends . . . but one spends no sympathy or time on them, too happy if he can but save his own life and legs."

SUNDAY MORNING COFFEE AT THE MARKET, NEW ORLEANS
(*From* Emerson's Magazine and Putnam's Monthly, v [*October, 1857*], *438, 440*)

"the quadroon girl, who sells that most delicious of drinks, coffee, made
surpassingly good."

SCENE AT THE MARKET ON SUNDAY MORNING
(*From* Emerson's Magazine and Putnam's Monthly, v [*October, 1857*], *438, 441*)

"Picturesque groups are often seen under the shadows of the markets, which the artist's will seize; not unlikely a party of Indian girls, ready to sell their small wares and willing to be gazed upon."

NEW ORLEANS CEMETERY

(*From* Emerson's Magazine and Putnam's Monthly, v [*October, 1857*], *443*)

"It is well known that in most parts of New Orleans water is found at the depth of two feet, which has brought about a custom of burying the dead in tombs and ovens, built above ground; you therefore find, in place of tombstones and tablets, intended to perpetuate the virtues of the departed, a City of the Dead."

LIVE OAK WITH SPANISH MOSS

(*From* Emerson's Magazine and Putnam's Monthly, v [*October, 1857*], *444*)

"Everywhere the hanging moss which covers the trees gives a wild and
picturesque character to the country."

SUGAR PLANTATION BELOW NEW ORLEANS
(*From* Emerson's Magazine and Putnam's Monthly, v [*October, 1857*], *436*)

FISHERMAN'S SHANTY NEAR THE MOUTH OF THE MISSISSIPPI
(*From* Emerson's Magazine and Putnam's Monthly, v [*October, 1857*], *434*)

"For a time no living thing breaks the profound solitude, or relieves the wide waste which spreads away on all sides; and you almost wonder that the bittern or the alligator should here continue to live. They are the only indications of life, till among the marsh grass of the ooze, a curling smoke, or the rude 'look-out,' tells of a fisherman's shanty. From this point he goes out in pursuit of fish, lobsters, and oysters, and along the gulf-shores, and its many bayous he gathers good spoil, with which the New Orleans Market is so well supplied."

SELF-PORTRAIT
(*From* Harper's New Monthly Magazine, xvi [*March, 1858*], 454)

HURRICANE AT NATCHEZ

―――――

[*Reported by J. H. Freligh, Captain of the steamboat* Prairie, *from New Orleans, May 16, 1840, to J. G. Bennett of the New York* Herald, *as reprinted in the St. Louis* Daily Commercial Bulletin, *June 9, 1840.*]

On the 7th inst., about 2 P.M., my boat was lying at the Natchez landing, taking cotton on board—we had been there about one and a half hours; the sky during that time was filled with heavy, dark clouds—in the distance was heard a continual dull roaring of what we supposed thunder, which gradually grew louder and more distinct. At intervals there were sharp, heavy claps, attended with the most vivid lightning. Gradually the clouds lowered still darker—the claps of thunder grew louder and seemed nearer—the lightning flashed still brighter—the distant rolling thunder assumed more the sound of moaning—every appearance indicated, as we supposed, a violent storm of rain. Many on board were attracted by the gloomy grandeur of the heavens, and were watching it with feelings of awe, which every manifestation of divine power so palpable to the senses is calculated to raise in the human breast. Suddenly the appearance of the sky changed, and showed by various signs the approach of a mighty wind. No time was then left for calculations or further observation of the terrific war of the elements. All were on the alert—additional lines were ordered to be got out to shore—the engineer ordered to be ready— the pilot summoned to the wheel, and every precaution taken to have the boat secure against the coming storm.

With one of the hands I ran to the roof to pay out a hawser to the forecastle. We had got the end out, and it was laid hold of by the men below, the hand and myself paying it out on the roof, when the storm burst on us. The roof was lifted, or started like. With the impulse of self-preservation, I sprang to the gangway leading to the boiler deck—plunged down it—and threw myself flat on my face on the boiler deck—grasped the edge of it to keep myself from being whirled away—looked up and saw the place I had just been standing on, and the entire upper works of the boat, swept away. The hand that was with me on the roof was precipitated to the forecastle uninjured. I lay, utterly incapable of motion from the violence of the wind about ten minutes. It then somewhat abated, and I was able to jump to the forecastle. The boat had parted all her moorings, and was turned stern up stream—her bow still being to the shore. She was again made fast, the waves pitching dreadfully. I looked around me—all was horror, desolation, ruin. Houses were laid level with the earth—the shore was entirely covered with the wreck of buildings, boats and goods. Two steamboats were sunk——fifty or more flat boats engulfed in the raging waters, with their contents and their crews. The forests opposite were transformed into mere stubble-fields of splinters. The surface of the river was covered with wrecks of various kinds. My own boat lay a dismantled and useless wreck, floating a shapeless hulk on the boiling and maddened waters. On examination, I found one young man a corpse, five or six badly hurt, and five missing.

A STORM SCENE ON THE MISSISSIPPI

T. B. THORPE

———

[*Among the many pictures of life on the Mississippi
sketched by Thomas Bangs Thorpe is this "Storm Scene,"
taken from the New York* Spirit of the Times, *March 26,
1842 (XII, 43–44).*]

In the year 18—— we found ourselves travelling "low down on
the Mississippi." The weather was intensely hot, and as we
threaded our way through the forests, and swamps, through
which the river flows, there seemed to be a stifled atmosphere, and
a silent one, such as required little wisdom to predict as the
forerunner of a storm. The insects of the woods were more than
usually troublesome, and venomous. The locust, would occasionally make its shrill sounds as on a merry day, then suddenly stop,
give a disquiet chirp or two, and relapse into silence. The venomous musquito, revelled in the dampness of the air, and suspending
its clamor of distant trumpets, seemed only intent to bite. The
crows scolded like unquiet housewives, high in the air, while
higher still, wheeled in graceful, but narrowed circles, the buzzard. The dried twigs in our path bent, instead of snapping, as the
weight of our horses' hoofs pressed upon them, while the animals
themselves, would put forward their ears, as if expecting soon to
be very much alarmed, and lastly, to make all these signs certain,
the rheumatic limbs of an old Indian guide, who accompanied us,
suddenly grew lame, for he went limping upon his delicately
formed feet, and occasionally looking aloft with suspicious eyes,
he would proclaim, that there would be "storm too much!"
    A storm in the forest is no trifling affair, the tree under
which you shelter yourself, may draw the lightning upon your
head, or its ponderous limbs, pressed upon by the wind, may drag
the heavy trunk to the earth, crushing you with itself, in its fall;

or some dead branch, that has for years protruded from among the green foliage, may on the very occasion of your presence, fall to the ground, and destroy you. The rain too, which in the forest, finds difficulty in soaking into the earth, will in a few hours, fill up the ravines, and water courses, wash away the trail you may be following, or destroy the road over which you journey. All these things, we were from experience aware of, and as we were some distance from our journey's end, and also from any "settlement," we passed forward to a "clearing" which was in our path, as a temporary stopping place, until the coming storm should have passed away.

Our resting place for the night, was on the banks of the Mississippi; it consisted of a rude cabin in the centre of a small garden spot, and field, and had been the residence of a squatter; now deserted, for causes unknown to us, it was most pleasantly situated, and commanded a fine view of the river, both up and down its channel. We reached this rude dwelling just as the sun was setting, and his disappearance behind the low lands of the Mississippi, was indeed glorious. Refracted by the humidity of the atmosphere into a vast globe of fire, it seemed to be kindling up the Cypress trees, that stretched out before us, into a light blaze, while the gathering clouds extended the conflagration far north and south, and carried it upwards far into the heavens. Indeed, so glorious for a moment was the sight, that we almost fancied that another Phaeton was driving the chariot of the Sun, and that, in its ungoverned course, its wheels were fired; and the illusion was quite complete, when we heard the distant thunder, echoing from those brilliant clouds, and saw the lightning, like silver arrows, flashing across the crimson heavens. A moment more, and the sun seemed extinguished in the waters, all light disappeared, and the sudden darkness that follows sunset as you approach the tropics surrounded us.

With the delightful consciousness of having already escaped the storm, we gathered round a pleasant blaze, formed of some dried twigs, kindled by flashing powder in the pan of an old fashioned gun. In the mean time the thunder was growing more and more distinct, the lightning flashed more brightly, and an occasional gust of wind, accompanied by sleet, would penetrate between the logs that composed our shelter. An old wood-chopper, who made one of our party, grew loquacious, as he became rested and comfortable, and he detailed with great effect, the woeful scenes he had been in at different times of his life the most awful of which had been preceded by just such signs of weather, as were then exhibiting themselves. Among other adventures, he had been wrecked, while acting as a "hand" on a flat boat, navigating the Mississippi. He said, he had come all the way from Pittsburg, at the head of the Ohio, to within two or three hundred miles of Orleans, without meeting with any other accident, than that of getting out of whiskey twice. But one night, the captain of the flat-boat said the weather was "crafty," a thing he thought himself, as it was most too quiet to last so, long. After detailing several other particulars he finished his story by being wrecked, as follows: "After the quiet weather I spoke of lasted a little, all of a sudden it changed, the river grew as rough as an alligator's back, thar was the tallest kind of a noise overhead, and the fire flew up thar, like fur in a cat fight. 'We'll put in shore,' said the captain, and we tried to do it, that's sartain, but the way we always walked off from a tree, whar we might have tied up, was a caution to steamboats. 'Keep the current,' said the captain, 'and let us sweat it out.' We went on this way some time, when I told the captain, said I captain, 'I have never been in these diggins 'afore, but if I havn't seen the same landscape three times, then I am a liar.' At this, the captain looked hard, and swore we were in an eddy, and doing nothing but whirling round. The lightning just at this time was very accommodating, and showed us a big tree in the river, that had stuck fast, and was bowing up and down, ready to receive us, and we found ourselves rushing straight on to it. The owner of the bakon was on board, and when he saw the 'sawyer,' he eyed it as hard as a small thief would a constable; says he, 'captain, if that ar fellow at the sweep,' (oar) 'fellow' meant me; said he, 'captain, if that ar fellow at the sweep, don't bear on it like ———, and keep us off that tree, I am a busted up pork merchant.' I did bear on it as hard as he suggested, but the current was too strong, and we went on the 'sawyer' all standing. The boat broke up, like a dried leaf would have done, pork and plunder scattered, and I swum half soaked to death, ashore. I lost in the whole operation just two shirts, eighteen dollars in wages, and half a box of Kentucky tobacker, beside two game cocks; I tell you what, a storm on that ar Mississippi, ain't to be sneezed at."

The wood-chopper's story, when concluded, would have occasioned a general laugh, had there not been outside our cabin, at this moment, a portentous silence, which alarmed us all. The storm had been upon us in its full fury, we thought, but we now felt that more was to come; in the midst of this expectation, a stream of fire rushed from the horizon upwards; when high overhead, could be seen its zig-zag course, then rushing downwards almost at our very feet, a few hundred yards from us, a tall oak dropped some of its gigantic limbs, and flashed into a light blaze. The rain however powerful previously, now descended in one continued sheet. The roof of our shelter seemed to gather rain rather than to protect us from it; little rivulets dashed across the floor, and then widening into streams, we were soon literally afloat. The descending floods, sounded about us like the roll-call of a muffled drum, the noise sometimes almost deafening us, then dying off in the distance, as the sweeping gusts of wind drove the clouds before them. The burning forest hissed and cracked and rolled up great columns of steam. The muddy water of the Mississippi in all this war of the elements, rushed on, save where it touched its banks, with a smooth, but mysterious looking surface, that resembled in the glare of the lightning, a mirror of bronze. And to heighten this almost unearthly effect, the forest trees that lined its shores, rose up like dark mountains, impenetrable darkness, against clouds burning with fire. The thunder cracked and echoed through the heavens, and the half-starved wolf, nearly dead with fear, mingled his cries of distress with the noises without, startling us with the full conviction that we heard the voices of men dying in the storm. Hours passed away, and the elements spent their fury; and although the rain continued falling in torrents, it was finally unaccompanied by lightning. So sudden indeed were the extremes, that with your eyes dilating with the glare of the heavens, you found yourself surrounded by the most perfect darkness. Confused, bewildered, and soaking wet, we followed the stoical example of our Indian guide, and settling down in a crouching attitude, waited most impatiently for the light of the morning. The rain continued to descend, and the same deep darkness was upon us; my companions soon fell asleep, and snored as soundly as if they were at home; the long drawn respirations added to my misery. Wound up to the highest pitch of impatience, I was about starting to my feet, to utter some angry complaint, when the Indian, who I thought was asleep, touched me on the arm, and with a peculiar sound, signified that I must listen. This I did do, but I heard nothing but the dull clattering of the rain, and after a while I said so. For some time the Indian made no reply, although I was conscious that he was intensely listening. Suddenly he sprang upon his feet, gave a loud grunt, and groped to the door. This intrusive noise awoke the wood-chopper, who instantly seizing his rifle, sang out, "Halloo, what's the matter, you red varmint, snorting in a man's face like a scared buffalo bull, what's the matter?"

"*River too near*," was the slow reply of the Indian.

"He's right, so help me ————," shouted the wood-chopper, "the banks of the Mississippi are caving in," and then with a spring he leaped through the door, and bid us follow. His advice was quickly obeyed. The Indian was the last to leave the cabin, and as he left its threshhold, *the weighty unhewn logs, that composed it, crumbled, along with the rich soil, into the swift rushing current of the Mississippi.*

This narrow escape made our fortunes somewhat bearable, and we waited with some little patience for day. At the proper time the sun rose gloriously bright, as if its smiling face was never obscured by a cloud. The little birds of the woods sang merrily, there was the greenness, and freshness, of a new creation on every thing; and the landscape of the previous night, was indeed altered. The long jutting point where stood the squatter's hut and "clearing," had disappeared, house, garden spot, fields, and fences, were gone; the water-washed banks lined with the ancient forest. The stranger would never have dreamed that the axe, and the plough, had been in the vicinity. The caving banks had obliterated all signs of humanity, and left every thing about in a wild, and primitive solitude.

T. B. T.

Note—The banks of the Mississippi are evidently formed of alluvial deposit from the river; we presume geologists would find the sub-stratum of these banks in all cases, sand, the swift current sometimes undermining hundreds of acres of bank which falls into the river. Plantations are in this way often ruined, and lives sometimes lost.

A SEVERE TIME ON THE MISSISSIPPI

CODDINGTON C. JACKSON

[*Yet another contributor to the New York* Spirit *of the* Times *who delighted readers with sketches of the Mississippi was Coddington C. Jackson, who used the pen name of "The Little 'Un." His "Severe Time on the Mississippi" appeared in the issue of June 14, 1851 (XXI, 194). His obituary was published in the* Spirit *in 1856 (XXV, 534).*]

Many of the readers of the *Spirit* are somewhat familiar with the *nom de plume* which has been attached to most of my "quail tracks" in the *Spirit*.

At the time the incidents (I am about to relate) occurred, I was, in reality, more of a "Little 'Un" than I am at this present writing—as the darkey would say, "Quite more mucher smaller," in fact, I was the "Little 'Un" of that crowd.

In the Fall of 184—— I took passage on board the steamer Annawan, at New Orleans, bound for St. Louis. I had at that time that interesting complaint, the "Every-other-day-ague," a complaint for which I have a most thorough contempt, from the fact that I can cure it in twenty-four hours (and if any of the "Spirit's" readers wish, I can furnish them with the recipe of an infallible remedy), and also because one day a person feels perfectly well, and the next as if he had been "dragged through a sick Frenchman." In my hurry at leaving I had neglected to provide myself with the necessary preventives, and a return of the ague was the consequence.

The next morning I observed considerable excitement among the passengers, and felt that the boat was very much jarred; on looking astern I saw the cause: another St. Louis boat was about a mile below us, doing her very tallest, and our captain, who wasn't one to be beaten without an effort, was cramming in the pine-knots, and crowding her hard. We had stopped at a wood-yard, and the crew and deck passengers were just finishing off the last cord, when the Captain (whom I had noticed standing aft, watching our rival,) started forward and rang the bell, and hailed the men to "drop that wood and jump aboard," and in a moment we were running down under a heavy head of steam to the other boat. We soon saw the cause of our captain's haste.

The other boat had run in to "wood" at a yard a short distance below us, when she struck a sawyer (under full headway), which passed through her forcas'le, boiler, and hurricane decks, and stuck up like a third chimney, for'ard the pilot house, thus preventing that part of the boat from sinking, while the ladies' saloon aft was under water, and when we hailed, they were cutting away the for'ard guard of the boiler deck to get a skiff into the cabin to save the baggage. She had on board a deck load of German emigrant passengers, whose entire property consisted of the money in their chests, then some twenty feet under water; and they in a strange land, unacquainted with our language; they were truly in a pitiable condition. Our captain offered every assistance, but the most he could do was to take her cabin passengers, which at that season of the year was necessarily a small number. The Germans refused to leave the spot. It appeared as if we were also doomed to meet with a series of accidents, the first of which occurred the next day, when the cry of "fire!" start[l]ed us, but it was soon put out, after burning the bedclothes of one berth. Two days after a snag raked off the starboard main deck guard; but the principal accident worthy of note, was the one that gave me the name I was known by among that crowd, and since among a larger crowd, the "Spirit's" readers.

We had tied up one night, in consequence of a thick fog, some hundred miles below the mouth of the Ohio river. I turned out about 4 P.M. to get a drink, as I had the fever on me *strong*. The pilot and engineer were sitting in the social hall talking, and I asked them how long before we should start? They said "in about half an hour," and I returned to my state-room, and turned into the lower berth. 'Tis a little singular that the day previous I had changed my state-room from the other side of the boat, as the room being against the wheel-house, was necessarily dark, and I was in the habit of lying in my berth in the day time, and reading until the ague came along and "gave me fits."

The next recollection I had, after turning in, was hearing

some one sing out, "Hello! where the devil are you, Little 'Un?" and feeling very cold and uncomfortably wet. Presently a lantern was poked in my face, and I found myself on top of a pile of salt, alongside of the engine, in my night dress only. The engineer picked me up, and carried me into the cabin, while the crowd kept asking, "Is that him?" "Found the Little 'Un yet?" "Where was he?" &c., &c.

I had a hard looking phiz. Imagine a fellow's hitting you a severe wipe over the countenance with a gridiron, every bar leaving its mark and starting the claret, and you will have a pretty good idea of the effect the slats of the upper berth had on our devoted mug. We had "tied up" to a bluff bank in the night, and just after I turned in a "landslip" had occurred, and with it came an immense dead tree, one fork of which raked us from the wheel-house, for'ard, taking the four state-rooms abaft the stairs, both larboard guards (boiler and main deck), knocking our wood all into the river, damaging the engine, and making a general smash, and converting the cabin floor into an inclined plain. No one was hurt but myself. The forward state-room (with four berths for the stewards) was vacant, the occupants being below getting breakfast underway. My room was second, the third empty, and the fourth contained a very fat man, and as his room was merely sloped down, he quietly rolled over and over until the salt pile brought him to, when he picked himself up and returned to the cabin.

It was fortunate that I had taken the under berth, as the mattress above was doubtless all that saved me, for the tree must have struck directly over my head, as on washing away the blood I found about half a pint of fine bark in my hair. My trunk was all "cove in," and most of my clothing missing. The clerk went down with a light, and brought up my coat, vest, pants, boots, and a very bad specimen of a "D'Arcy's best plug," which, in the vernacular, is supposed to mean a "cady," otherwise a hat. I found my pocket-book safe in an inside pocket, a gold pencil in my vest pocket was broken, (it was mended in N. Y., and a subscriber of the "Spirit" has it to this day). Some Catholic priests were on board, and were very kind to me; one washed my head with brandy (pleasant senation that!), and dressed my wounds, another brought me a shirt that trailed on the floor, and a pair of drawers that would go around twice and button behind, and a pair of woollen stockings, that only needed waistbands to make me a pair of pantaloons. The captain and clerk supplied me with a cap, suspenders, and cravat, and the accident knocked the ague into fits for the time being. Some tarpaulins were rigged up for a side to the cabin, the floors propped up, and we were all snug again, though a very hard looking craft, you can suppose.

Soon after passing the mouth of the Ohio, and entering the upper Mississippi, we came to the "Graveyard," so named, I believe, from the number of accidents that have occurred there. Here we found several boats aground, waiting for a rise. We took a keel boat as we passed Cairo, at the mouth of the Ohio, in case we should need it; and we did, for a bar (which I won't pretend to spell right), pronounced "Tiwoppitie," brought us up all standing, and for three days we lay hard and fast, during which time I took *just a few* lessons in Euchre, and "so forth," and I *paid* for *that* quarter's schooling—well, I did! A slight rise in the river induced our captain to try his hand at getting off. Lightening her as much as possible, by transferring freight to the keel boat, a kedge was carried out into the channel, and the keel boat cast off; of course she swung into deeper water. A hawser was then carried out to a perfect snorter of a snag, and the other end passed several times around the shaft, with a watch tackle to take in the slack. When all was ready, the Captain gave the word to "go ahead slow," and we had the satisfaction to feel her move. We took our keel boat in tow as soon as praticable, and after a passage of thirteen days, reached St. Louis.

When I arrived, I was taken sick, and lay five weeks, two of which I was as crazy as was at all pleasant to my neighbors, and when I recovered I turned towards "Old Gotham," and I am inclined to think that I got enough on the "Big Muddy" to last me as long as I am

"The Little 'Un."

THE BURNING OF THE *GENERAL PRATTE*

[As reported in the St. Louis *Missouri Republican*]

[*Missouri Republican*, December 2, 1842]

ANOTHER TERRIBLE
STEAM BOAT ACCIDENT

Mr. Papin, Clerk of the *Gen. Pratte*, arrived here this morning; from him we learn the following painful particulars:

On Thursday morning, the 24th ult., about 2 o'clock, when about 12 miles above Memphis, the steam boat *Gen. Pratte* was discovered to be on fire, between the wheel house and privy. The fire originated from the sparks. The wind was blowing very strong at the time. Captain Casey, Clerk, Mate, and Carpenter, were all up at the time. An effort was made to extinguish it by water from buckets, but it soon became apparent that this was impossible.

The Captain then ordered her to be run ashore, and the passengers to be awakened. So rapidly did the flames spread, that there was hardly time to arouse the passengers before she was a complete sheet of flames. Fortunately, the Pilot and Engineer retained their presence of mind, and stuck to their posts. One wheel was unshipped, and she was run on to the foot of Beef Island. It so happened, that she had a long flat in tow at the time, which lay in between the boat and the shore, and to this is ascribed the preservation of the lives of the passengers.

The *Pratte* had on board about twenty cabin and about five hundred deck passengers. It was with great difficulty that numbers of them, especially the children were aroused in time to save them, and it is believed that if the Captain and his officers had not exerted themselves at the risk of their own lives, many of them would have perished. As it was, every one on board, it was believed is saved. A few of the passengers got out their trunks and a little baggage, but by far the greater number saved nothing at all.

The deck passengers were all German emigrants, who came over in the ships *Indiana*, *Columbus*, and a vessel whose name is not remembered. The weather was extremely cold.

There was on board about 175 tons of freight, consisting of dry goods and groceries, for this port, all of which was lost. The books, papers, and money of the boat, and the letters on board, were lost; consequently, there is no means of arriving at the owners of the goods.

The Captain and some of the passengers returned to Memphis—a portion of the passengers came up on the Walnut Hills to the mouth of the Ohio—the residue were on the island when the Clerk left.

The destitute condition of most of the emigrants, appeals loudly for sympathy and some immediate relief. Several families have not even clothing suitable for the season.

It is due to the Pilot, Samuel Donnel, and to the Engineer, Oliver Fairchild, that their steady, composed, and heroic conduct should be remembered. Both, though surrounded by the flames and in imminent danger all the time, remained firm and unwavering, and to them is due the credit of having brought the boat safely into shore. When they had fully discharged the responsibilities of their respective places, and not until then, did they leave the wreck.

Captain Casey several times rushed through the flames to rescue children who had been overlooked. He saved two young ladies who were asleep, after the boat had been abandoned by the passengers.

The entire hull of the boat was burnt out. She broke in two and sunk in about fifteen feet water.

The clerk states that nearly every trunk and box which was got ashore was broken open and robbed of its contents by the passengers. In some cases they were opened in the presence of the owner, but there was no power sufficient to prevent the robbery.

The boat was owned by P. Chouteau, Jr., & Co., Berthold, Tesson & Co., Chas. Mulliken, Pratte & Cabanne, and Capt. Casey. The two first insured, the others not.

[*Missouri Republican*, December 5, 1842]

BURNING OF THE *GEN. PRATTE*.

Capt. Casey, of the *Gen. Pratte*, arrived in the city yesterday, having met with a second accident on his way up. He was on board the *Boston* when she sunk. Below we give his statement of the burning of the *Pratte*.

Several of the passengers arrived in this city yesterday on the *Ohio*.

To A. B. Chambers, *Editor of the Republican*:

Dear Sir: It becomes my painful task to record the loss of the steamer *Gen. Pratte*, and as this is the only statement given by me for publication, I will give all the details—nothing extenuated —and leave the community to be our judges if any censure can be attached to myself and crew.

We left New Orleans on Saturday, 19th November, at half past 5 o'clock, P.M., bound for St. Louis, with upwards of 130 tons freight, consisting in part of groceries, dry goods, and baggage of German emigrants on board. We took from on board of ship *Columbus*, say 110 persons; ship *Johannes*, 140 to 150; ship *Diana*, 114 grown persons and several children. Not having collected their passage, the exact number is not known. We had 18 or 20 cabin passengers, including three ladies and three children.

We had ascended 12 miles above Memphis, when at 20 minutes past 2 A.M., the 24th ult., a fire broke out on the starboard side, forward of the wheel-house. The mate (Stephen G. Cochran) and watchman being on the hurricane deck at the time. I had just left the pilothouse, and was in the social hall. I ran out, and was handed by the mate a bucket of water, which was thrown upon it—and for the moment seemed subsided: still 10 or 15 more were thrown by Mr. Button, the carpenter, Mr. Papin, 2d clerk, and myself—our buckets being all filled with water at the time of the accident. Our efforts proved unavailing; and when convinced of said fact, I ran forward and told Mr. S. T. Donalds, pilot, to land her, as she could not be saved. He spoke to the engineer, O. H. Fairchild, through the trumpet, not to be alarmed but throw out the starboard wheel; which was done. She was run ashore and the engine stopped. They both remaining at their posts as long as their services could avail anything.

We had three tiers of berths in the engine room, together with the after guards, filled with deck passengers; also the boiler deck forward of the chimneys, and the curtains lashed down to protect them from the weather. After speaking to the pilot, I tore down the curtain–dragged two women to the larboard gang-way, the rest followed, not knowing where they were going; 60 or 70 persons must have been sleeping there. When they reached the bow, the plank was ashore, and measures taken to fasten her by a chain; which was done. Returning from the gangway, I rushed into the ladies cabin, whither Mr. O. M. White, first clerk, had preceded me, having bursted open the doors gave the alarm of fire, and endeavored to persuade Mr. Meyer and two daughters ashore; they, not understanding English, would not stir. I had two children placed under my care; those, with the two Miss Myers, I forced ashore. I entreated the father to follow, but he rushed back, and nothing but force prevented the daughters from following. We thought they had perished in the flames, but with a presence of mind which few men of his age possess, he forced open the door on the guard (not being able to follow us through the cabin, it being enveloped in flames,) and threw his wife and child into the yawl, Dr. Malone having preceded him; the yawl was suspended on that side, and thus were they timely saved. Had the engine remained running, the yawl would, no doubt, have sunk. One man only jumped into the river; he reached the yawl and, as far as could be ascertained, not *one life* was lost. Nineteen of our firemen slept in the run, (after part of the hold;) they were saved.

We had several aged men and women, who had to be carried from on board the ships; they were all carried out, and some children on board *not one month old*. From the lamentations of the emigrants, I supposed that every family had lost some relative, and it was not until late next morning that the children could be found; they were placed indiscriminately around the fires, (seventeen in number being made,) as it froze very hard that night. From the best source that could be ascertained, (twenty of our men speaking German,) they reported no lives lost, but nearly all their baggage and provisions; fortunately, they never undress on board, and most of them had even their shoes on.

Mr. White, not being called until all hopes of extinguishing the fire was given up, did not save the *books*, *papers*, or *funds* of the boat, but rushed into the cabin, with his clothes on his arm. The *iron chest* fell on the lower guard, and was taken on shore by the exertions of *Mr. Button*, (carpenter,) and *Adrian Louet*, (cook,) the latter having a lid of a chest on his head, to prevent the falling timbers from burning him, the water being thrown on him *step by step*. Nothing short of the preservation of life would have induced any other men to run such a risk. The safe was locked, for, in the presence of J. C. Scott, who had placed $2050 in it, I forced the hinges off with a pick-axe; there was in it, viz:

Bag gold, half burnt, $2050 J. C. Scott.
Do do. not damaged, wet, $3000 Meyers
Do. silver do.   wet, $ 400 more or less, J. and
                                     E. Welsh
Letter half burnt—consignee, care Smith, Brothers & Co.,
                                     $7 50 100 [sic]
Letter and paper, Custom-house Bonds—Burnt to cinders.

Also, some other paper, the contents not known or discernible. The portfolio of the boat was crisped; but the contents being wet, was saved. All the funds in the drawer were lost, together with the clothes of Mr. White, O. H. Fairchild, engineer, and myself, save what we had on. Had self interest been taken into consideration by any of the crew, half the lives on board would have perished; for at that hour of the night, in the middle of the river, more than 450 souls asleep—and from the time of the alarm given, such was the progress of the fire, in five minutes the whole cabin was in flames, and in four hours not a vestige remained to tell that such a boat as the *Pratte* had ever floated, save a few floating embers. Nothing but the interposition of Providence, and the presence of mind displayed by the Pilot, Engineer, and Mate, with the untiring exertions of the crew, could have saved so many lives; and it must ever remain a proud remembrance that their efforts proved successful. I tender them my best and hearty thanks, being all I have to offer: they ask no more. Hoping I may never again witness such a scene,

I remain, Yours
T. J. Casey

P.S. Messrs. Pratte & Cabanne, C. Mullikin, and T. J. Casey, were not insured.

[*Missouri Republican*, December 5, 1842]

We, the undersigned, cabin passengers on board of the steamer *Gen. Pratte*, at the time of her unfortunate destruction by fire, deem it our duty to state that Capt. Casey, and the officers who were on duty at the time, deserve great credit as well as the gratitude of all on board, for the cool and judicious manner in which they landed the boat and exerted themselves to save the lives of the passengers, when there was no longer any prospect of saving the boat or any part of the cargo, and that without regard for their individual interest. We presume it will not be going too far to assert that there never was a boat burned with 450 persons on board and no lives lost—and that too in the *dead of night*.

We learn that Capt. Casey's all was embarked in her, and truly and deeply sympathize with his loss.

Sam'l B Malone, Columbus, Mo.; E Winston, La Grange, Tenn, J C Scott, Columbia, Mo.; L C Evans, Mo; T H Johns, Tenn; N Yates, New Orleans; J Meyer and Lady; Miss C Meyer; Miss E Meyer; S W Miles; Jules Chenie.

[*Missouri Republican*, December 9, 1842]

Merited Compliment. We yesterday mentioned the just tribute paid by the Chamber of Commerce of this city to Captain Casey, and the officers and crew of the *Gen Pratte*, for the gallant discharge of their duties in the conflagration of that boat. We now present the correspondence, which is published by order of the Chamber.

Chamber of Commerce,
St. Louis, Dec. 7, 1842.

Captain T. J. Casey, late commander of the steamboat *General Pratte*:

Dear Sir—The agreeable duty has been committed to us, of communicating to you a copy of the following resolution, which was unanimously passed by the Chamber of Commerce at its meeting last evening.

Resolved, That, in the recent destruction, by fire, of the steamboat *General Pratte*, of St. Louis, at the dead of night, in the Mississippi river, the rescue of all the passengers on board (in number nearly five hundred) must be principally attributed to the coolness, judgment, decision, and intrepidity of the Captain and Officers of the boat; and that the acknowledgments of this Chamber are due to Captain T. J. Casey, Mr. S. T. Donald, Pilot, and Mr. O. H. Fairchild, Engineer, for their admirable discharge of their respective duties.

We are also instructed by the Chamber, to request you to express to the other officers and crew of the boat, the high sense entertained by the Chamber of their fearless and disinterested efforts for the safety of the passengers.

The resolution needs no commentary. It is a tribute to courage, under circumstances the most appalling, and to coolness and self-possession, when the lives of hundreds depended on their exercise; but at a moment, when of all others, there was the greatest combination of causes, to create confusion and dismay. There are few men destined to such an ordeal as you have passed; and none who could have met it with greater honor. Of all the requisites for the successful prosecution of your profession, there are perhaps none more important than coolness in danger, promptitude of decision, energy of action, and entire devotion to the passengers who have placed their lives and property under your protection. These chivalric virtues you have evinced in a remarkable manner, and we trust they will not only be rewarded by public approbation, but ensure for you the fullest confidence of travelers, and render any vessel that you command, a public favorite.

That your future success may so recompense you for your pecuniary loss on this occasion, is our ardent wish

With cordial respect,

Your Ob't servants,

J C Dinnes, G K McGunnegle, Wm Morrison, Committee.

To Messrs. J. C. Dinnies, G. K. McGunnegle, Wm. M. Morrison, Committee:

Gentlemen—Your letter, which I received last evening, containing a copy of the resolutions passed by the "Chamber of Commerce," complimentary to the manner in which the duties that devolved upon myself, Mr. S. T. Donalds, Pilot, Mr. O. H.

Fairchild, Engineer, and the crew, were discharged during the conflagration of the steamer *Gen. Pratte*, was as highly gratifying as unexpected to me.

The consciousness of possessing and deserving the confidence and sympathies of my fellow-citizens, alleviates, in a great degree, my loss; and with the wish that my future actions may merit your commendations,

I remain, with respect, your Ob't. servant,

Thomas J. Casey.

Thursday morning, Dec. 8, 1842

EXPLOSION OF THE STEAMER
PENNSYLVANIA

—————

[*At six o'clock on Sunday morning, June 13, 1858, the
steamboat* Pennsylvania *exploded at Ship Island, seventy
miles below Memphis. Of three hundred and fifty-five passengers and eighty crew aboard more than two hundred
were killed or missing. Among the injured was the third
clerk, who was badly scalded and later died—poor fellow,
the newspaper did not even spell his name correctly, for the
Henry Clements of the first newsstory was the young
brother about whom Mark Twain wrote in* Life on the Mississippi (*Chapter 20*). *The rather brief first report in the
St. Louis* Missouri Republican *on June 15 was followed
the next day by a much fuller statement (reprinted here)
from two of the survivors, W. G. Mepham of St. Louis and
Henry Spencer, the bar-keeper.*]

Additional Particulars
of the
Explosion and Burning of the
PENNSYLVANIA!

Two Hundred Lost and Missing.
STATEMENT OF PASSENGERS.
Incidents of the Disaster, &c.

We published yesterday morning a telegraphic statement of the
late terrible disaster to the steamer *Pennsylvania*, bound from
New Orleans to this port.

From passengers of the *Pennsylvania* who arrived in this
city by railroad last evening, we have received full statements, to
be found below. They embrace all that was known here last
evening concerning this awful calamity, but give very few additional names of the lost, missing or saved.

STATEMENT OF MR. W. G. MEPHAM.

The steamer *Pennsylvania* left New Orleans on the 9th inst. with one hundred and twenty-five cabin passengers and one hundred and fifty-eight deckers. She afterwards took on board, at Baton Rouge, Natchez and Vicksburg, 62 passengers, and at Napoleon 10. There were 40 deck hands and firemen; 24 of the steward's crew, and 16 officers—making in all 450 souls.

Out of this number, 182 were rescued by a wood boat, and about 70 others escaped in various ways. These numbers include the wounded and scalded. About 200 are lost and missing.

At about 6 o'clock on the morning of the 13th inst., when the boat was about 70 miles below Memphis, she exploded four of her boilers, while under way. At the time of the explosion, she was near 300 yards from shore. The cabin was torn to pieces forward of her wheel houses. Very few of the passengers were out of their staterooms at the time. The passengers in the after part of the cabin—men, women and children—rushed out, and the utmost confusion ensued among them, all supposing the boat was on fire, from the smoke and steam which came rushing through the cabin.

After close examination it was ascertained that the boat was not on fire, and the excitement was in some degree quelled.

After the explosion the boat commenced drifting down with the current, and an anchor was thrown overboard for the purpose of checking the boat, for at that time we were of opinion that we could prevent the boat from taking fire. But the water being so deep and the current so swift, the anchor dragged and the boat continued to drift down. As quickly as possible Capt. KLINEFELTER and two or three of his men made an attempt to carry a line ashore by the yawl, but from the line being too short, or some other cause, they did not succeed. Without losing a moment's time the Captain ordered the yawl turned down stream to a Mr. HARRIS' wood-yard, for the purpose of bringing an empty wood-boat, which was lying there, to the rescue. This boat was not supplied with oars, and it was an exceedingly difficult matter to accomplish this purpose, but by dint of skill and hard labor the Captain succeeded in getting it alongside.

In from three to five minutes from the time the wood-boat

touched the steamer it was discovered that the *Pennsylvania* was on fire.

The fire appeared to issue from about the after end of the boilers, and in one minute from the time of the alarm, the boat was wrapped in flames. Passengers and crew immediately rushed from the burning boat upon the wood-boat, and filled it as full as they could stand. Captain KLINEFELTER was the last man that jumped from the steamer to the wood-boat, as it was being pushed off, with its living freight, from the burning boat. The most intense excitement prevailed on board the wood-boat, as we endeavored to propel it from the burning mass—as we had only a few boards, in place of oars, and the crowd rendered it almost impossible to work them with success. But we finally succeeded in getting her bow turned out, so that the current struck her stern and swung the wood-boat around, and by that means we cleared the burning boat, and she drifted by, but not until many of the passengers were severely scorched. By turning our backs, and with the aid of a few counterpanes and quilts which were saved, we screened ourselves from the heat, as much as possible, and finally succeeded, after drifting one mile, in reaching an island or tow-head, called Ship Island, where the wood-boat was made fast to some trees.

After shoving the wood-boat from the steamer there were a good many deck passengers seen rushing out with their trunks, boxes, &c., in the hope of saving their little stack of plunder, and by trying to save their effects, they lost their lives, for it was impossible for us to render them any assistance. I remember seeing one man and woman, who, from their appearance, were German emigrants, hanging to a line from the stern of the boat—the man holding the line with one hand and his chest with the other, and as the boat swung around they disappeared from view. They, doubtless, remained in this position until they were compelled, by the heat of the flames, to loose their hold, and drown. The cabin passengers, with the exception of one or two, behaved with great coolness and decision, and rendered one another every assistance in their power, but among the deck passengers the greatest excitement prevailed. It seemed that all they cared for was to save their plunder, throwing it over the guards into the wood-boat not heeding where it fell. A number of the passengers in the wood-boat were bruised and injured by the falling of the trunks and boxes into the boat. From this disposition to save baggage, many of the deckers were lost, who would otherwise have saved their lives.

About twenty-five of the wounded escaped on the wood-boat, amongst them were the 1st mate, 2nd engineer, two Frenchmen late of the Theatre d'Orleans, Col. Parris of Arkansas, badly scalded, and others very badly cut and bruised—mostly deck passengers. They suffered very much in consequence of their being no medical attendance to dress their wounds, and no means of procuring any for the space of two hours. But at length neighboring planters, from the Arkansas shore, brought some Linseed Oil and Linament which with the aid of cotton taken from the quilts, gave some relief to the wounded. The scalded victims suffered much from the heat of the sun, as the whole country was overflowed, and we could not succeed in getting the boat to the main land, and in this condition we were obliged to remain under a broiling sun for fully eight hours. The women and children who were unhurt also suffered excessively from the heat of the sun and hunger. After remaining on the Island eight hours the steamer *Imperial* bound down came to our relief, and after giving us a good dinner, put us on board of the *Kate Frisbee* and *Diana*, bound up. Too much praise cannot be given to the officers of these boats for the kindness they extended to us.

The *Diana* being crowded with passengers, very few of us came on her, the greater portion of our company going on the *Frisbee*, which the *Diana* left behind. It was the intention of the Captain of the *Frisbee* when we left, to try and save all he could, and pick up scattering passengers along the shore. The *Diana* brought up fifteen of the wounded to Memphis to be taken to the hospital. The passengers on the *Diana* raised a subscription of between two and three hundred dollars towards defraying the expenses of the sufferers in Memphis. They also made up several purses for destitute women who were aboard. Altogether, they acted very magnanimously in the way of supplying the women and children, who were scantily dressed with garments.

Mrs. Witt of St. Louis, who was lost, occupied with her daughter, Mrs. Fulton, room No. 8, in the gentlemen's cabin. Mrs. Witt was taken from the ruins just as the fire broke out, perfectly blind, and in a dying condition; by that time the woodboat had left the steamer, and a young man, who was endeavoring to rescue her, was compelled to jump overboard, and swim to the wood-boat to save his own life. Mrs. FULTON was not seen after the explosion. There was a man buried in the wreck who, from his expressions, must have been either a sugar or cotton Planter—as in his despair he said he had money, negroes, and a plantation, and would give all to save his life.

He was covered deeply in the ruins and the fire coming on so rapidly it was impossible to rescue him.

A gentleman passenger had gone to the boiler deck just before the explosion, and the next thing he recollected was being precipitated to the main deck amongst fragments of the boat, and pinioned to the deck by the boat's bell, which in falling, caught him around the neck, which, together with other fragments, rendered it impossible for him to move. By the timely aid of passengers he was rescued from his perilous position and escaped without much damage.

At the time of the explosion, Capt. KLINEFELTER was in the barber shop being shaved, and at the explosion the barber says— the Captain exclaimed—"Oh, my God! what is that?" He hurried out through the back door and climbed upon the hurricane roof, as all the forward part of the boat was blown to pieces. Too much credit cannot be awarded to Capt. KLINEFELTER for his daring and gallant conduct in endeavoring to save both life and property.

Nearly all the deck hands were either killed or missing— First and second mates, so badly injured, as to render them helpless. First clerk, Mr. BLACK, and Mr. BROWN, Pilot, both missing, the Captain had to assume the whole charge of the boat, under the trying circumstances. Of the firemen on watch at the time of the explosion, only one was saved, and he stated to me that they had just hauled the coals from the ash pan, and had neglected in some measure to replenish the fire. At that time the Engineer came around, and called on them saying, "Shove her up boys, for we are scarcely stemming the current," and he states that they had scarcely put any wood into the fire doors before the explosion occurred. By some miracle this man escaped with a slight scald in the back.

From the report of those engaged in trying to keep down the fire, barrels of turpentine or some other combustible liquid must have taken fire in the hold from the rapidity with which the flames enveloped the whole boat, so soon after the alarm of fire. If not for the timely aid of the wood-boat, or if it had been delayed five minutes, there would not have been fifty of us left to tell the tale.

A number of passengers were saved by the skiffs of the neighboring woodmen, who acted very promptly and gallantly in coming to the rescue and picking up those adrift on pieces of the wreck, planks, &c.

One of the wounded musicians states that he had 20,000 francs on board, which were lost. Of course, all the boat's money, books and papers were lost.

A Mr. A. L. BARTLETT, of New York, had $800 in gold in a small box in his trunk, but in the confusion the money was forgotten. Not a trunk or piece of clothing, save what they had on, was saved by any cabin passenger, and most of them were left without funds. Those who had money divided with those who had none, and all seemed perfectly satisfied to have escaped with their lives.

The wreck floated down about two and a half miles, and landed on the point of a tow-head, where it burned to the water's edge. All that could be seen of it, when we left, were some portions of the machinery and one of the boilers. When the river falls, the wreck will be left high and dry.

Capt. KLINEFELTER remarked to me before I left on the *Diana*, that he would stay by the wreck and save all he could, both of life and property until he could be of no further service.

The cook of the boat tells us that he and five others were in the cook-house at the time of the explosion, but all escaped without injury.

One of the female passengers informed us that she escaped with the loss of two trunks and all her wardrobe except the clothing she wore. She represented that all the passengers found it impossible to save anything—they barely escaped with their lives.

We were very happy to meet WASHINGTON KING among the passengers. It appears that it was erroneously supposed that he was on the *Pennsylvania*. He did not reach the scene of the disaster until some hours after it occurred.

STATEMENT OF HENRY SPENCER.

At the time of the occurrence of the accident, which was at six o'clock Sunday morning, I was inside of the bar and talking with the Captain, who had just been shaved. The explosion took place and the saloon was immediately filled with steam and smoke. We made our way out through the water closet passage and climbed on the hurricane deck. The Captain, with the barber and one of the cabin boys, at once launched the life-boat, while I broke the skylight to let the steam and smoke out of the cabin to prevent those inside from suffocating as I feared they would from their screaming. The boat was entirely unmanageable and drifting rapidly. An attempt was made to carry a line to the shore, but without success. At this moment the Captain discovered an empty flat-boat fastened to the shore, and had the life-boat manned and sent to the flat to bring it as expeditiously as possible to the wreck. This prompt measure on the part of the Captain proved the means of saving more than half of the passengers, who were taken off. The fact of the boat not taking fire for more than half an hour after the explosion, served to allay the terror of the passengers and give them self-possession enough to dress, as many of them were in their berths. There was time enough for them to get off, and nearly all did through the calm conduct of the Captain. Nearly all who were lost died from the immediate effect of the explosion. What exceptions there were, were deck passengers, who endangered themselves by an over anxiety to secure their baggage and effects. The cabin passengers generally abandoned their baggage and were content to save their lives. As to the number of persons, no correct list can be supplied, as the register was lost. The cabin berthed 120, and it was entirely full. An approximate estimate of the deck can be arrived at only by considering the amount collected of them, which was $476, and that on the first day out. The price of passage for each was $3. This would make nearly 160 persons. We took on besides 20 coalboatmen at Baton Rouge. One of the number told me that only six of the twenty were alive after the explosion. They were from Louisville. Officer and crew numbered 80. This would make in all 380 persons on board of the steamer, and the number is by no means overstated. Of those saved I counted 181 on the flat. Twenty-five more were taken to the shore by the life-boat, part of them from the flat to lighten her up before this count was made. Twenty were picked up by the *Diana*, making 226 saved, and 154 lost or missing. Some of the latter may have got on shore.

Mr. DENNIS of New Orleans, formerly editor of the *Delta*, but some three months back established the *Magnet*, a Sunday journal. He had retired from this likewise, and was on the way, I think, to Memphis with the intention of proceeding East from that city. A few moments before the explosion I saw him, and think he must have gone to the forward part of the boat.

Col. TALBOTT, from Mississippi, had a negro boy with him, who was blacking his boots. Neither were ever seen after the accident.

A gambler from Texas, a tall, fine-looking man who wore spectacles and was slightly bald was lost. Two other gamblers were on board, and were lost, unless they got off at Helena, thirty miles below, which they may have done. One, I think, lived there, as he spoke of his wife being there.

Of the Steward's force it is remarkable that but one was lost, and he was the second steward. Not one of the others was even seriously hurt. They happened to be preparing breakfast and were about the pantry, a locality not much exposed to danger. About twenty-five persons were under his direction. EMORY (colored) second steward, passed forward and was never seen again.

Another Priest besides Father DELCROSS (lost) was so seriously injured that no hopes were entertained of his recovery. He was put off at Memphis and his cousin got off there to attend to him. He was scalded terribly, and his lower extremities were literally boiled, and he was dying, in fact, when last seen. He was going, I think, to some College in Maryland, and was a talented and learned man. He was so scorched and scalded that he looked like a negro.

The telegraphic account confuses the names as well as the fate of the 1st and 2nd Engineers. It was JAMES DORRIS, the 1st Engineer, who was fatally hurt. His brother, FRANCIS DORRIS, the second, escaped with little injury. The same account mentions WILLIAM JACKSON as bar-keeper. I was bar-keeper and JACKSON, who is quite a lad, was my assistant. He was unhurt.

I knew the names only of those I chanced to come in contact with. There were very many lost I did not know, and whose names will never be learned. All the cabin passengers, situated beyond the centre passage of the boat, were saved.

A gentleman and his wife, who occupied a room forward of the cabin division, died most horribly, having burned alive. In the fall of the rubbish caused by the explosion, they were caught under a heap of ruins of the fallen rooms, and a boiler fell on that.

He implored the others to extricate them, and offered all he was worth. The attempt was made, but it was impossible to save them, as the boat was on fire.

One of the French Opera Troupe was injured so that he will die. I do not know which one. Another, a large man, was injured by scalds on the hands. He had on nothing at the time but a red shirt. A pair of pantaloon were given him. He soon recovered his cheerfulness, and inquired of a Doctor, with some solicitude, when his hands would get well.

The wounded were transferred to the flat and then taken on board of the *Frisbee* and *Diana*, where they received every care and attention that humanity could devise. A card was signed by the passengers of the *Diana*, expressing their sense of the magnanimous conduct of Capt. STURGEON and Mr. SMITH the Clerk, who was likewise unremitting in his exertions to alieviate the sufferings of the wounded. No charge was made against the survivors, and they were also provided with free tickets over the Illinois Central and the Ohio and Mississippi Railroads to St. Louis. Capt. KLINEFELTER and the surviving officers of the *Pennsylvania* remained in the neighborhood of the wreck for the purpose of taking care of all property belonging to the passengers that might come in their way.

FEVER, FATIGUE, AND DEATH

TIMOTHY FLINT

―――――――

[*Floating down the river, Timothy Flint noted elsewhere in his* Recollections of the Last Ten Years in the Valley of the Mississippi (*Boston, 1826*), *often seemed glamorous to those living quietly ashore, but the pain and difficulty often to be endured Flint could sum up in a few pages from his own unhappy experience* (*pp. 284–88*).]

Soon after we left the St. Francis, both our hands were taken ill of fever and ague, and we were obliged to leave them behind. We were now left with none but my own family, in the midst of the wilderness, the heavy current of the Mississippi against us, and more than four hundred miles still before us. The river was so low, that steam-boats were scarce on it, and the few that attempted to ascend it were aground on the sand bars. In fact, no boats were seen ascending or descending, and it seemed impossible for us to procure hands in lieu of those who had left us on account of sickness. The wind generally blew up the stream, and was favourable for sailing, except in the curves, or bends of the river, which were often so deep as to cause that the wind, which was directly in favour at one point of the bend, would be directly against us at the other. We made use of our sail, when it would serve, and of our cordelle, when it would not; and in this way we went on cheerfully, though with inexpressible fatigue to myself, to the point between the first and the middle Chickasaw bluff. In arriving here, we had the most beautiful autumnal evenings that I ever witnessed. We were "a feeble folk," alone in the wilderness. The owls, forty in concert, and in every whimsical note, from the wailings of an infant babe, to the deep grunt of a drunken German, gave us their serenade. Ever and anon, a wolf would raise his prolonged and dismal howl in the forests. The gabbling of numberless water fowls of every description on the sand-bars, was a kind of tambourine to the grand accompaniment of the owls and the wolves. The swan you know naturally plays the trumpet. My family had the ague, and the paroxysm creates a kind of poetical excitement, so that a person who is just rising from the fit, is in the highest degree capable of enjoyment, in a state of mind not unlike that produced by the agency of opium. Then, when we were made fast in a cove on the wide sand-bar; when the moon, with her circumference broadened and reddened by the haze and smoke of Indian summer, rose, and diffused, as Chateaubriand so beautifully says, the "great secret of melancholy over these ancient forests;" after our evening prayers, and the favourite hymn, "The day is past and gone," &c. I have spent hours in traversing the sand-bars entirely alone.

But I hasten to matters more appropriate to my narrative. I could describe to you two days of excessive fatigue, in which we made repeated attempts to pass a rapid place in the river, too rapid to be passed with oars, too muddy to afford bottom for poles, and the shore a quagmire for a mile in extent, and of course not admitting the use of a cordelle. We tried to surmount this place for two days, and failed, exhausted in every attempt. We crossed the river, and attempted to ascend on the bend side, to a point, where fallen-in timber forbade our going higher. We then recrossed, and both times fell below the impassable place. Discouraged and wearied out, we gave up the attempt, and expected to lie there, until a rise in the river should enable us to pass the place, or until a passing steam-boat might tow us up. How often do we find relief at a moment of the deepest despondency! Just as we had agreed to lie by, and had resigned ourselves to our lot, a fine breeze sprang up, we hoisted our sail, and passed the difficult place with perfect ease.

A difficulty still more formidable now awaited us. We had expected to be able each day to replenish our stock of provisions from the descending boats. The season was sultry, and we took with us no more than could be preserved from day to day. We were in this wilderness eight days without seeing a single boat pass. You can easily imagine what followed. Fortunately we at length described a flat boat descending; we hailed her, and she told us to come on board. We did, and were lashed beside her. She instantly discovered our situation, and made her own calculations; and we paid thirty dollars for a barrel of pork and one of flour, meanwhile descending the river three miles, which we were obliged, with great toil, to remount, in order to gain the point where we hailed the boat.

We arrived opposite to the second Chickasaw bluff on the twenty-sixth of November. The country on the shore receives and deserves the emphatic name of "wilderness." At ten in the morning we perceived indications of a severe approaching storm. The air was oppressively sultry. Brassy clouds were visible upon all quarters of the sky. Distant thunder was heard. We were upon a wide sand bar far from any house. Opposite to us was a vast cypress swamp. At this period, and in this place, Mrs. F. was taken in travail. My children, wrapped in blankets, laid themselves down on the sand-bar. I secured the boat in every possible way against the danger of being driven by the storm into the river. At eleven the storm burst upon us in all its fury. Mrs. F. had been salivated during her fever, and had not yet been able to leave her couch. I was alone with her in this dreadful situation. Hail, and wind, and thunder, and rain in torrents poured upon us. I was in terror, lest the wind would drive my boat, notwithstanding all her fastenings, into the river. No imagination can reach what I endured. The only alleviating circumstance was her perfect tranquillity. She knew that the hour of sorrow, and expected that of death, was come. She was so perfectly calm, spoke with such tranquil assurance about the future, and about the dear ones that were at this moment " 'biding the pelting of the pitiless storm" on the sand-bar, that I became calm myself. A little after twelve the wind burst in the roof of my boat, and let in the glare of the lightning, and the torrents of rain upon my poor wife. I could really have expostulated with the elements in the language of the poor old Lear. I had wrapped my wife in blankets, ready to be carried to the shelter of the forest, in case of the driving of my boat into the river. About four the fury of the storm began to subside. At five the sun in his descending glory burst from the dark masses of the receding clouds. At eleven in the evening Mrs. F. was safely delivered of a female infant, and notwithstanding all, did well. The babe, from preceding circumstances, was feeble and sickly, and I saw could not survive. At midnight we had raised a blazing fire. The children came into the boat. Supper was prepared, and we surely must have been ungrateful not to have sung a hymn of deliverance. There can be but one trial more for me that can surpass the agony of that day, and there can never be on this earth a happier period than those midnight hours. The babe staid with us but two days and a half, and expired. The children, poor things, laid it deeply to heart, and raised a loud lament. We were, as I have remarked, far away from all human aid and sympathy, and left alone with God. We deposited the body of our lost babe—laid in a small trunk for a coffin—in a grave amid the rushes, there to await the resurrection of the dead. The prayer made on the occasion by the father, with the children for concourse and mourners, if not eloquent, was, to us at least, deeply affecting. The grave is on a high bank opposite to the second Chickasaw bluff, and I have since passed the rude memorial which we raised on the spot; and I passed it, carrying to you my miserable and exhausted frame, with little hope of its renovation, and in the hourly expectation of depositing my own bones on the banks of the Mississippi. But enough, and too much, of all this.

THE "PILGRIMS"

TIMOTHY FLINT

—————

[*Nothing was too strange to be found on the river, as witness this description of the "wretched remains of a singular class of enthusiasts, known in this country by the name of the 'Pilgrims!' " Other travelers at this time* (ca. *1820*) *reported seeing this remnant of fanatics but none so vividly as Timothy Flint did in his* Recollections of the Last Ten Years in the Valley of the Mississippi (*Boston, 1826*), *275–80.*]

Before I left the country, I crossed the river to view the wretched remains of that singular class of enthusiasts, known in this country by the name of the "Pilgrims." This whole region, it is true, wears an aspect of irreligion; but we must not thence infer, that we do not often see the semblance and the counterfeit of religion. There is no country where bigotry and enthusiasm are seen in forms of more glaring absurdity, and, at the same time, of more arrogant assumption. There were, I think, six persons of them left, the "prophet," so called, and his wife, and another woman, and perhaps three children. They were sick and poor; and the rags with which they were originally habited to excite attention, and to be *in keeping* with their name and assumption, were now retained from necessity. The "prophet" was too sick to impart much information, and the others seemed reluctant to do it. But from the wife of the prophet I gleaned the information which follows, of their origin, progress, and end. I have collated her information with the most authentic notices of them, which I obtained at every stage on the Mississippi where they were seen, and where they stopped.

It seems that the fermenting principle of the society began to operate in Lower Canada. A few religious people began to talk about the deadness and the unworthiness of all churches, as bodies, and they were anxious to separate from them, in order to compound a more perfect society. The enthusiasm caught in other minds like a spark fallen in flax. A number immediately sold every thing, and prepared to commence a course towards the southwest. In their progress through Vermont they came in contact with other minds affected with the same longing with themselves. There can be no doubt that most of these were perfectly honest in their purpose. The "prophet," a compound, like the character of Cromwell, of hypocrite and enthusiast, joined himself to them, and from his superior talents or contributions to the common stock of the society, became their leader. They went on accumulating through New York, where their numbers amounted to nearly fifty. Here they encountered the Shakers, and as they had some notions in common, a kind of coalition was attempted with them. But the Shakers are industrious and neat to a proverb, and are more known to the community by these traits, than any other. But industry made little part of the religion of the Pilgrims, and neatness still less; for it was a maxim with them to wear the clothes as long as they would last on the body, without washing or changing; and the more patched and particoloured the better. If they wore one whole shoe, the other one—like the pretended pilgrims of old time—was clouted and patched. They made it a point, in short, to be as ragged and dirty as might be. Of course, after a long debate with the Shakers, in which they insisted upon industry, cleanliness, and parting from their wives, proving abundantly and quoting profusely that it ought to be so; and the Pilgrims proving by more numerous and apposite quotations, that they ought to cleave to their dirt, rags, laziness, and wives, and that they ought to go due southwest to find the New Jerusalem, the logamachy terminated as most religious disputes do; each party claimed the victory, and lamented the obduracy, blindness, and certain tendency to everlasting destruction of the other; and they probably parted with these expectations of each other's doom.

I knew nothing of their course from that place to New Madrid below the mouth of the Ohio. They were then organized to a considerable degree, and had probably eight or ten thousand dollars in common stock. The prophet was their ruler, spiritual and temporal. He had visions by night, which were expounded in the morning, and determined whether they should stand still or go on; whether they should advance by land or water; in short every thing was settled by immediate inspiration. Arrived at New Madrid, they walked ashore in Indian file, the old men in front, then the women, and the children in the rear. They chanted a kind of tune, as they walked, the burden of which was "Praise God! Praise God!"

Their food was mush and milk, prepared in a trough, and they sucked it up, standing erect, through a perforated stalk of cane. They enjoined severe penances, according to the state of grace in which the penitent was. For the lower stages the penance was very severe, as to stand for four successive days without reclining or sitting, to fast one or two days. In fact fasting was a primary object of penance, both as severe in itself, and as economical. They affected to be ragged, and to have different stripes in their dresses and caps, like those adopted in penitentiaries as badges of the character of the convicts. So formidable a band of ragged Pilgrims, marching in perfect order, chanting with a peculiar twang the short phrase "Praise God! Praise God!" had in it something imposing to a people, like those of the West, strongly governed by feelings and impressions. Sensible people assured me that the coming of a band of these Pilgrims into their houses affected them with a thrill of alarm which they could hardly express. The untasted food before them lost its savour, while they heard these strange people call upon them, standing themselves in the posture of statues, and uttering only the words, "Praise God, repent, fast, pray." Small children, waggish and profane as most of the children are, were seen to shed tears, and to ask their parents, if it would not be fasting enough, to leave off one meal a day. Two of their most distinguished members escaped from them at New Madrid, not without great difficulty, and having been both of them confined to prevent their escape. One of them, an amiable and accomplished woman, whose over-wrought imagination had been carried away by their imposing rites, died soon after, worn down by the austerities and privations which she had endured. The husband had an emaciated look, like the Shakers, a sweet voice for sacred music, and was preaching in union with the Methodists. At Pilgrim Island, thirty miles below, and opposte the Little Prairie, they staid a long time.

Here dissensions began to spring up among them. Emaciated with hunger, and feverish from filth and the climate, many of them left their bones. They were ordered by the prophet, from some direct revelation which he received, to lie unburied; and their bones were bleaching on the island when we were there. Some escaped from them at this place, and the sheriff of the county of New Madrid, indignant at the starvation imposed as a discipline upon the little children, carried to them a pirogue of provisions, keeping off with his sword the leaders, who would fain have prevented these greedy innocents from satiating their appetites.

While on this island, a great number of boatmen are said to have joined, to take them at their profession of having no regard for the world, or the things of it, and robbed them of all their money, differently stated to be between five and ten thousand dollars. From this place, reduced in number by desertion and death, in their descent to the mouth of the Arkansas, there were only the numbers surviving, which I saw. When I asked the wife of the prophet, why, instead of descending in the summer to the sickly country, they had not ascended to the high and healthy regions of Cape Girardeau, in order to acclimate themselves before their descent; their answer was, that such calculations of worldly wisdom were foreign to their object; that they did not study advantage, or calculate to act as the world acts upon such subjects, but that suffering was a part of their plan. When I asked them, why they deserted their station at the mouth of the Arkansas on the Mississippi; they answered, that they could neither get corn, pumpkins, nor milk, at the mouth of the river, as the people there had neither fields nor cows; that they could obtain all these things in the region where they were, and had come thither for this purpose. When I observed to them that this was reasoning precisely of a character with that, which I had been recommending to them, in respect to ascending the river to Cape Girardeau, and that, unknown to themselves, they were acting upon the universal principle of attempting to better their condition; they discovered that they had committed themselves, and had proved, that they acted from motives contrary to their avowed principles, and replied, that they were not used to such discussions, and that they reasoned as differently from the world, as they acted. This history of the delusion and destruction of between thirty and forty people, most of them honest and sincere, left a deep and melancholy impression of the universal empire of bigotry, and its fatal influences in all ages and countries. To this narrative I shall only add, that I heard an aged man, with a long beard, preaching, as they called it, at New Madrid. He descended the Mississippi a year after these unfortunate people, and he also called himself a Pilgrim. He was as wild and visionary as they were, and talked and acted like a maniac. He was descending the Mississippi, as he said, to the *real* Jerusalem in Asia. He appeared deeply impressed, that by going on in that direction he should finally reach that city. There was a numerous audience, and I heard many of them expressing their admiration of his preaching. Let none think that the age of fanaticism has gone by.

REMINISCENCE

OF NATCHEZ "UNDER-THE-HILL"

"My Grandmother's Trick."

WILLIAM C. HALL

[*The brief sketch of Natchez-under-the-hill in its notorious days by William C. Hall first appeared in the New York* Spirit of the Times, *December 11, 1843 (XIII, 523) over the signature "Yazoo."*]

Landing at Natchez in the winter of 1824–5, about ten o'clock in the evening, I thought I would stop for a few minutes Under-the-hill, with the view of ascertaining, if possible, what peculiarity it was, that had made *"Natchez under-the-hill,"* so celebrated throughout the Union. I walked up the street, and entered the first door I saw open. The room into which I entered, was a brilliantly lighted saloon, around which, two gaily dressed, sylph-like forms were whirling in the waltz. A few spectators had, at this early hour, collected to witness the extraordinary scenes that were nightly enacted at these places. They appeared to be principally Kentucky boatmen, and were wedged in the corners, or stuck around the room flat against the wall, affording as large a space in the centre as possible, for the dancers. On an elevated platform, serving as an orchestra, sat some four or five musicians; two violins, a clarionet, and bass drum, I noticed particularly; and in front of these as a kind of figure-head, stood a black boy of some 12 or 13 years of age, dressed *à la Turk*, who flourished and beat a tamboureen in the most fantastic manner, producing sounds that would in all probability, have slept until the Day of Judgment, but for the skill and *genius* of this performer. On my entrance the waltz was stopped, and an exciting reel struck up by the band, while the imp of the tamboureen redoubled his exertions, grinning and chaunting in melodious cadence some stanzas of which I caught but the concluding line of each verse:

"The old woman she ——— hid in the haymow."

One of the beautiful creatures I have mentioned, came up to me, and desired me to dance with her, while others equally beautiful, and as gawdily dressed, came flocking in, with a like request to those standing about the room. The invitation to dance I declined——— "Then d——n you, treat me," said she, which I instantly did, and *retreated* into an adjoining room, the door of which stood invitingly open. Here a scene presented itself which made a lasting impression upon me. Immediately in front, as I entered, stood a Roulette table, revolving like the flood wheel of a tubmill, from which I ever and anon heard the ominous exclamation of "double O black!" On the right, around a table, sat some half dozen or more persons betting at Faro. Some bet with silver coin, some with bank notes, and a few who seemed to be the largest betters, with "checks" or counters.

"Split again, by ———!" said one, as the dealer cried "Jacks a pair," who took one half the stakes upon the Jack, and continued———. "Ace, Tray—Ten, Four."

"D——n that catharpen, it has twice split me wide open," said another of the betters; a third cursed the Queen as a "faithless ———," whilst a fourth lost [in] sullen silence. I observed, however, one who was betting with counters, to win several large bets in succession without lifting his money from the table. The checks, which were circular pieces of bone or ivory, were paid him and piled up, one above another, to a great height. The large amount now pending induced the banker to ask the bettor whether he "went" the whole amount. "Yes, by ———, I'll pile my paralee to the ceiling," replied the desperate gamester.

Just at this moment my attention was attracted to a different part of the room, where the proprietor appeared to be endeavoring to eject some person from the house who was greatly intoxicated. "I won't go," said the drunken man, "until I have won five hundred dollars, or lost my pile." "You're a fool," said the landlord; "put your money up, and go home." "If I'm a fool my money aint," replied he, and he offered to bet any amount, on any thing. In one hand he held five $100 bank notes, and in the other a deck of cards. The money he scattered about the room seemingly regardless of its value—falling himself against the counter and sometimes upon the floor. His money was picked up, and handed to him by the considerate landlord, who urged him by every argument in his power, to put up his money, and go home: this he declined doing, and as a dernier resort, the landlord proposed to me, who was looking on with some interest at the strange scene, to win his money and return it to him, when sober.

"If you don't," said he, "some gambler will, and keep it."

This seemed reasonable and looked kind in the landlord, and I felt half disposed to put the scheme in execution. The drunken man had laid out three cards, and placed $500 as a stake upon the counter, which he offered to bet, that he *could name and turn any of the three cards*, or he would bet the same amount no one else could do so. The cards he had previously shown, and were the Jack of Clubs, the Tray of Spades, and the Nine of Diamonds. He was now about to add to his beastly intoxication, by taking another drink, and in doing so, had partially turned his back upon the cards he had laid out. At this stage of the game, a plainly dressed man, whom I took to be a farmer from the neighborhood, stepped up to me, and said he would join me in carrying out the suggestion of the landlord; that it was a charitable act, and one that we ought not to hesitate to perform for our fellow men. The gentleman put his hand into his pocket for the money to stake, but immediately recollected that he had left his pocket book at the hotel where he stopped, to avoid the risk of having his pocket picked while *under-the-hill*. He then appealed to me to furnish the money for so praiseworthy an object, alledging that he would not have me do so, if the game was not a certain one; and to make assurance doubly sure, he lifted one of the cards, while the man's back was turned towards us, and turned up one of the corners, shewing me that it was the *Nine of Diamonds*, which, said he, "you can name and turn for the bet—the bent corner will not be observed and you can win the money without risk."

I had taken out my pocket book, not for the purpose of staking the money, but merely to see if my money was safe, and as I ran over the notes, my companion and friend, as he seemed to be, half soliciting and half forcing, took from my hand five notes of $100 each, and placed them with the $500 already on the counter, observing with a wink, that he would hold the stakes. He now desired me to name and turn a card for the money; this I was about to do, when the drunken man asked the privilege of shuffling the three cards, which was of course granted, and with the dexterity of Signor Blitz, or the "wonder working Adrian," he smoothed down the corner which had been turned up, and turned up the corner of one of the black cards, in precisely the same manner—this of course I did not observe. "Now," said he, "name and turn a card for the money staked." I examined the backs and turned the card with the corner bent; it proved to be the *Jack of Clubs*! I cast my eyes towards the holder of the stakes—he was in the act of handing them over to the winner, who had suddenly become quite sober, and who, as he pocketed the money, coolly informed me that it was "*all fair;*" and that I had lost my money, upon "*My Grandmother's Trick.*"

I turned to leave the den. The Roulette was still whirling its endless round, the small ivory ball vainly endeavoring to enter the *compressed compartments upon which the bettors had staked;* Faro was catching in hockley, and "splitting open" more victims, and as I passed through the ball-room the little nigger was still thumping the tamboureen and singing.

"The old woman she ——— hid in the haymow."

Yazoo.

GAMBLERS AND SUCKERS

JONATHAN H. GREEN

———

[*Jonathan H. Green, whose* Gambling Unmasked! or the Personal Experience of Jonathan H. Green, the Reformed Gambler . . . written by Himself *was first published in Philadelphia in 1844 and a third edition—"improved"—in 1848, had run away from home in Lawrenceburg, Indiana, in 1829 at the age of sixteen. After a career at gambling on the steamboats and in the river towns he made a second lecturing over the United States billed as "the Reformed Gambler." In the passages below, from the 1857 printing of his book (pp. 123–36) he exposes some of the tricks played on suckers in Silver Street, Natchez-under-the-hill, and on board the boats, the "Spanish burying," for example, as well as the hazard gamblers had to chance of "waking up the wrong passenger."*]

I have known the gamblers to perpetrate the greatest outrages in disposing of their victims. One day, while the fraternity were lounging in a Silver street coffee-house, a young man came in and was soon engaged in conversation. He said he had some fifteen hundred dollars, which he would like to invest in some profitable business. They proposed that he should purchase a certain hotel, which, by the way, was the head-quarters of the gamblers. It belonged, they told him, to a man by the name of Clifton. He and this Mr. Clifton were soon brought together, and a bargain was closed. The young man paid down fifteen hundred dollars for the furniture and the kitchen apparatus, and on the following morning was to take possession. Morning came; but what was the surprise of the purchaser to find that Clifton was only a bartender, and that he had left the city the night before; having been discharged by the proprietor of the hotel! The young man saw that his money was gone, and frantic with his loss, he hastened to tell his *friends* how Clifton had swindled him. They heard his story; and then one of them, with great seriousness, inquired if he had taken possession of the establishment?

"Why," said he, "the man declared the property was his, and told me the sooner I was missing the better it would be for me."

"And you took the hint, did you?" asked the waggish gambler.

"I did," was the reply; "for the man out with a bowie-knife, sixteen inches long, and declared he would whistle that fellow down on my head and cut off my ears."

Seeing they had caught a *green* one, they determined to dispose of him as quickly as possible, and give Clifton a chance to return. So they wrote a letter, signing it with Clifton's name, and sealing it. This was delivered to the young man, as if it had been left for him by Clifton. It read nearly as follows:

FRIEND REED

Owing to certain afflictive circumstances in my father's family in New Orleans, I feel compelled to leave for that place this evening. When you come to know fully the reasons which induced me to take your money, I know you will not curse me, as you now do. Be assured I shall regard the fifteen hundred dollars as a loan, and will endeavour to repay you soon. But if I can persuade you to invest it in a hotel, now owned by a brother of mine, and where you will find me, I shall do both him and you a good service. The hotel is on Silver street. Excuse haste. Come on without delay.

Yours, truly,
J. W. CLIFTON.

The young man was fool enough to be taken in again. He started for New Orleans in the first boat; but of his history afterwards I know nothing. I venture to say, however, that he never forgot *Silver street*, or *Natchez-under-the-hill*.

Clifton soon returned. He was a hard case, having hugged the *whipping-post* once or twice before he came to Silver street to graduate. By this last piece of villany, he realized about five hundred dollars. But his good fortune excited the envy of some of the brotherhood, and a plan was put on foot to swindle him out of his money. Clifton was remarkably swift on foot, and prided himself upon it greatly. They remarked that it was impossible for any man to run one hundred yards in twelve seconds. Clifton said he could. A stranger who was present offered to bet a thousand dollars that he could not run sixty-five yards in twelve seconds.

Clifton said he would take it, and turned round to find some one to go him halves. A young "hoosier" gambler was ready to do him the favor, and a thousand dollars were put up. Clifton was to run that night, for the stranger said he must leave in the next boat. The distance having been measured to the satisfaction of all concerned, Clifton started and ran; but when he had gone about half the distance, he fell, as if he had been shot dead. In a few moments, as soon as he recovered from the first shock of the fall, he sprang to his feet, shouting, "Five hundred for the man who hit me with that brickbat! Don't give up the stakes, Mr. Stakeholder. I was knocked down with a brickbat."

"No, sir," said the "hoosier" gambler, "no one threw a brickbat; but some of those rascals have stretched a bed-cord across the street, and it is that which threw you down."

The stakes were given up; but there is good reason to believe the young "hoosier" got his five hundred dollars back, and two hundred and fifty out of Clifton's. Clifton was enraged against the stakeholder, and wanted revenge. He suggested that a *Spanish burying* should be held for the express purpose of chastising the stakeholder. The others approved of it; but the "hoosier" observed, that, in order to prevent suspicion on the part of the stakeholder, which would defeat the whole plan, they must get in some stranger, and have things look as if they were going to whip him. Clifton said he would get in some country chap. He did so, and the ceremony began. It is necessary that I should here give the reader some description of this *Spanish burying*—as it is called. It is one of those plays, or exercises, which the gamblers use partly to make their victims afraid to give them further trouble, and partly to gratify their own cruel and hellish passions. It is but a specimen of their brutal sports. To play it, requires some ten or twenty men; all of whom join their force against one poor fellow. Some one of the fraternity invites him to play a small game for liquor. If he objects, or says he does not understand it, which is generally the case, the gambler tells him to come and learn. "It is a very simple thing—we shall be sure to beat them; but if our side loses, why, I will pay the liquor. Come, bear a hand." The poor fellow may make all kinds of excuses; but they will scarcely ever fail to get him in.

The play begins by their joining hands and forming a ring, within which is laid, flat on his back, one of their largest and strongest men. A handkerchief is laid over his face, and he is called *the dead man*. Then they march around him with a kind of ceremony, which neither they nor anybody else understand. Suddenly halting, they say—*Salute the dead*. Each one then goes and kisses, or pretends to kiss, the supposed corpse. But when it comes the turn of the victim of their brutal play to kiss the corpse, he suddenly finds himself clutched fast by the *dead man*, while the rest beat him with their handkerchiefs, which have been tied full of knots on purpose, and twisted so as to be almost as hard as cow-skins. The poor fellow flounders, and swears, and kicks, but all to no purpose. In the course of fifteen seconds, five hundred blows will be administered. When permitted to get up, the enraged man demands an explanation, upon which some mean wretch, a real carrion-crow, will step up and address him in such a strain as this:

"Most worthy brother, I am happy to inform you that, through your expert and manly efforts, the side which chose you are entitled to a gallon of brandy, at the expense of the opposite side; some of which brandy will be applied to your blistered back. The Spanish Burying Club also wish you to understand that you have just been initiated into their honorable fraternity. Furthermore, that fifteen degrees are due you; and that if you remain within their reach, one or two degrees will be given at a time, till you have received the whole. Fourteen of the degrees will be conferred in the same manner as the one you have already received, with this exception—in conferring the last seven, the honorable fraternity will tie bullets in their handkerchiefs, and eight of their number will use cowhides, which must be purchased by the candidate. The last degree, which will constitute you a *grand-master* in the honorable body, will be simply shaving off those red ears of yours. We trust you will continue among us a faithful brother, &c."

During such an explanation, the poor fellow's blood will boil in every vein. His reply will sometimes be one thing, sometimes another; but will generally conclude with his cursing the whole affair, and cutting his connection with the fraternity.

It was by means of this game that Clifton sought to be revenged on the stakeholder. The ceremony began; but when it came Clifton's turn to salute the dead, he was clutched and held fast. The fraternity gave him about five hundred blows, and then let him get up. He jumped to his feet, the tears streaming from his eyes, "Gentlemen," said he, "what have I done to merit this foul treatment?" The "hoosier" told him he supposed they were mistaken. "But how could you make such a horrible mistake?" he asked. *The dead man* then came up, and declared that it was a great mistake, and that having the handkerchief over his eyes he could not see; but supposed he was to take the touch of the lip as a signal to grasp the man.

Being satisfied that the mistake was not intentional, Clifton determined to try again, and to have the stakeholder whipped. The young "hoosier" gambler said it would be a great satisfaction to him to see it well done. All things being ready, the play began again. And again Clifton was grasped and held down by the *dead man*. He shouted lustily—"Hold, hold, it is me; it is Clifton;" but the fraternity did not choose to hear him till they had administered several hundred blows. When released, he jumped up, frothing and foaming with rage. The "hoosier" was full of sympathy. "Friend Clifton," said he, "have they hurt you?"

"I reckon they have," he replied, "and you are the only man that sympathizes with me."

"Certainly I am," said the "hoosier;" when at the same time it was the young "hoosier" that had stretched the rope and planned the whole series of Clifton's misfortunes. Clifton immediately left the brotherhood.

Such is the thirst of gamblers for unnatural excitement, that when tired of cards, they often seek it in such brutal sports as this. In order to kill time, they are ready to sacrifice the last vestige of principle, or of human feeling in their hearts. And when their interest is concerned in the result, as is usually the case, it gives their fiend-like sport a double relish. The reader may like to know to what class of gamblers this applies. I have known those who are upheld as respectable sportsmen, or gentlemanly faro dealers, to engage in such brutalizing scenes; and I warn every inexperienced youth to beware how he comes within the circle of their influence.

For the permission of such acts of outrageous villany, the citizens were often to blame. At the date to which the events narrated above belong, steamboat travelling upon our southern and western waters was actually dangerous. Thousands of accidents occurred while the officers were at the card-table. And it is a lamentable fact, that many splendid steamers are still under the command of gamblers, or of those who are in league with them. All the ports between New Orleans and Pittsburg are infested with villains of the blackest dye; who are perfectly at home on board these boats, and whose gambling, and thieving, and other deeds of villany, are connived at by the officers. Sometimes they will be introduced to the passengers as if they were, or had lately been, officers of the boat. In the spring of the year, you will see thousands of men coming up from New Orleans, Natchez, and other southern ports. Ask them where they are bound, and they reply, to the upper country for our health. In the fall, you see them crowding south, and for their health, they say. There are some exceptions, of course; but, as a general thing, these men are villains, gamblers, and pickpockets. If they cannot swindle, they will rob, and the captains, and clerks, and pilots of many boats are ready to second their attempts. I write from experience, for I have spent years on those rivers, and won thousands and tens of thousands on those boats. It is my decided opinion, that a law ought to be enacted, making the captain and his employers, who permit *faro*, *twenty-one*, *roulette*, and other swindling games to be played on board, responsible for the money swindled from the inexperienced. I have known some of the most respectable men in the country basely plundered, with the consent, too, of some of those river captains. To the inexperienced I would say—shun those gambling boats as you would the plague; and, on board of any western steamboat, beware of any marked expressions of friendship from a stranger. Be afraid of "*waking up the wrong passenger*." The first time I heard that phrase used, I well recollect, and will give the circumstances.

I had been in Natchez from the time of Mose Way's horse-race until poor Clifton received his second Spanish burying. I left on board of the *Tippecanoe*, a snug little boat, running in the cotton-trade between Natchez and Princeton, and commanded by Captain Simon Miller, of Louisville. As gamblers are accustomed to do, soon after going on board, I endeavored to ascertain what the prospects were for game. The usual way of doing this is by going around and forming acquaintances among the players in a friendly game of *whist, eucher, boston, seven-up*, or *old-sledge*. This is done to draw in the unsuspecting, to see who plays, and what amount of money they carry upon their persons. Then, if

they cannot get the money by gambling, there are but few who
will not try to secure it in another way.

I soon found that my prospects were dull enough, for I could
not start a game, even for amusement. So I took my berth, thinking I would sleep upon it. A curious set of passengers, thought I,
afraid to play with a beardless boy. But as I lay in my berth,
thinking over the matter, the boat stopped her engines—passengers had hailed her. The yawl was sent out, and two elderly men,
planters in appearance, came on board. They were evidently
under the influence of liquor. They had scarcely reached the boat
before they sung out, "Bar-keeper, have you any cards on board?"
Being answered in the affirmative, they asked if there were any
gentlemen that would play? The bar-keeper could not inform
them; but remarked they could satisfy themselves by inquiry.
Upon this, they advanced to where several persons were seated,
whom I had annoyed very much, by urging them to play. They all
refused again. "But you must play," said one of the old men; "we
will have a game." Some one of them pointed to my berth, and
said, there was a gentleman there who would probably be happy
to accommodate them. He was right, and if they had not called
upon me, I would soon have called upon them, to accommodate
them with a game of poker. The old man turned round and felt
his way along to the berth where I lay, as he supposed, asleep.
But "all men do not sleep when their eyes are shut." He gave me a
hearty shake, crying out, "Halloo! get up, get up." I affected the
sleeping man, muttered out my surprise, asked him if the boat
was sinking, and so forth. He was perfectly deceived, and continued to bawl out, "Get up, get up, and play poker."

"Well, if I must, I must," said I. "Go and get the table and
cards ready, and I will be with you as soon as possible." I soon
heard him giving orders to the steward to bring a table and cards.
While things were making ready, I was very busy in finding and
arranging my wearing apparel, and saw, from the run of their
conversation, that they were expecting a rich treat, and had
agreed to play against me in partnership. Their agreement I
overheard. Said one of them, "You, sir, set your foot on mine, and
for one pair, kick me once; for two pairs, twice; for three, three
times; for four, four times; and for "a full," once very hard. I
knew that, with this arrangement, unless I should counterplay,
they would soon fleece me. Soon after the game began, I found

them feeling for feet, and being of an accommodating disposition, I gave them a foot a piece. Kick after kick did I get, and answer; and soon found myself winner by six hundred dollars, and my opponents in a very disagreeable mood for amusement players, as they assured me they were. We had about forty dollars in silver to play with, and as fast as I won it, they would give me banknotes in exchange. When I had won the six hundred dollars, and all the silver, they wished to play upon credit. This I refused; and as they were getting very quarrelsome, I determined to close. They objected to this, and insisted that if I did quit, I should leave the silver. I did so, and they soon were playing high against each other. It is a natural consequence that, when two gamblers in partnership have been unsuccessful, they will turn upon one another. I lay in my berth, well pleased with my night's work. Unpleasant and harsh words passed between the old men.

"You did not play the game according to bargain, Mr. ———."

"I not play! Do you mean me, Mr.?"

"I mean you, ———."

"Don't say that, Mr. ———. No, sir, it will not do to accuse me, when you did not kick me right one time during the whole night."

"Hold! hold! Did you kick me according to the arrangement? Mr. ———, we are neighbors, and I thought friends, till this evening's play; but I must confess I am somewhat ———"

"Ashamed of yourself, I suppose," said ———, taking the words out of his mouth.

"No, sir; one proposition, and leave the balance until to-morrow."

"Propose," said ———.

"That we settle our play to-night, and leave the matter of the incorrect kicking to be settled at another time."

"Very willing; how do you say we stand?"

"I owe you one hundred and seventy-five dollars," said ———.

"You are a correct man, sir."

"That I am, and this settlement will prove it; but let me ask how you like our night's play?" said ———.

"Don't like it at all," said ———.

"And the boy that played, what do you think of him?"

"I think just this, Mr. ———; I think we *waked up the wrong passenger!*"

"I think so, too; we are perfectly agreed, Mr. ———. And now, neighbor ———, you know I have a great respect for you, and hope you may not lose; but I must cast up my account against you, and see how much you are indebted to me."

"Account against me!" exclaimed ———; "I will submit to no such thing, I assure you."

"Just look over that list, and—keep cool, friend ———, keep cool, sir—it says you owe me two hundred and twenty-five dollars; bringing you in my debt fifty dollars. Is not that right?"

"Too late to rectify mistakes, sir."

"But you are bound to rectify this one. What do you think of that?"

"I think as I did of the boy—that I *waked up the wrong passenger*," said he, at the same time sliding his claim from the table, badly beaten.

These two old men had come on board on purpose to fleece some inexperienced card-player, while they pretended that *amusement* was all they wanted in playing. I was, probably, the only individual on board whom they could not have beaten. Beware of the men who say they play merely for amusement. Beware, too, of those who advocate such playing; for, while here and there one may do it from ignorance, it is generally done by dishonest, unprincipled men, as a cloak for their own knavery and crime. The only safe course is total abstinence. Touch not, handle not the implements of the gambler.

THIMBLERIG, THE RIVERBOAT GAMBLER

DAVID CROCKETT

––––––

[*It may well be that David Crockett did not write this account of a gambler on the Mississippi, for it was published in 1836 as Chapters VI and VII of* Col. Crockett's Exploits and Adventures in Texas. *But whoever did provided a lively picture of riverboat gamblers.*]

There was a considerable number of passengers on board the boat, and our assortment was somewhat like the Yankee merchant's cargo of notions, pretty particularly miscellaneous, I tell you. I moved through the crowd from stem to stern, to see if I could discover any face that was not altogether strange to me; but after a general survey, I concluded that I had never seen one of them before. There were merchants and emigrants and gamblers, but none who seemed to have embarked in that particular business that for the time being occupied my mind—I could find none who were going to Texas. All seemed to have their hands full enough of their own affairs, without meddling with the cause of freedom. The greater share of glory will be mine, thought I, so go ahead, Crockett.

I saw a small cluster of passengers at one end of the boat, and hearing an occasional burst of laughter, thinks I there's some sport started in that quarter, and having nothing better to do, I'll go in for my share of it. Accordingly I drew nigh to the cluster, and seated on a chest was a tall lank sea sarpent looking blackleg, who had crawled over from Natchez under the hill, and was amusing the passengers with his skill at thimblerig; at the same time he was picking up their shillings just about as expeditiously as a hungry gobbler would a pint of corn. He was doing what might be called an average business in a small way, and lost no time in gathering up the fragments.

I watched the whole process for some time, and found that he had adopted the example set by the old tempter himself, to get the weathergage of us poor weak mortals. He made it a point to let his victims win always the first stake, that they might be tempted to go ahead; and then, when they least suspected it, he would come down upon them like a hurricane in a cornfield, sweeping all before it.

I stood looking on, seeing him pick up the chicken feed from the green horns, and thought if men are such darned fools as to be cheated out of their hard earnings by a fellow who had just brains enough to pass a pea from one thimble to another, with such slight of hand, that you could not tell under which he had deposited it; it is not astonishing that the magician of Kinderhook should play thimblerig upon the big figure, and attempt to cheat the whole nation. I thought that "the Government" was playing the same game with the deposites, and with such address too, that before long it will be a hard matter to find them under any of the thimbles where it is supposed they have been originally placed.

The thimble conjurer saw me looking on, and eyeing me as if he thought I would be a good subject, said carelessly, "Come, stranger, won't you take a chance?" the whole time passing the pea from one thimble to the other, by way of throwing out a bait for the gudgeons to bite at. "I never gamble, stranger," says I, "principled against it; think it a slippery way of getting through the world at best." "Them are my sentiments to a notch," says he; "but this is not gambling by no means. A little innocent pastime, nothing more. Better take a hack by way of trying your luck at guessing." All this time he continued working with his thimbles; first putting the pea under one, which was plain to be seen, and then uncovering it, would show you the pea was there; he would then put it under the second thimble, and do the same, and then under the third; all of which he did to show how easy it would be to guess where the pea was deposited, if one would only keep a sharp look-out.

"Come, stranger," says he to me again, "you had better take a chance. Stake a trifle, I don't care how small, just for the fun of the thing."

"I am principled against betting money," says I, "but I don't mind going in for drinks for the present company, for I'm as dry as one of little Isaac Hill's regular set speeches."

"I admire your principles," says he, "and to show that I play with these here thimbles just for the sake of pastime, I will take that bet, though I'm a whole hog temperance man. Just say when, stranger."

He continued all the time slipping the pea from one thimble to another; my eye was as keen as a lizard's, and when he stopped, I cried out, "Now; the pea is under the middle thimble." He was going to raise it to show that it wasn't there, when I interfered, and said, "Stop, if you please," and raised it myself, and sure enough the pea was there; but it mought have been otherwise if he had had the uncovering of it.

"Sure enough you've won the bet," says he. "You've a sharp eye, but I don't care if I give you another chance. Let us go fifty cents this bout; I'm sure you'll win."

"Then you're a darned fool to bet, stranger," says I; "and since that is the case, it would be little better than picking your pocket to bet with you; so I'll let it alone."

"I don't mind running the risk," said he.

"But I do," says I, "and since I always let well enough alone, and I have had just about glory enough for one day, let us all go to the bar and liquor."

This called forth a loud laugh at the thimble conjurer's expense; and he tried hard to induce me to take just one chance more, but he mought just as well have sung psalms to a dead horse, for my mind was made up; and I told him, that I looked upon gambling as about the dirtiest way that a man could adopt to get through this dirty world; and that I would never bet any thing beyond a quart of whisky upon a rifle shot, which I considered a legal bet, and gentlemanly and rational amusement. "But all this cackling," says I, "makes me very thirsty, so let us adjourn to the bar and liquor."

He gathered up his thimbles, and the whole company followed us to the bar, laughing heartily at the conjurer; for, as he had won some of their money, they were sort of delighted to see him beaten with his own cudgel. He tried to laugh too, but his laugh wasn't at all pleasant, and rather forced. The barkeeper placed a big-bellied bottle before us; and after mixing our liquor, I was called on for a toast, by one of the company, a chap just about as rough hewn as if he had been cut out of a gum log with a broad axe, and sent into the market without even being smoothed off with a jack plane—one of them chaps who, in their journey through life, are always ready for a fight or a frolic, and don't care the toss of a copper which.

"Well, gentlemen," says I, "being called upon for a toast, and being in a slave-holding state, in order to avoid giving offence and running the risk of being Lynched, it may be necessary to premise that I am neither an abolitionist nor a colonizationist, but simply Colonel Crockett of Tennessee, now bound for Texas." When they heard my name they gave three cheers for Colonel Crockett; and silence being restored, I continued, "Now, gentlemen, I will offer you a toast, hoping, after what I have started, that it will give offence to no one present; but should I be mistaken, I must imitate the 'old Roman,' and take the responsibility. I offer, gentlemen, The abolition of slavery: Let the work first begin in the two houses of Congress. There are no slaves in the country more servile than the party slaves in Congress. The wink or the nod of their masters is all sufficient for the accomplishment of the most dirty work."

They drank the toast in a style that satisfied me, that the Little Magician might as well go to a pigsty for wool, as to beat round in that part for voters; they were all either for Judge White or Old Tippecanoe. The thimble conjurer having asked the barkeeper how much was to pay, was told that there were sixteen smallers, which amounted to one dollar. He was about to lay down the blunt, but not in Benton's metallic currency, which I find has already become as shy as honesty with an office holder, but he planked down one of Biddle's notes, when I interfered, and told him that the barkeeper had made a mistake.

"How so?" demanded the barkeeper.

"How much do you charge," said I, "when you retail your liquor?"

"A fip a glass."

"Well, then," says I, "as Thimblerig here, who belongs to the temperance society, took it in wholesale, I reckon you can afford to let him have it at half price?"

Now, as they had all noticed that the conjurer went what is called the heavy wet, they laughed outright, and we heard no more about temperance from that quarter. When we returned to the deck the blackleg set to work with his thimbles again, and bantered me to bet; but I told him that it was against my principle, and as I had already reaped glory enough for one day, I would just let well enough alone for the present. If the "old Roman" had done the same in relation to the deposites and "the monster," we should have escaped more difficulties than all the cunning of the Little Flying Dutchman, and Dick Johnson to boot, will be able to repair. I shouldn't be astonished if the new Vice President's head should get wool gathering before they have half unravelled the knotted and twisted thread of perplexities that the old General has spun, in which case his charming spouse will no doubt be delighted, for then they will be all in the family way. What a handsome display they will make in the White House. No doubt the first act of Congress will be to repeal the duties on Cologne and Lavender waters, for they will be in great demand about the Palace, particularly in the dog days.

One of the passengers hearing that I was on board of the boat, came up to me, and began to talk about the affairs of the nation, and said a good deal in favor of "the Magician," and wished to hear what I had to say against him. He talked loud, which is the way with all politicians educated in the Jackson school; and by his slang-whanging drew a considerable crowd around us. Now, this was the very thing I wanted, as I knew I should not soon have another opportunity of making a political speech; he no sooner asked to hear what I had to say against his candidate, than I let him have it, strong and hot as he could take, I tell you.

My speech was received with great applause, and the politician, finding that I was better acquainted with his candidate than he was himself, for I wrote his life, shut his fly trap, and turned on his heel without saying a word. He found that he had barked up the wrong tree. I afterward learnt that he was a mail contractor in those parts, and that he also had large dealings in the Land office, and therefore thought it necessary to chime in with his penny whistle, in the universal chorus. There's a large band of the same description, but I'm thinking Uncle Sam will some day find out that he had paid too much for the piper.

After my speech, and setting my face against gambling, poor Thimblerig was obliged to break off conjuring for want of customers, and call it half a day. He came and entered into conversation with me, and I found him a good-natured intelligent fellow, with a keen eye for the main chance. He belonged to that numerous class, that it is perfectly safe to trust as far as a tailor can sling a bull by the tail—but no farther. He told me that he had been brought up a gentleman; that is say, he was not instructed in any useful pursuit by which he could obtain a livelihood, so that when he found he had to depend upon himself for the necessaries of life, he began to suspect, that dame nature would have conferred a particular favour if she had consigned him to the care of any one else. She had made a very injudicious choice when she selected him to sustain the dignity of a gentleman.

The first bright idea that occurred to him as a speedy means of bettering his fortune, would be to marry an heiress. Accordingly he looked about himself pretty sharp, and after glancing from one fair object to another, finally his hawk's eye rested upon the young and pretty daughter of a wealthy planter. Thimblerig run his brazen face with his tailor for a new suit, for he abounded more in that metallic currency than he did in either Benton's mint drops or in Biddle's notes; and having the gentility of his outward Adam thus endorsed by his tailor—an important endorsement, by-the-way, as times go—he managed to obtain an introduction to the planter's daughter.

Our worthy had the principle of going ahead strongly developed. He was possessed of considerable address, and had brass enough in his face to make a wash-kettle; and having once got access to the planter's house, it was no easy matter to dislodge him. In this he resembled those politicians who commence life as office holders; they will hang on tooth and nail, and even when death shakes them off, you'll find a commission of some kind crumpled up in their clenched fingers. Little Van appears to belong to this class—there's no beating his snout from the public crib. He'll feed there while there's a grain of corn left, and even then, from long habit, he'll set to work and gnaw at the manger.

Thimblerig got the blind side of the planter, and every thing to outward appearances went on swimmingly. Our worthy boasted to his cronies that the business was settled, and that in a few weeks he should occupy the elevated station in society that nature had designed him to adorn. He swelled like the frog in the fable, or rather like Johnson's wife, of Kentucky, when the idea occurred to her of figuring away at Washington. But there's many a slip 'twixt the cup and the lip, says the proverb, and suddenly Thimblerig discontinued his visits at the planter's house. His friends inquired of him the meaning of this abrupt termination of his devotions.

"I have been treated with disrespect," replied the worthy, indignantly.

"Disrespect! in what way?"

"My visits, it seems, are not altogether agreeable."

"But how have you ascertained that?"

"I received a hint to that effect; and I can take a hint as soon as another."

"A hint—and have you allowed a hint to drive you from the pursuit? For shame. Go back again."

"No, no, never! a hint is sufficient for a man of my gentlemanly feelings. I asked the old man for his daughter."

"Well, what followed? what did he say?"

"Didn't say a word."

"Silence gives consent all the world over."

"So I thought. I then told him to fix the day."

"Well, what then?"

"Why, then he kicked me down stairs, and ordered his slaves to pump upon me. That's hint enough for me, that my visits are not properly appreciated; and blast my old shoes if I condescend to renew the acquaintance, or notice them in any way until they send for me."

As Thimblerig's new coat became rather too seedy to play the part of a gentleman much longer in real life, he determined to sustain that character upon the stage, and accordingly joined a company of players. He began, according to custom, at the top of the ladder, and was regularly hissed and pelted through every gradation until he found himself at the lowest rowel. "This," said he, "was a dreadful check to proud ambition;" but he consoled himself with the idea of peace and quietness in his present obscure walk; and though he had no prospect of being elated by the applause of admiring multitudes, he no longer trod the scene of mimic glory in constant dread of becoming a target for rotten eggs and oranges. "And there was much in that," said Thimblerig. But this calm could not continue for ever.

The manager, who, like all managers who pay salaries regularly, was as absolute behind the scenes as the "old Roman" is in the White House, had fixed upon getting up an eastern spectacle, called the Cataract of the Ganges. He intended to introduce a fine procession, in which an elephant was to be the principal feature. Here a difficulty occurred. What was to be done for an elephant? Alligators were plenty in those parts, but an elephant was not to be had for love or money. But an alligator would not answer the purpose, so he determined to make a pasteboard elephant as large as life, and twice as natural. The next difficulty was to find members of the company of suitable dimensions to perform the several members of the pasteboard star. The manager cast his eye upon the long, gaunt figure of the unfortunate Thimblerig, and cast him for the hinder legs, the rump, and part of the back of the elephant. The poor player expostulated, and the manager replied, that he would appear as a star of the occasion, and would no doubt receive more applause than he had during his whole career. "But I shall not be seen," said the player. "All the better," replied the manager, "as in that case you will have nothing to apprehend from eggs and oranges."

Thimblerig, finding that mild expostulation availed nothing, swore that he would not study the part, and accordingly threw it up in dignified disgust. He said that it was an outrage upon the feelings of the proud representative of Shakespeare's heroes, to be compelled to play pantomime in the hinder parts of the noblest animal that ever trod the stage. If it had been the fore quarters of the elephant, it might possibly have been made a speaking part; at any rate he might have snorted through the trunk, if nothing more; but from the position he was to occupy, damned the word could he utter, or even roar with propriety. He therefore positively refused to act, as he considered it an insult to his reputation to tread the stage in such a character; and he looked upon the whole affair as a profanation of the legitimate drama. The result was, our worthy was discharged from the company, and compelled to commence hoeing another row.

He drifted to New Orleans, and hired himself as marker to a gambling table. Here he remained but a few months, for his ideas of arithmetic differed widely from those of his employer, and accordingly they had some difficulty in balancing the cash account; for when his employer, in adding up the receipts, made it nought and carry two, Thimblerig insisted that it should be nought and carry one; and in order to prove that he was correct, he carried himself off, and left nothing behind him.

He now commenced professional blackleg of his own hook,

and took up his quarters in Natchez under the hill. Here he remained, doing business in a small way, until Judge Lynch commenced his practice in that quarter, and made the place too hot for his comfort. He shifted his habitation, but not having sufficient capital to go the big figure, he practised the game of thimblerig until he acquired considerable skill, and then commenced passing up and down the river in the steamboats; and managed, by close attention to business, to pick up a decent livelihood in the small way, from such as had more pence in their pockets than sense in their noddles.

I found Thimblerig to be a pleasant talkative fellow. He communicated the foregoing facts with as much indifference as if there had been nothing disgraceful in his career; and at times he would chuckle with an air of triumph at the adroitness he had displayed in some of the knavish tricks he had practised. He looked upon this world as one vast stage, crowded with empirics and jugglers; and that he who could practise his deceptions with the greatest skill was entitled to the greatest applause.

I asked him to give me an account of Natchez and his adventures there, and I would put it in the book I intended to write, when he gave me the following, which betrays that his feelings were still somewhat irritated at being obliged to give them leg bail when Judge Lynch made his appearance. I give it in his own words.

"Natchez is a land of fevers, alligators, niggers, and cotton bales: where the sun shines with force sufficient to melt the diamond, and the word ice is expunged from the dictionary, for its definition cannot be comprehended by the natives: where to refuse grog before breakfast would degrade you below the brute creation; and where a good dinner is looked upon as an angel's visit, and voted a miracle: where the evergreen and majestic magnolia tree, with its superb flower, unknown to the northern climes, and its fragrance unsurpassed, calls forth the admiration of every beholder; and the dark moss hangs in festoons from the forest trees like the drapery of a funeral pall: where bears, the size of young jackasses, are fondled in lieu of pet dogs; and knives, the length of a barber's pole, usurp the place of toothpicks: where the filth of the town is carried off by buzzards, and the inhabitants are carried off by fevers: where nigger women are knocked down by the auctioneer, and knocked up by the purchaser: where the poorest slave has plenty of yellow boys, but not of Benton's mintage; and indeed the shades of colour are so varied and mixed, that a nigger is frequently seen black and blue at the same time. And such is Natchez.

"The town is divided into two parts, as distinct in character as they are in appearance. Natchez on the hill, situated upon a high bluff overlooking the Mississippi, is a pretty little town with streets regularly laid out, and ornamented with divers handsome public buildings. Natchez under the hill—where, O where, shall I find words suitable to describe the peculiarities of that unholy spot? 'Tis, in fact, the jumping off place. Satan looks on it with glee, and chuckles as he beholds the orgies of his votaries. The buildings are for the most part brothels, taverns, or gambling houses, and fequently the whole three may be found under the same roof. Obscene songs are sung at the top of the voice in all quarters. I have repeatedly seen the strumpets tear a man's clothes from his back, and leave his body beautified with all the colors of the rainbow.

"One of the most popular tricks is called the 'Spanish burial.' When a greenhorn makes his appearance among them, one who is in the plot announces the death of a resident, and that all strangers must subscribe to the custom of the place upon such an occasion. They forthwith arrange a procession; each person, as he passes the departed, kneels down and pretends to kiss the treacherous corpse. When the unsophisticated attempts this ceremony the dead man clinches him, and the mourners beat the fellow so entrapped until he consents to treat all hands; but should he be penniless, his life will be endangered by the severity of the castigation. And such is Natchez under the hill.

"An odd affair occurred while I was last there," continued Thimblerig. "A steamboat stopped at the landing, and one of the hands went ashore under the hill to purchase provisions, and the adroit citizens of that delectable retreat contrived to rob him of all his money. The captain of the boat, a determined fellow, went ashore in the hope of persuading them to refund—but that cock wouldn't fight. Without farther ceremony, assisted by his crew and passengers, some three or four hundred in number, he made fast an immense cable to the frame tenement where the theft had been perpetrated, and allowed fifteen minutes for the money to be forthcoming; vowing if it was not produced within that time, to put steam to his boat, and drag the house into the river. The money was instantly produced.

"I witnessed a sight during my stay there," continued the thimble conjuror, "that almost froze my blood with horror, and will serve as a specimen of the customs of the far south. A planter, of the name of Foster, connected with the best families of the state, unprovoked, in cold blood, murdered his young and beautiful wife, a few months after marriage. He beat her deliberately to death in a walk adjoining his dwelling, carried the body to the hut of one of his slaves, washed the dirt from her person, and, assisted by his negroes, buried her upon his plantation. Suspicion was awakened, the body disinterred, and the villain's guilt established. He fled, was overtaken, and secured in prison. His trial was, by some device of the law, delayed until the third term of the court. At length it came on, and so clear and indisputable was the evidence, that not a doubt was entertained of the result; when, by an oversight on the part of the sheriff, who neglected swearing into office his deputy who summoned the jurors, the trial was abruptly discontinued, and all proceedings against Foster were suspended, or rather ended.

"There exists throughout the extreme south, bodies of men who style themselves Lynchers. When an individual escapes punishment by some technicality of the law, or perpetrates an offence not recognized in courts of justice, they seize him, and inflict such chastisement as they conceive adequate to the offence. They usually act at night, and disguise their persons. This society at Natchez embraces all the lawyers, physicians, and principal merchants of the place. Foster, whom all good men loathed as a monster unfit to live, was called into court, and formally dismissed. But the Lynchers were at hand. The moment he stept from the court-house he was knocked down, his arms bound behind him, his eyes bandaged, and in this condition was marched to the rear of the town, where a deep ravine afforded a fit place for his punishment. His clothes were torn from his back, his head partially scalped, they next bound him to a tree; each Lyncher was supplied with a cow skin, and they took turns at the flogging until the flesh hung in ribands from his body. A quantity of heated tar was then poured over his head, and made to cover every part of his person; they finally showered a sack of feathers on him, and in this horrid guise, with no other apparel than a miserable pair of breeches, with a drummer at his heels, he was paraded through the principal streets at midday. No disguise was assumed by the Lynchers; the very lawyers employed upon his trial took part in his punishment.

"Owing to long confinement his gait had become cramped, and his movements were very faltering. By the time the procession reached the most public part of the town, Foster fell down from exhaustion, and was allowed to lie there for a time, without exciting the sympathies of any one—an object of universal detestation. The blood oozing from his stripes had become mixed with the feathers and tar, and rendered his aspect still more horrible and loathsome. Finding him unable to proceed further, a common dray was brought, and with his back to the horse's tail, the drummer standing over him playing the rogue's march, he was reconducted to prison, the only place at which he would be received.

"A guard was placed outside of the jail to give notice to the body of Lynchers when Foster might attempt to escape, for they had determined on branding him on the forehead and cutting his ears off. At two o'clock in the morning of the second subsequent day, two horsemen with a led horse stopped at the prison, and Foster was with difficulty placed astride. The Lynchers wished to secure him; he put spurs to his beast, and passed them. As he rode by they fired at him; a ball struck his hat, which was thrown to the ground, and he escaped; but if ever found within the limits of the state, he will be shot down as if a price was set on his head.

"Sights of this kind," continued Thimblerig, "are by no means unfrequent. I once saw a gambler, a sort of friend of mine, by-the-way, detected cheating at faro, at a time when the bets were running pretty high. They flogged him almost to death, added the tar and feathers, and placed him aboard a dug-out, a sort of canoe, at twelve at night; and with no other instruments of navigation than a bottle of whisky and a paddle, set him adrift in the Mississippi. He has never been heard of since, and the presumption is, that he either died of his wounds or was run down in the night by a steamer. And this is what we call Lynching in Natchez."

Thimblerig had also been at Vicksburg in his time, and entertained as little liking for that place as he did for Natchez. He had luckily made his escape a short time before the recent clearing-out of the slight-of-hand gentry; and he reckoned some time would elapse before he would pay them another visit. He said they must become more civilized first. All the time he was talking to me he was seated on a chest, and playing mechanically with his pea and thimbles, as if he was afraid that he would lose the slight unless he kept his hand in constant practice. Nothing of any consequence occurred in our passage down the river, and I arrived at Natchitoches in perfect health, and in good spirits.

THE BIG BEAR OF ARKANSAS

T. B. THORPE

[*Many of the feature stories published or reprinted in the* New York Spirit of the Times, *however heightened by the gifted journalists who composed them, were at bottom a vivid reporting of life on the western waters and the plains. Whether literally true or not, Thorpe's masterpiece, "The Big Bear of Arkansas," must be in any book concerned with the lore of the Mississippi. For the life of this most effective of American frontier writers before Mark Twain see Milton Rickels,* Thomas Bangs Thorpe, Humorist of the Old Southwest (*Baton Rouge, Louisiana State University Press, 1962*). The Big Bear made its original appearance in the Spirit *on March 27, 1841.*]

A steamboat on the Mississippi frequently, in making her regular trips, carries between places varying from one to two thousand miles apart; and as these boats advertise to land passengers and freight at "all intermediate landings," the heterogeneous character of the passengers of one of these up-country boats can scarcely be imagined by one who has never seen it with his own eyes. Starting from New Orleans in one of these boats, you will find yourself associated with men from every state in the Union, and from every portion of the globe; and a man of observation need not lack for amusement or instruction in such a crowd, if he will take the trouble to read the great book of character so favourably opened before him. Here may be seen jostling together the wealthy Southern planter, and the pedlar of tin-ware from New England—the Northern merchant, and the Southern jockey—a venerable bishop, and a desperate gambler—the land speculator, and the honest farmer—professional men of all creeds and characters—Wolvereens, Suckers, Hoosiers, Buckeyes, and Corn-crackers, beside a "plentiful sprinkling" of the half-horse and half-alligator species of men, who are peculiar to "old Mississippi," and

who appear to gain a livelihood simply by going up and down the
river. In the pursuit of pleasure or business, I have frequently
found myself in such a crowd.

On one occasion, when in New Orleans, I had occasion to
take a trip of a few miles up the Mississippi, and I hurried
on board the well-known "high-pressure-and-beat-every-thing"
steamboat *Invincible*, just as the last note of the last bell was
sounding; and when the confusion and bustle that is natural to a
boat's getting under way had subsided, I discovered that I was
associated in as heterogeneous a crowd as was ever got together.
As my trip was to be of a few hours' duration only, I made no
endeavours to become acquainted with my fellow passengers,
most of whom would be together many days. Instead of this, I
took out of my pocket the "latest paper," and more critically than
usual examined its contents; my fellow passengers at the same
time disposed themselves in little groups. While I was thus busily
employed in reading, and my companions were more busily employed in discussing such subjects as suited their humours best,
we were startled most unexpectedly by a loud Indian whoop,
uttered in the "social hall," that part of the cabin fitted off for a
bar; then was to be heard a loud crowing, which would not have
continued to have interested us—such sounds being quite common
in that place of spirits—had not the hero of these windy accomplishments stuck his head into the cabin and hallooed out, "Hurra
for the Big Bar of Arkansaw!" and then might be heard a confused hum of voices, unintelligible, save in such broken sentences
as "horse," "screamer," "lightning is slow," &c. As might have
been expected, this continued interruption attracted the attention
of every one in the cabin; all conversation dropped, and in the
midst of this surprise the "Big Bar" walked into the cabin, took a
chair, put his feet on the stove, and looking back over his shoulder, passed the general and familiar salute of "Strangers, how are
you?" He then expressed himself as much at home as if he had
been at "the Forks of Cypress," and "perhaps a little more so."
Some of the company at this familiarity looked a little angry, and
some astonished; but in a moment every face was wreathed in a
smile. There was something about the intruder that won the heart
on sight. He appeared to be a man enjoying perfect health and
contentment: his eyes were as sparkling as diamonds, and good-
natured to simplicity. Then his perfect confidence in himself was

irresistibly droll. "Perhaps," said he, "gentlemen," running on without a person speaking, "perhaps you have been to New Orleans often; I never made *the first visit before*, and I don't intend to make another in a crow's life. I am thrown away in that ar place, and useless, that ar a fact. Some of the gentlemen thar called me *green*—well, perhaps I am, said I, *but I arn't so at home*; and if I ain't off my trail much, the heads of them perlite chaps themselves wern't much the hardest; for according to my notion, they were real *know-nothings*, green as a pumpkin-vine—couldn't, in farming, I'll bet, raise a crop of turnips: and as for shooting, they'd miss a barn if the door was swinging, and that, too, with the best rifle in the country. And then they talked to me 'bout hunting, and laughed at my calling the principal game in Arkansaw poker, and high-low-jack. 'Perhaps,' said I, 'you prefer chickens and rolette'; at this they laughed harder than ever, and asked me if I lived in the woods, and didn't know what *game* was? At this I rather think I laughed. 'Yes,' I roared, and says, 'Strangers, if you'd asked me *how we got our meat* in Arkansaw, I'd a told you at once, and given you a list of varmints that would make a caravan, beginning with the bar, and ending off with the cat; that's *meat* though, not game.' Game, indeed, that's what city folks call it; and with them it means chippen-birds and shite-pokes; maybe such trash live in my diggens, but I arn't noticed them yet: a bird any way is too trifling. I never did shoot at but one, and I'd never forgiven myself for that, had it weighed less than forty pounds. I wouldn't draw a rifle on any thing less than that; and when I meet with another wild turkey of the same weight I will drap him."

"A wild turkey weighing forty pounds!" exclaimed twenty voices in the cabin at once.

"Yes, strangers, and wasn't it a whopper? You see, the thing was so fat that it couldn't fly far; and when he fell out of the tree, after I shot him, on striking the ground he bust open behind, and the way the pound gobs of tallow rolled out of the opening was perfectly beautiful."

"Where did all that happen?" asked a cynical-looking Hoosier.

"Happen! happened in Arkansaw: where else could it have happened, but in the creation state, the finishing-up country—a state where the *sile* runs down to the centre of the 'arth, and

government gives you a title to every inch of it? Then its airs—
just breathe them, and they will make you snort like a horse. It's a
state without a fault, it is.

"Excepting mosquitoes," cried the Hoosier.

"Well, stranger, except them; for it ar a fact that they are
rather *enormous*, and do push themselves in somewhat troublesome. But, stranger, they never stick twice in the same place; and
give them a fair chance for a few months, and you will get as
much above noticing them as an alligator. They can't hurt my
feelings, for they lay under the skin; and I never knew but one
case of injury resulting from them, and that was to a Yankee: and
they take worse to foreigners, any how, than they do to natives.
But the way they used that fellow up! first they punched him until
he swelled up and busted; then he su-per-a-ted, as the doctor called
it, until he was as raw as beef; then he took the ager, owing to the
warm weather, and finally he took a steamboat and left the country. He was the only man that ever took mosquitoes to heart that I
know of. But mosquitoes is natur, and I never find fault with her.
If they ar large, Arkansaw is large, her varmints ar large, her
trees ar large, her rivers ar large, and a small mosquito would be
of no more use in Arkansaw than preaching in a cane-brake."

This knock-down argument in favour of big mosquitoes
used the Hoosier up, and the logician started on a new track, to
explain how numerous bear were in his "diggins," where he
represented them to be "about as plenty as blackberries, and a
little plentifuler."

Upon the utterance of this assertion, a timid little man near
me inquired if the bear in Arkansaw ever attacked the settlers in
numbers.

"No," said our hero, warming with the subject, "no,
stranger, for you see it ain't the natur of bar to go in droves; but
the way they squander about in pairs and single ones is edifying.
And then the way I hunt them the old black rascals know the
crack of my gun as well as they know a pig's squealing. They
grow thin in our parts, it frightens them so, and they do take the
noise dreadfully, poor things. That gun of mine is perfect *epi-
demic among bar*; if not watched closely, it will go off as quick on
a warm scent as my dog Bowie-knife will: and then that dog—
whew! why the fellow thinks that the world is full of bar, he finds
them so easy. It's lucky he don't talk as well as think; for with his

natural modesty, if he should suddenly learn how much he is acknowledged to be ahead of all other dogs in the universe, he would be astonished to death in two minutes. Strangers, the dog knows a bar's way as well as a horse-jockey knows a woman's: he always barks at the right time, bites at the exact place, and whips without getting a scratch. I never could tell whether he was made expressly to hunt bar, or whether bar was made expressly for him to hunt: any way, I believe they were ordained to go together as naturally as Squire Jones says a man and woman is, when he moralizes in marrying a couple. In fact, Jones once said, said he, 'Marriage according to law is a civil contract of divine origin; it's common to all countries as well as Arkansaw, and people take to it as naturally as Jim Doggett's Bowie-knife takes to bar.' "

"What season of the year do your hunts take place?" inquired a gentlemanly foreigner, who, from some peculiarities of his baggage, I suspected to be an Englishman, on some hunting expedition, probably at the foot of the Rocky Mountains.

"The season for bar hunting, stranger," said the man of Arkansaw, "is generally all the year round, and the hunts take place about as regular. I read in history that varmints have their fat season, and their lean season. That is not the case in Arkansaw, feeding as they do upon the *spontenacious* productions of the sile, they have one continued fat season the year round: though in winter things in this way is rather more greasy than in summer, I must admit. For that reason bar with us run in warm weather, but in winter, they only waddle. Fat, fat! it's an enemy to speed; it tames everything that has plenty of it. I have seen wild turkeys, from its influence, as gentle as chickens. Run a bar in this fat condition, and the way it improves the critter for eating is amazing; it sort of mixes the ile up with the meat, until you can't tell t'other from which. I've done this often. I recollect one perty morning in particular, of putting an old fellow on the stretch, and considering the weight he carried, he run well. But the dogs soon tired him down, and when I came up with him wasn't he in a beautiful sweat—I might say fever; and then to see his tongue sticking out of his mouth a feet, and his sides sinking and opening like a bellows, and his cheeks so fat he couldn't look cross. In this fix I blazed at him, and pitch me naked into a briar patch if the steam didn't come out of the bullet-hole ten foot in a straight line. The fellow, I reckon, was made on the high-pressure system, and the lead sort of bust his biler."

"That column of steam was rather curious, or else the bear must have been *warm*," observed the foreigner, with a laugh.

"Stranger, as you observe, that bar was WARM, and the blowing off of the steam show'd it, and also how hard the varmint had been run. I have no doubt if he had kept on two miles farther his insides would have been stewed; and I expect to meet with a varmint yet of extra bottom, who will run himself into a skinfull of bar's grease: it is possible, much onlikelier things have happened."

"Whereabouts are these bears so abundant?" inquired the foreigner, with increasing interest.

"Why, stranger, they inhabit the neighbourhood of my settlement, one of the prettiest places on old Mississippi—a perfect location, and no mistake; a place that had some defects until the river made the 'cut-off' at 'Shirt-tail bend,' and that remedied the evil, as it brought my cabin on the edge of the river—a great advantage in wet weather, I assure you, as you can now roll a barrel of whiskey into my yard in high water from a boat, as easy as falling off a log. It's a great improvement, as toting it by land in a jug, as I used to do, *evaporated* it too fast, and it became expensive. Just stop with me, stranger, a month or two, or a year if you like, and you will appreciate my place. I can give you plenty to eat; for beside hog and hominy, you can have bar-ham, and bar-sausages, and a mattrass of bar-skins to sleep on, and a wildcat-skin, pulled off hull, stuffed with corn-shucks, for a pillow. That bed would put you to sleep if you had the rheumatics in every joint in your body. I call that ar bed a *quietus*. Then look at my land—the government ain' got another such a piece to dispose of. Such timber, and such bottom land, why you can't preserve any thing natural you plant in it unless you pick it young, things thar will grow out of shape so quick. I once planted in those diggins a few potatoes and beets: they took a fine start, and after that an ox team couldn't have kept them from growing. About that time I went off to old Kentuck on bisiness, and did not hear from them things in three months, when I accidentally stumbled on a fellow who had stopped at my place, with an idea of buying me out. 'How did you like things?' said I. 'Pretty well,' said he; 'the cabin is convenient, and the timber land is good; but that bottom land ain't worth the first red cent.' 'Why?' said I. ' 'Cause,' said he. ' 'Cause what?' said I. ' 'Cause it's full of cedar stumps and Indian mounds,' said he, *'and it can't be cleared.'*

'Lord,' said I, 'them ar "cedar stumps" is beets, and them ar "Indian mounds" ar tater hills.' As I expected, the crop was overgrown and useless: the sile is too rich, *and planting in Arkansaw is dangerous.* I had a good-sized sow killed in that same bottom land. The old thief stole an ear of corn, and took it down where she slept at night to eat. Well, she left a grain or two on the ground, and lay down on them: before morning the corn shot up, and the percussion killed her dead. I don't plant any more: natur intended Arkansaw for a hunting ground, and I go according to natur."

The questioner who thus elicited the description of our hero's settlement, seemed to be perfectly satisfied, and said no more; but the "Big Bar of Arkansaw" rambled on from one thing to another with a volubility perfectly astonishing, occasionally disputing with those around him, particularly with a "live Sucker" from Illinois, who had the daring to say that our Arkansaw friend's stories "smelt rather tall."

In this manner the evening was spent; but conscious that my own association with so singular a personage would probably end before morning, I asked him if he would not give me a description of some particular bear hunt; adding that I took great interest in such things, though I was no sportsman. The desire seemed to please him, and he squared himself round towards me, saying, that he could give me an idea of a bar hunt that was never beat in this world, or in any other. His manner was so singular, that half of his story consisted in his excellent way of telling it, the great peculiarity of which was, the happy manner he had of emphasizing the prominent parts of his conversation. As near as I can recollect, I have italicized them, and given the story in his own words.

"Stranger," said he, "in bar hunts *I am numerous,* and which particular one, as you say, I shall tell, puzzles me. There was the old she devil I shot at the Hurricane last fall—then there was the old hog thief I popped over at the Bloody Crossing, and then— Yes, I have it! I will give you an idea of a hunt, in which the greatest bar was killed that ever lived, *none excepted*; about an old fellow that I hunted, more or less, for two or three years; and if that ain't a particular bar hunt, I ain't got one to tell. But in the first place, stranger, let me say, I am pleased with you, because you ain't ashamed to gain information by asking, and listening, and that's what I say to Countess's pups every day when I'm home; and I have got great hopes of them ar pups, because they are continually *nosing* about; and though they stick it sometimes in the wrong place, they gain experience any how, and may learn something useful to boot. Well, as I was saying about this big bar, you see when I and some more first settled in our region, we were drivin to hunting naturally; we soon liked it, and after that we found it an easy matter to make the thing our business. One old chap who had pioneered 'afore us, gave us to understand that we had settled in the right place. He dwelt upon its merits until it was affecting, and showed us, to prove his assertions, more marks on the sassafras trees than I ever saw on a tavern door 'lection time. 'Who keeps that ar reckoning?' said I. 'The bar,' said he. 'What for?' said I. 'Can't tell,' said he; 'but so it is: the bar bite the bark and wood too, at the highest point from the ground they can reach, and you can tell, by the marks,' said he, 'the length of the bar to an inch.' 'Enough,' said I; 'I've learned something here a'ready, and I'll put it in practice.'

"Well, stranger, just one month from that time I killed a bar, and told its exact length before I measured it, by those very marks; and when I did that, I swelled up considerable—I've been a prouder man ever since. So I went on, larning something every day, until I was reckoned a buster, and allowed to be decidedly the best bar hunter in my district; and that is a reputation as much harder to earn than to be reckoned first man in Congress, as an iron ramrod is harder than a toadstool. Did the varmints grow over-cunning by being fooled with by green-horn hunters, and by this means get troublesome, they send for me as a matter of course; and thus I do my own hunting, and most of my neighbours'. I walk into the varmints though, and it has become about as much the same to me as drinking. It is told in two sentences—a bar is started, and he is killed. The thing is somewhat monotonous now—I know just how much they will run, where they will tire, how much they will growl, and what a thundering time I will have in getting them home. I could give you this history of the chase with all particulars at the commencement, I know the signs so well—*Stranger, I'm certain*. Once I met with a match though, and I will tell you about it; for a common hunt would not be worth relating.

"On a fine fall day, long time ago, I was trailing about for bar, and what should I see but fresh marks on the sassafras trees, about eight inches above any in the forests that I knew of. Says I, 'them marks is a hoax, or it indicates the d——t bar that was ever grown.' In fact, stranger, I couldn't believe it was real, and I went on. Again I saw the same marks, at the same height, and *I knew the thing lived.* That conviction came home to my soul like an earthquake. Says I, 'here is something a-purpose for me: that bar is mine, or I give up the hunting business.' The very next morning what should I see but a number of buzzards hovering over my cornfield. 'The rascal has been there,' said I, 'for that sign is certain:' and, sure enough, on examining, I found the bones of what had been as beautiful a hog the day before, as was ever raised by a Buckeye. Then I tracked the critter out of the field to the woods, and all the marks he left behind, showed me that he was *the bar.*

"Well, stranger, the first fair chase I ever had with that big critter, I saw him no less than three distinct times at a distance: the dogs run him over eighteen miles and broke down, my horse gave out, and I was as nearly used up as a man can be, made on *my* principle, *which is patent.* Before this adventure, such things were unknown to me as possible; but, strange as it was, that bar got me used to it before I was done with him; for he got so at last, that he would leave me on a long chase *quite easy.* How he did it, I never could understand. That a bar runs at all, is puzzling; but how this one could tire down and bust up a pack of hounds and a horse, that were used to overhauling everything they started after in no time, was past my understanding. Well, stranger, that bar finally got so sassy, that he used to help himself to a hog off my premises whenever he wanted one; the buzzards followed after what he left, and so between *bar and buzzard,* I rather think I was *out of pork.*

"Well, missing that bar so often took hold of my vitals, and I wasted away. The thing had been carried too far, and it reduced me in flesh faster than an ager. I would see that bar in every thing I did: *he hunted me,* and that, too, like a devil, which I began to think he was. While in this fix, I made preparations to give him a last brush, and be done with it. Having completed every thing to my satisfaction, I started at sunrise, and to my great joy, I discovered from the way the dogs run, that they were near him; finding his trail was nothing, for that had become as plain to the pack as a turnpike road. On we went, and coming to an open country, what should I see but the bar very leisurely ascending a hill, and the dogs close at his heels, either a match for him in speed, or else he did not care to get out of their way—I don't know which. But wasn't he a beauty, though? I loved him like a brother.

"On he went, until he came to a tree, the limbs of which formed a crotch about six feet from the ground. Into this crotch he got and seated himself, the dogs yelling all around it; and there he sat eyeing them as quiet as a pond in low water. A green-horn friend of mine, in company, reached shooting distance before me, and blazed away, hitting the critter in the centre of his forehead. The bar shook his head as the ball struck it, and then walked down from that tree as gently as a lady would from a carriage. 'Twas a beautiful sight to see him do that—he was in such a rage that he seemed to be as little afraid of the dogs as if they had been sucking pigs; and the dogs warn't slow in making a ring around him at a respectful distance, I tell you; even Bowie-knife, himself, stood off. Then the way his eyes flashed—why the fire of them would have singed a cat's hair; in fact that bar was in a *wrath all over*. Only one pup came near him, and he was brushed out so totally with the bar's left paw, that he entirely disappeared; and that made the old dogs more cautious still. In the mean time, I came up, and taking deliberate aim as a man should do, at his side, just back of his foreleg, *if my gun did not snap*, call me a coward, and I won't take it personal. Yes, stranger, *it snapped*, and I could not find a cap about my person. While in this predicament, I turned round to my fool friend—says I, 'Bill,' says I, 'you're an ass—you're a fool—you might as well have tried to kill that bar by barking the tree under his belly, as to have done it by hitting him in the head. Your shot has made a tiger of him, and blast me, if a dog gets killed or wounded when they come to blows, I will stick my knife into your liver, I will————' my wrath was up. I had lost my caps, my gun had snapped, the fellow with me had fired at the bar's head, and I expected every moment to see him close in with the dogs, and kill a dozen of them at least. In this thing I was mistaken, for the bar leaped over the ring formed by the dogs, and giving a fierce growl, was off—the pack, of course, in full cry after him. The run this time was short, for coming to the edge of a lake the varmint jumped in, and swam to a little island in the lake, which it reached just a moment before the dogs. 'I'll have him now,' said I, for I had found my caps in the *lining of my coat*—so, rolling a log into the lake, I paddled myself across to the island, just as the dogs had cornered the bar in a thicket. I rushed up and fired—at the same time the critter leaped over the dogs and came within three feet of me, running like mad; he jumped into the lake, and tried to mount the log I had just deserted, but every time he got half his body on it, it would roll over and send him under; the dogs, too, got around him, and pulled him about, and finally Bowie-knife clenched with him, and they sunk into the lake together. Stranger, about this time, I was excited, and I stripped off my coat, drew my knife, and intended to have taken a part with Bowie-knife myself, when the bar rose to the surface. But the varmint staid under—Bowie-knife came up alone, more dead than alive, and with the pack came ashore. 'Thank God,' said I, 'the old villain has got his deserts at last.' Determined to have the body, I cut a grape-vine for a rope, and dove down where I could see the bar in the water, fastened my queer rope to his leg, and fished him, with great difficulty, ashore. Stranger, may I be chawed to death by young alligators, if the thing I looked at wasn't a *she bar, and not the old critter after all*. The way matters got mixed on that island was onaccountably curious, and thinking of it made me more than ever convinced that I was hunting the devil himself. I went home that night and took to my bed—the thing was killing me. The entire team of Arkansaw in barhunting, acknowledged himself used up, and the fact sunk into my feelings like a snagged boat will in the Mississippi. I grew as cross as a bar with two cubs and a sore tail. The thing got out 'mong my neighbours, and I was asked how come on that individu-al that never lost a bar when once started? and if that same individ-u-al didn't wear telescopes when he turned a she bar, of ordinary size, into an old he one, a little larger than a horse? 'Perhaps,' said I, 'friends'—getting wrathy—'perhaps you want to call somebody a liar,' 'Oh, no,' said they, 'we only heard such things as being *rather common* of late, but we don't believe one word of it; oh, no,'—and then they would ride off and laugh like so many hyenas over a dead nigger. It was too much, and I determined to catch that bar, go to Texas, or die—and I made my preparations accordin'. I had the pack shut up and rested. I took my rifle to pieces and iled it. I put caps in every pocket about my person, *for fear of the lining*. I then told my neighbours, that on Monday morning—naming the day—I would start THAT BAR, and bring him home with me, or they might divide my settlement among them, the owner having disappeared. Well, stranger, on the morning previous to the great day of my hunting expedition, I went into the woods near my house, taking my gun and Bowie-knife along, just *from habit*, and there sitting down also from habit, what should I see, getting over my fence, but *the bar*! Yes, the old varmint was within a hundred yards of me, and the way he walked *over that fence*—stranger, he loomed up like a *black mist*, he seemed so large, and he walked right towards me. I raised myself, took deliberate aim, and fired. Instantly the varmint wheeled, gave a yell, and *walked through the fence* like a falling tree would through a cobweb. I started after, but was tripped up by my inexpressibles, which either from habit, or the excitement of the moment, were about my heels, and before I had really gathered myself up, I heard the old varmint groaning in a thicket near by, like a thousand sinners, and by the time I reached him he was a corpse. Stranger, it took five niggers and myself to put that carcase on a mule's back, and old long-ears waddled under the load, as if he was foundered in every leg of his body, and with a common whopper of a bar, he would have trotted off, and enjoyed himself. 'Twould astonish you to know how big he was: I made a *bed-spread of his skin*, and the way it used to cover my bar mattress, and leave several feet on each side to tuck up, would have delighted you. It was in fact a creation bar, and if it had lived in Samson's time, and had met him, in a fair fight, it would have licked him in the twinkling of a dice-box. But, strangers, I never like the way I hunted, and *missed him*. There is something curious about it, I could never understand—and I never was satisfied at his giving in so easy at last. Prehaps, he had heard of my preparations to hunt him the next day, so he jist come in, like Capt. Scott's coon, to save his wind to grunt with in dying; but that ain't likely. My private opinion is, that that bar was an *unhuntable bar, and died when his time come*."

When the story was ended, our hero sat some minutes with his auditors in a grave silence; I saw there was a mystery to him connected with the bear whose death he had just related, that had evidently made a strong impression on his mind. It was also evident that there was some superstitious awe connected with the affair,—a feeling common with all "children of the wood," when they meet with any thing out of their everyday experience. He was the first one, however, to break the silence, and jumping up, he asked all present to "liquor" before going to bed—a thing which he did, with a number of companions, evidently to his heart's content.

Long before day, I was put ashore at my place of destination, and I can only follow with the reader, in imagination, our Arkansas friend, in his adventures at the "Forks of Cypress" on the Mississippi.

THE DISGRACED SCALP LOCK

or

Incidents on the Western Waters

T. B. THORPE

[*Though but few of the adventures recounted of Mike Fink
by journalists in the decades after his death can be established as fact, this frontier character who came to be hailed
as the "king of the keelboatmen" must inevitably be represented in any collection sampling life on the Mississippi in
the early days. To the July 16, 1842 number of the New
York* Spirit of the Times (*XII, 229–30*), *Thomas Bangs
Thorpe contributed the following story about one of his exploits. For the full history of the literature concerning Mike
Fink see Walter Blair and Franklin J. Meine*, Mike Fink,
King of the Mississippi Keelboatmen (*New York, Henry
Holt, 1933*) *and their* Half Horse, Half Alligator: The
Growth of the Mike Fink Legend (*Chicago, the University
of Chicago Press, 1956*).]

Occasionally may be seen on the Ohio and Mississippi rivers
singularly hearty looking men, that puzzle a stranger as to their
history and age. Their forms always exhibit a powerful development of muscle and bone; their cheeks are prominent, and you
would pronounce them men, enjoying perfect health, in middle
life, were it not for their heads, which, if not bald, will be sparsely
covered with grey hair. Another peculiarity about these people is,
that they have a singular knowledge of all the places on the river,
every bar and bend is spoken of with precision and familiarity—
every town is recollected before it was half as large as the present,
or no town at all. Innumerable places are marked out, where once
was an Indian fight, or a rendezvous of robbers. The manner, the
language, and the dress of these individuals are all characteristic
of sterling common sense; the manner modest, yet full of self
reliance, the language strong and forcible, from superiority of

mind rather than from education, the dress studied for comfort rather than fashion; on the whole, you insensibly become attached to them, and court their society. The good humor, the frankness, the practical sense, the reminiscences, the powerful frame, all indicate a character at the present day extinct and anomalous; and such indeed is the case, for your acquaintance will be one of the few remaining people now spoken of as the "last of the flat-boat-men."

Thirty years ago the navigation of the Western waters was confined to this class of men; the obstacles presented to the pursuit in those swift running and wayward waters had to be overcome by physical force alone; the navigator's arm grew strong as he guided his rude craft past the "snag" and "sawyer," or kept off the no less dreaded bar. Besides all this, the deep forests that covered the river banks concealed the wily Indian, who gloated over the shedding of blood. The qualities of the frontier warrior associated themselves with the boatman, while he would, when at home, drop both these characters in the cultivator of the soil. It is no wonder, then, that they were brave, hardy, and open-handed men; their whole lives were a round of manly excitement, they were hyperbolical in thought and in deed, when most natural, compared with any other class of men. Their bravery and chivalrous deeds were performed without a herald to proclaim them to the world—they were the mere incidents of a border life, considered too common to outlive the time of a passing wonder. Obscurity has obliterated nearly the actions and the men—a few of the latter still exist, as if to justify their wonderful exploits, which now live almost exclusively as traditions.

Among the flat-boatmen, there were none that gained the notoriety of Mike Fink: his name is still remembered along the whole of the Ohio as a man who excelled his fellows in everything, particularly in his rifle shot, which was acknowledged to be unsurpassed. Probably no man ever lived who could compete with Mike Fink in the latter accomplishment; strong as Hercules, free from all nervous excitement, possessed of perfect health, and familiar with his weapon from childhood, he raised the rifle to his eye, and having once taken sight, it was as firmly fixed as if buried in a rock. It was Mike's pride, and he rejoiced on all occasions where he could bring it into use, whether it was turned against the beast of prey, or the more savage Indian, and in his

day these last named were the common foe with which Mike and
his associates had to contend. On the occasion that we would
particularly introduce Mike to the reader, he had bound himself
for a while to the pursuits of trade, until a voyage from the head
waters of the Ohio, and down the Mississippi, could be completed; heretofore he had kept himself exclusively to the Ohio, but
a liberal reward, and some curiosity, prompted him to extend his
business character beyond his ordinary habits and inclinations. In
accomplishment of this object, he was lolling carelessly over the
big "sweep" that guided the "flat" on which he officiated; the
current of the river bore the boat swiftly along, and made his
labor light; his eye glanced around him, and he broke forth in
extacies [*sic*] at what he saw and felt. If there is a river in the
world that merits the name of beautiful, it is the Ohio, when its
channel is

"Without o'erflowing, full."

The scenery is everywhere soft—there are no jutting rocks,
no steep banks, no high hills, but the clear and swift current laves
beautiful and undulating shores, that descend gradually to the
water's edge. The foliage is rich and luxuriant, and its outlines in
the water are no less distinct than when it is relieved against the
sky. Interspersed along its route are islands, as beautiful as ever
figured in poetry as the land of fairies; enchanted spots indeed,
that seem to sit so lightly on the water, that you almost expect
them as you approach to vanish into dreams. So late as when
Mike Fink disturbed the solitudes of the Ohio with his rifle, the
canoe of the Indian was hidden in the little recesses along the
shore; they moved about in their frail barks like spirits, and
clung, in spite of the constant encroachments of civilization, to the
places which tradition had designated as the happy places of a
favored people.

Wild and uncultivated as Mike appeared, he loved nature,
and had a soul that sometimes felt, while admiring it, an exalted
enthusiasm. The Ohio was his favorite stream; from where it runs
no stronger than a gentle rivulet, to where it mixes with the
muddy Mississippi, Mike was as familiar as a child could be with
the meanderings of a flower garden. He could not help noticing
with sorrow the desecrating hand of improvement as he passed
along, and half soliloquizing, and half addressing his compan-

ions, he broke forth, "I knew these parts afore a squatter's axe had blazed a tree; 'twas'nt them pulling a———sweep to get a living, but pulling the trigger done the business. Those were times, to see; a man might call himself lucky. What's the use of improvements? When did cutting down trees make deer more plenty? Who ever cotched a bar by building a log cabin, or twenty on 'em? Who ever found wild buffalo, or a brave Indian in a city? Where's the fun, the frolicking, the fighting? Gone! gone! The rifle won't make a man a living now—he must turn nigger and work. If forests continue to be used up, I may yet be smothered in a settlement. Boys, this 'ere life won't do—I'll stick to the broad horn 'cordin' to contract, but once done with it, I'm off for a frolic. If the Choctas, or Cherokees, or the Massassip don't give us a brush as we pass along, I shall grow as poor as a strawed wolf in a pit-fall. I must, to live peaceably, point my rifle at something more dangerous than varmint. Six months, and no Indian fight, would spile me worse than a dead horse on a prairie." Mike ceased speaking; the then beautiful village of Louisville appeared in sight; the labor of landing the boat occupied his attention—the bustle and confusion that in those days followed such an incident ensued, and Mike was his own master by law until his employers ceased trafficking, and again required his services.

At the time we write of, there were a great many renegade Indians who lived about the settlements, and which is still the case in the extreme South-west. These Indians generally are the most degraded of the tribe, outcasts, who, for crime or dissipation, are no longer allowed to associate with their people; they live by hunting or stealing, and spend their precarious gains in intoxication. Among the throng that crowded on the flat-boat on its arrival, were a number of these unfortunate beings; they were influenced by no other motive than that of loitering round, in idle speculation at what was going on. Mike was attracted towards them at sight, and as he too was in the situation that is deemed most favorable to mischief, it struck him that it was a good opportunity to have a little sport at the Indians' expense. Without ceremony, he gave a terrific war-whoop, and then mixing the language of the aborigines and his own together, he went on savage fashion, and bragged of his triumphs and victories on the war path, with all the seeming earnestness of a real "brave." Nor were taunting words spared to exasperate the poor creatures, who, perfectly helpless, listened to the tales of their own greatness, and their own shame, until wound up to the highest pitch of impotent exasperation. Mike's companions joined in, thoughtless boys caught the spirit of the affair, and the Indians were goaded until they in turn made battle with their tongues. Then commenced a system of running against them, pulling off their blankets, together with a thousand other indignities; finally they made a precipitate retreat ashore, amidst the hooting and jeering of an unfeeling crowd, who considered them poor devils, destitute of feeling and humanity. Among this crowd of outcasts was a Cherokee, who bore the name of Proud Joe; what his real cognomen was no one knew, for he was taciturn, haughty, and in spite of his poverty, and his manner of life, won the name we have mentioned. His face was expressive of talent, but it was furrowed by the most terrible habits of drunkenness; that he was a superior Indian was admitted, and it was also understood that he was banished from his mountainous home, his tribe being then numerous and powerful, for some great crime. He was always looked up to by his companions, and managed, however intoxicated he might be, to sustain a singularly proud bearing, which did not even depart from him while prostrated on the ground. Joe was filthy in his person and habits; in these respects he was behind his fellows; but one ornament of his person was attended to with a care which would have done honor to him if surrounded by his people, and in his native woods. Joe still wore with Indian dignity his scalp lock; he ornamented it with taste, and cherished it, as report said, that some Indian messenger of vengeance might tear it from his head, as expiatory of his numerous crimes. Mike noticed this peculiarity, and reaching out his hand, plucked from it a hawk's feather, which was attached to the scalp lock. The Indian glared horribly on Mike as he consummated the insult, snatched the feather from his hand, then shaking his clenched fist in the air, as if calling on heaven for revenge, retreated with his friends. Mike saw that he had roused the savage's soul, and he marvelled wonderfully that so much resentment should be exhibited, and as an earnest to proud Joe that the wrong he had done him should not rest unrevenged, he swore he would cut the scalp lock off close to his head the first convenient opportunity he got, and then he thought no more of the matter.

The morning following the arrival of the boat at Louisville

was occupied in making preparations to pursue the voyage down the river; nearly everything was completed, and Mike had taken his favorite place at the sweep, when looking up the river bank, he beheld at some distance Joe and his companions, and from their gesticulations, they were making him the subject of conversation. Mike thought instantly of several ways in which he could show them all together a fair fight, and then whip them with ease; he also reflected with what extreme satisfaction he would enter into the spirit of the arrangement, and other matters to him equally pleasing, when all the Indians disappeared, save Joe himself, who stood at times viewing him in moody silence and then staring round at passing objects. From the peculiarity of Joe's position to Mike, who was below him, his head and upper part of his body relieved boldly against the sky, and in one of his movements he brought his profile face to view; the prominent scalp lock and its adornments seemed to be more striking than ever, and it again roused the pugnacity of Mike Fink; in an instant he raised his rifle, always loaded and at command, brought it to his eye, and before he could be prevented, drew sight upon proud Joe and fired. The rifle ball whistled loud and shrill, and Joe, springing his whole length into the air, fell upon the ground. The cold blooded murder was noticed by fifty persons at least, and there arose from the crowd an universal cry of horror and indignation at the bloody deed. Mike himself seemed to be much astonished, and in an instant reloaded his rifle, and as a number of white persons rushed towards the boat, Mike threw aside his coat, and taking his powder horn between his teeth, leaped, rifle in hand, into the Ohio, and commenced swimming for the opposite shore. Some bold spirits present determined Mike should not so easily escape, and jumping into the only skiff at command, pulled swiftly after him. Mike watched their movements until they came within a hundred yards of him, then turning in the water, he supported himself by his feet alone, and raised deadly rifle to his eye; the muzzle, if it spoke hostilely, was as certain to send a messenger of death through one or more of his pursuers as if it were the lightning, and they knew it; dropping their oars, and turning pale, they bid Mike not to fire. Mike waved his hand towards the little village of Louisville, and again pursued his way to the opposite shore.

The time consumed by the firing of Mike's rifle, the pursuit, and the abandonment of it, required less time than we have taken to give the details, and in that time to the astonishment of the gaping crowd around Joe, they saw him rising with a bewildered air; a moment more and he recovered his senses, and stood up—*at his feet lay his scalp lock*! The ball had cut it clear from his head; the cord around the root of it, in which were placed feathers and other ornaments, held it together; the concussion had merely stunned its owner; farther he had escaped all bodily harm! A cry of exultation rose at this last evidence of the skill of Mike Fink; the exhibition of a shot that established his claim, indisputably, to the eminence he ever afterwards held; the unrivalled marksman of all the flat-boatmen of the Western waves. Proud Joe had received many insults, he looked upon himself as a degraded, worthless being, and the ignominy heaped upon him, he never, except by reply, resented; but this last insult, was like seizing the lion by the mane, or a Roman senator by the beard—it roused the slumbering demon within, and made him again thirst to resent his wrongs, with an intensity of emotion that can only be felt by an Indian. His eye glared upon the jeering crowd around; like a fiend, his chest swelled and heaved, until it seemed that he must suffocate. No one noticed this emotion, all were intent upon the exploit that had so singularly deprived Joe of his war lock; and smothering his wrath he retreated to his associates, with a consuming fire at his vitals; he was a different man from an hour before, and with that desperate resolution on which a man stakes his all, he swore by the Great Spirit of his forefathers that he would be revenged.

An hour after the disappearance of Joe, both he and Mike Fink were forgotten. The flat-boat, which the latter had deserted, was got under way, and dashing through the rapids in the river opposite Louisville, wended on its course. As is customary when night sets in, the boat was securely fastened in some little bend or bay in the shore, where it remained until early morn. Long before the sun had fairly risen, the boat was pushed again into the stream, and it passed through a valley presenting the greatest possible beauty and freshness of landscape, the mind can conceive. It was Spring, and a thousand tints of green developed themselves in the half formed foliage and bursting buds. The beautiful mallard skimmed across the water, ignorant of the danger of the white man's approach; the splendid spoonbill decked the shallow places near the shore, while myriads of singing birds filled the air with their unwritten songs. In the far reaches down the river, there occasionally might be seen a bear, stepping along the ground as if dainty of its feet, and sniffing the intruder on his wild home, he would retreat into the woods. To enliven all this, and give the picture the look of humanity, there might also be seen, struggling with the floating mists, a column of blue smoke, that came from a fire built on a projecting point of land, around which the current swept rapidly, and carried every thing that floated on the river. The eye of a boatman saw the advantage of the situation which the place rendered to those on shore, to annoy and attack, and as wandering Indians, in those days, did not hesitate to rob, there was much speculation as to what reception the boat would receive from the builders of the fire. The rifles were all loaded, to be prepared for the worst, and the loss of Mike Fink lamented, as a prospect of a fight presented itself, where he could use his terrible rifle. The boat in the mean time, swept round the point, but instead of an enemy, there lay in a profound sleep, Mike Fink with his feet toasting at the fire, his pillow was a huge bear, that had been shot on the day previous, while at his sides, and scattered in profusion around him, were several deer and wild turkeys. Mike had not been idle; after picking out a place most eligible to notice the passing boat, he had spent his time in hunting, and he was surrounded by trophies of his prowess. The scene that he presented, was worthy of the time and the man, and would have thrown Landseer into a delirium of joy, could he have witnessed it. The boat, owing to the swiftness of the current, passed Mike's resting place, although it was pulled strongly to the shore. As Mike's companions came opposite to him, they raised such a shout, half in exultation of meeting him, and half to alarm him with the idea that Joe's friends were upon him. Mike, at the sound sprang to his feet, rifle in hand, and as he looked around, he raised it to his eyes, and by the time he discovered the boat, he was ready to fire. "Down with your shooting iron, you wild critter," shouted one of the boatmen. Mike dropped the piece, and gave a loud halloo, that echoed among the solitudes like a piece of artillery. The meeting between Mike and his fellows was characteristic. They joked, and jibed him, with their rough wit, and he parried it off, with a most creditable ingenuity. Mike soon learned the extent of his rifle shot—he seemed perfectly indifferent to the fact that Proud Joe was not dead. The only sentiment he uttered, was regret that he did not fire at the vagabond's head, and if he hadn't hit it, why he made the first bad shot in twenty years. The dead game was carried on board of the boat, the adventure was forgotten, and everything resumed the monotony of floating in a flat-boat down the Ohio.

A month or more elapsed, and Mike had progressed several hundred miles down the Mississippi; his journey had been remarkably free from incident; morning, noon, and night, presented the same banks, the same muddy water, and he sighed to see some broken land, some high hills, and he railed, and swore that he should have been such a fool as to desert his favorite Ohio for a river that produced nothing but alligators, and was never at best half-finished. Occasionally, the plentifulness of game put him in spirits, but it did not last long, he wanted more lasting excitement, and declared himself as perfectly miserable, and helpless, as a wild cat without teeth or claws.

In the vicinity of Natchez, rises a few, abrupt hills, which tower above the surrounding lowlands of the Mississippi like monuments; they are not high, but from their loneliness, and rarity, they create sensations of pleasure and awe. Under the shadow of one of these bluffs, Mike and his associates made the customary preparations to pass the night. Mike's enthusiasm knew no bounds at the sight of land again; he said it was as pleasant as "cold water to a fresh wound;" and, as his spirits rose, he went on making the region round about, according to his notions, an agreeable residence. "The Choctas live in these diggins," said Mike, "and a cursed time they must have of it. Now, if I lived in these parts, I'd declare war on 'em, just to have something to keep me from growing dull; without some such business, I'd be as musty as an old swamp moccasin. I could build a cabin on that ar hill yonder, that could from its location, with my rifle repulse a whole tribe, if they came after me. What a beautiful time I'd have of it. I never was particular, about what's called a fair fight, I just ask a half a chance, and the odds against me; and if I then don't keep clear of snags and sawyers, let me spring a leak, and go to the bottom. Its natur that the big fish should eat the little ones. I've seen trout swallow a perch, and a cat would come along and swallow the trout, and prehaps on the Massissip, the alligators use up the cat, so on until the end of the row. Well,

I walk tall into varmint and Indian, it's a way I've got, and it comes as natural as grinning to a hyena. I'm a regular tornado, tough as a hickory withe, long winded as a nor'-wester. I can strike a blow like a falling tree, and every lick makes a gap in the crowd that lets in an acre of sunshine. Whew, boys," shouted Mike, twirling his rifle, like a walking stick around his head, at the ideas suggested in his mind. "Whew, boys! if the Chocta devils in them ar woods, thar, would give us a brush, just as I feel now, I'd call them gentlemen. I must fight something, or I'll catch the dry rot, burnt brandy won't save me." Such were some of the expressions which Mike gave utterance to, and in which his companions heartily joined; but they never presumed to be quite equal to Mike, for his bodily prowess, as well as his rifle were acknowledged to be unsurpassed. These displays of animal spirits generally ended in boxing, and wrestling matches, in which falls were received, and blows struck without being noticed, that would have destroyed common men. Occasionally angry words and blows were exchanged; but like the summer storm, the cloud that emitted the lightning purified the air, and when the commotion ceased, the combatants, immediately made friends, and became more attached to each other than before the cause that interrupted the good feelings occurred. Such were the conversation and amusements of the evening, when the boat was moored under one of the bluffs we have alluded to; as night wore on, one by one of the hardy boatmen fell asleep, some in the confined interior, and other protected by a light covering in the open air. The moon rose in beautiful majesty, her silver light behind the high lands, gave them a powerful and theatrical effect, as it ascended, and as its silver rays grew perpendicular, they finally kissed gently the summit of the hills, and poured down their full light upon the boat, with almost noonday brilliancy. The silence, with which the beautiful changes of darkness and light were produced, made it mysterious. It seemed as if some creative power was at work, bringing form, and life out of darkness. In the midst of the witchery of this quiet scene, there sounded forth the terrible rifle, and the more terrible war-whoop of the Indian. One of the flatboat men, asleep on the deck, gave a stifled groan, turned upon his face, and with a quivering motion ceased to live. Not so with his companions—they in an instant, as men accustomed to danger and sudden attacks, sprang ready armed to their feet; but before they could discover their foes, seven sleek, and horribly painted savages, leaped from the hill into the boat. The firing of the rifle was useless, and each man singled out a foe, and met him with the drawn knife. The struggle was quick and fearful, and deadly blows were given, screams and imprecations rent the air. Yet the voice of Mike Fink could be heard in encouraging shouts above the clamor, "Give it to them, boys," he cried, "cut their hearts out, choke the dogs, here's hell afire, and the river rising!" then clenching with the most powerful of the assailants, he rolled with him upon the deck of the boat. Powerful as Mike was, the Indian seemed nearly a match for him; the two twisted, and writhed like serpents, now one seeming to have the advantage and then the other. In all this confusion there might occasionally be seen glancing in the moonlight the blade of a knife, but at whom the thrusts were made, or who wielded it, could not be discovered.

The general fight lasted less time than we have taken to describe it. The white men gained the advantage, two of the Indians lay dead upon the boat, and the living, escaping from their antagonists leaped ashore, and before the rifle could be brought to bear, they were out of its reach. While Mike was yet struggling with his antagonist, one of his companions cut the boat loose from the shore, and with powerful exertion, managed to get its bows so far into the current, that it swung round and floated, but before this was accomplished, and before anyone interfered with Mike, he was on his feet, covered with blood, and blowing like a porpoise; by the time he could get his breath, he commenced talking. "Ain't been so busy in a long time," said he, turning over his victim with his foot, "that fellow fou't beautiful; if he's a specimen of the Chocta, that live in these parts, they are screamers, the infernal sarpents, the d——d possums." Talking in this way, he with others took a general survey of the killed and wounded. Mike himself was a good deal cut up with the Indian's knife, but he called his wounds mere blackberry scratches; one of Mike's associates, was severely hurt, the rest escaped comparatively harmless. The sacrifice was made at the first fire, for beside the dead Indians, there lay one of the boat's crew, cold and dead, his body perforated with four different balls; that he was the chief object of attack seemed evident, yet no one of his associates knew of his having a single fight with Indians. The soul of Mike was affected, and taking the hand of his deceased friend between his own, he raised his bloody knife towards the bright moon, and swore, that he would desolate "the nation," that claimed the Indians who had made war upon them that night, and turning to his stiffened victim, that, dead as it was, retained the expression of implacable hatred and defiance, he gave it a smile of grim satisfaction, and then joined in the general conversation, which the occurrences of the night would naturally suggest. The master of the "broad horn" was a business man, and had often been down the Mississippi; this was the first attack he had received, or knew to have been made, from the shores inhabited by the Choctas, except by the white man, and he, among other things, suggested the keeping of the dead Indians, until daylight, that they might have an opportunity to examine their dress and features, and see with certainty who were to blame for the occurrences of the night. The dead boatman was removed with care to a respectful distance, and the living, except the person at the sweep of the boat, were soon buried in profound slumber. Not until after the rude breakfast was partaken of, and the funeral rites of the dead boatman were solemnly performed, did Mike and his companions disturb the corses of the red men. When both these things had been leisurely, and gently got through with, there was a different spirit among the men. Mike was astir, and went about his business with alacrity; he stripped the bloody blanket from the corpse of the Indian he had killed, as if it enveloped something disgusting, and required no respect; he examined carefully the mocasin on the Indian's feet, pronouncing them at one time Chickasas, at another time Shawnese; he stared at the livid face, but could not recognize the style of the paint that covered it. That the Indians were not strictly national in their adornments was certain, for they were examined by practised eyes, that could have told the nation of the dead, if such had been the case, as readily as a sailor could distinguish a ship by its flag. Mike was evidently puzzled, and as he was about giving up his task as hopeless, the dead body he was examining, from some cause turned on its side. Mike's eyes distended, as some of his companions observed, "like a choked cat," and became rivitted; he drew himself up in a half serious, and half comic expression, and pointing at the back of the dead Indian's head, there was exhibited a dead warrior in his paint destitute of his scalp lock, the small stump which was only left, being stiffened with *red paint;* those who could read Indian symbols, learned a volume of deadly resolve, in what they saw. The body of Proud Joe was stiff and cold before them.

The last and best shot of Mike Fink, cost a brave man his life; the corpse so lately interred, was evidently taken in the mood-light by Proud Joe and his party, as that of Mike's, and they had resigned their lives, one and all, that he might with certainty be sacrificed. Nearly a thousand miles of swamps had been threaded, large and swift running rivers had been crossed, hostile tribes passed through by Joe, and his friends, that they might revenge the fearful insult, of destroying, *without the life*, the sacred scalp-lock.

T.B.T.

Louisiana, June, 1842.

SKETCHES FROM THE SAGA OF JACK PIERCE

Flatboatman and Ram-Butter

MENRA HOPEWELL

[*In Mississippi rowdy lore Jack Pierce has never won the popular place that Mike Fink did, but if we can credit Menra Hopewell's* Legends of the Missouri and Mississippi (*London, 1874?*), *he was a worthy confrere of that notorious bully and on one occasion beat him up. Hopewell's literary career is but faintly known; for four or five years he was listed in St. Louis directories as an M. D. and during this period collaborated with Richard Edwards on Edward's* Great West and her Commercial Metropolis. . . . (*St. Louis, 1860*). Legends *was in all probability written in St. Louis about this time. The following passages are from pp. 387–89, 391–97, 398–99, 400–401.*]

One day while he was seated among his companions, who should come in but a mulatto fellow, who lived in New Orleans, and was known by the name of Nigger Jim. He was the bully of that town, with huge limbs more like those of a horse than a man, and in his many contests, in all of which he came off victorious, he used rarely his fists in striking, but would butt his antagonist in so severe a manner that on three occasions death ensued.

This was the first visit of Nigger Jim to St. Louis, and among the flat-boatmen his arrival created quite a sensation, and some most marvellous stories were told of his prodigious strength, and of the fights of which he was the hero. The negro did not bear his honours meekly, but, as all other negroes do, when made too much of, grew impudent and imperious. On this occasion he sat down and commenced boasting of some of his exploits, and because one of the boatmen ventured to differ with him in opinion in some unimportant part of the narrative, the negro threw back his tremendous head, and brought it with such force against that of the boatman, that the latter was tumbled from his seat, and remained stretched senseless upon the earthen

floor. No one appeared to have the courage to resent the unprovoked and brutal attack, when Jack Pierce rose to his feet, and
made a tremendous blow at the negro, striking him upon his nasal
organ, and making the dark blood stream from it in a rill. Following up his advantage, Jack Pierce struck the negro again with all
his strength fairly upon the temple, and expected that the negro
would topple over upon the earth, but was surprised to find the
blow was of no avail, his fist rebounded from it as from a block of
wood. The combatants then closed, and rolled together out of the
door of the groggery, and the boatmen quickly formed a ring to
witness a fight between so redoubted champions. The fight was a
terrible one, and the negro seemed proof against the powerful
blows of his antagonist, who likewise bore with impunity, greatly
to the astonishment of the negro, the butts which were given upon
his head, and which he thought would have finished the fight.
Jack Pierce at length reeled under a powerful butt from the
negro, which took effect at the back of the ear, which caused him
to stagger some distance, and strange lights flashed before him,
and he was sensible of a reeling sensation, and struck wildly
about him.

A hoarse and triumphant laugh escaped from the negro, and
he aimed a tremendous blow with his head at the temple of Jack
Pierce, who, unexpectedly to the negro, presented his head to the
shock, and stood it unmoved. The heads sounded at the concussion like two pieces of solid timber brought into collision.

"That is it, Jack; butt him, butt him," said two of his
friends, who had witnessed how successful was Jack Pierce in
standing the butts of the negro; and Jack Pierce, as if in obedi-
ence to their request, when the negro ran back so as to give
greater momentum to his blow, did the same thing, and, all
breathless, the spectators beheld the two bounding forward, and
the two heads met in mid-space with a tremendous shock. Jack
Pierce remained unmoved, but the negro rebounded several
paces, then reeled and fell. A shout of triumph arose from Jack
Pierce's friends, and the negro, foaming with rage, and somewhat
recovering himself, got up, came forward again, and endeavoured
to grapple with his adversary; but Jack Pierce, who had on what
are called double-soled stogies, well nailed to prevent wearing,
inflicted a kick upon the shin of a [the] negro which would have
been creditable to the strongest stallion.

This new mode of attack was too much for the philosophy of the negro. He fell upon his knees, the tears coursed down his cheeks, every vestige of manly courage left him, and he begged not to be hurt any more.

Negro Jim lost his laurels in that fight, and returned to New Orleans much crest-fallen. All of his arrogance had left him, and the name of Jack Pierce was blessed by hundreds for flogging the negro into humility and politeness. . . .

Jack Pierce went and engaged himself to take command of a flat-boat laden with wheat, and destined for the Orleans market. It was necessary for him to engage two or three others to navigate the boat, and for that purpose he went to one of the little groggeries where the flat-boatmen were accustomed to congregate, for the purpose of engaging those he wished. As was usual, he saw many of his companions, was welcomed on all sides, and invited to drink; but, true to the promise that he had made his mother, he had determined to avoid all intoxicating fluids, and refused the invitation. Some of his comrades were surprised, and some piqued by the refusal, and at length one of them said:

"Come, Jack, and drink with Mike Fink; you have never met him before, though he has often been in St. Louis, but at the very time you were not here. There ain't a better man than Mike Fink ever stood in a flat-boat on the Mississippi."

The individual alluded to as Mike Fink was a heap of flesh and blood, nerve and muscle, so firm, hard, and coarse in his general make-up, that he looked of the consistence of iron. He had the reputation of being the strongest man that boated on the Mississippi, except Jack Pierce, and between the two, who was the strongest and best fighter, opinion was equally divided. Mike Fink glared upon Jack Pierce with his small grey eye, that had all the brilliancy and fierceness of that of the adder. He had heard of his immense strength, his fame as a fighter, and of his last triumph over the renowned Negro Jim. He was envious of his growing fame, which had commenced to overshadow his, and he determined on the first opportunity to provoke a quarrel with him that might lead to a collision.

Jack Pierce guessed by the expression of Mike Fink's countenance what was passing within, and determined to avoid any difficulty with him, having promised his mother to leave off all vicious habits, went over to Mike Fink, and took his hand in token of friendship.

Mike Fink then brought all his iron nerve to bear upon the hand of Jack Pierce, but the bones and sinews were unyielding. The grip was then returned by Jack Pierce, and though the countenance of Mike Fink changed not, he felt a pain from the grasp that he never felt before, and it increased the prejudice, and the hate to the man whose deeds were already eclipsing the fame which he had won in many a hard-contested fight. Envy touched his heart with her poisoned fang, and he determined to force him into a fight, relying on his experience and muscular strength. Should he prove the victor, of which he felt confident, he would then stand alone as the champion of the Mississippi.

Jack Pierce then drank, and touched his glass with Mike Fink, and the conversation turned upon Negro Jim of New Orleans. Mike Fink took it upon himself particularly to eulogize the negro, declaring with an oath that with fair play the negro, with the exception of him, Mike Fink, could whop any man that lived between St. Louis and New Orleans.

This was a direct insult to Jack Pierce, and was intended as such, and there was a look of surprise among the rough spirits there congregated to see Jack Pierce pocket the insult. Mike Fink then said that he could throw down any man that boated on the Mississippi, looking significantly at the same time towards Jack Pierce, and then, to show that the challenge was expressly meant for him, he advanced towards him, and laying his heavy hand upon his shoulder, said, "Jack Pierce, you are a strapping young fellow, have you got pluck enough to take a wrestle with me?"

The blood of Jack Pierce boiled in his veins at this second insult, and the fire of battle was in his eye, when he recollected his promise to his mother. In an instant he calmed his fury, rose to his feet, and, throwing off a sort of round jacket worn by people of his class at that day, said, "I'll try you, Mike Fink."

It was in the afternoon in the month of September, and the party then went on the "Hill," as it was then called, to the square now occupied by the Gaol and Court-house, and which then had not been built upon. After some preliminaries, the combatants took their holds. They were nearly equally matched, but Mike Fink was broader across the shoulders, and his muscles appeared firm and knotted as a gnarled oak. Jack Pierce had less brawn, was more youthful and active, and though his brute force was not as great, he had more activity and intelligence than his adversary, and possessed a skill which the other could never acquire.

They both stood a few seconds with their arms locked, and legs as far out as possible, in a colossal position. Then the feints commenced, succeeded by tugs, and twists of their bodies, and then, as if desiring to bring the contest to an issue, each drew his adversary's body towards him, and each tried to raise his antagonist, and neither was successful. At length Mike Fink made a desperate effort, and Jack Pierce suddenly yielded to it a moment, and, as he was rising, got his right leg between his opponent's, and, swinging himself around with all his strength, brought Mike Fink to the ground with a fall that made the earth shake, falling heavily upon him.

It was the first time that Mike Fink ever was thrown, and when he arose his small grey eyes flashed like meteors, and he foamed at the mouth like an enraged bull.

"Now, Jack Pierce, you have got to fight," said he. "There is no cheating in fighting—the best man takes the day, each one doing his best, and in his own way."

"I won't fight you, Mike Fink," replied Jack Pierce. "If you want to know why, I tell you I promised the old woman, my mother, to be quiet for some time, and I want to keep my promise."

"By God, I'll make you," replied this desperado of the Mississippi, advancing in a threatening attitude towards Jack Pierce.

"I'll fight you some other day, Mike Fink, but not now," said the latter. "Don't strike."

"Wait, Mike," cried several of his friends, interfering—"another time. He has promised to fight you another time—that is all you can ask. He ain't ready now."

"I guess he will ask the old woman to give him leave," said Mike Fink, with a coarse laugh, "and I will whip her baby so that he will never leave her side again."

Jack Pierce replied not, but took his jacket, that was held by one of the bystanders, and putting it on, and accompanied by some of his friends, went back to the village, determining to keep the pledge he had given his mother.

He had scarcely arrived at the cabin of his mother when he found one of the neighbours relating to her an accident that had occurred to a young man that morning from an attack made upon him by a vicious ram as he was crossing the common, and the owner of the ram, having heard of it, came to the cabin at that moment to solicit Jack Pierce's assistance to capture the vicious animal. They went to the common, and on approaching the ram, the animal, by his movements, showed that he was ready to give battle.

"Fight him his own way, Jack," said one of his companions, laughing; "your head is as hard as his horns."

"I'll do it," replied Jack Pierce, feeling in one of his dare-devil moods, and immediately approached the ram, which, giving an angry bleat, made towards him.

To the astonishment of his companions, who thought he had been jesting, Jack Pierce dropped on all fours, and stooping his head to avoid the direct blow of the ram, raised it just in time to strike him under the lower jaw; and so sudden was the shock, that the animal's neck was broken.

This novel feat in twenty-four hours became the topic of conversation of the whole village, and such was the curiosity to witness a similar one, that quite a sum of money was made up to induce Jack Pierce to give battle to another ram. The feat came off in presence of a large multitude of persons, Jack Pierce breaking the neck of the ram as he did in the battle with the first.

Whatever may be said of the strong will—of the power of resisting temptation—of the option between good and evil—man, after all, is much the creature of surrounding influences. They will trammel him as a network, nor can he break loose from them at will.

Jack Pierce found it impossible to resist the temptations by which he was surrounded. Though he was successful in many instances, in some unguarded moments he would yield to them, and becoming discouraged in his efforts at reformation, he no more tried to avert the moral ruin to which he was fast approaching. He again caroused at the drinking-shops, and indulged in all the vices incident to a flat-boatman's life, yet strove to keep continually employed so that his mother should have every comfort during her helplessness. His happiest moments were when he laid the money he had received for his wages upon her pillow, and whatever might have been his frailties, no unkind look or word added to the sufferings of his parent.

Mike Fink left St. Louis for some months, after his wrestling-match with Jack Pierce, and returned to New Orleans with his flat-boat. During the whole time, the mortification of his defeat by Jack Pierce was rankling at his heart, and goading him to revenge. He determined to force him to a fight, and felt a demon-like joy as he anticipated the bloody horrors of the fight.

Again business required him to ascend the Mississippi to St. Louis, and, acting on his premeditated design, directly he met with Jack Pierce, before he gave him any greeting, and in the presence of a number of flat-boatmen, he walked to him whilst he was sitting, and with the back of his hand struck him a powerful blow in the face, saying, "How does mamma's baby now?"

Jack Pierce rose to his feet, retreated a few steps, and pulled off his coat, remarking, "I am in for a big fight," and advanced towards Mike Fink, who, in a fighting attitude, was awaiting him.

"Go out of the house," cried several voices, and the combat-ants silently acquiescing walked out of the door, and both cau-tiously as belligerent tigers approached each other.

The first blow was attempted to be given by Mike Fink, which was successfully parried by his opponent, who planted his large fist between his peepers with such effect that he staggered backwards, and stars of every hue danced before his reeling vision. He recovered himself in a moment, and with his face flushed and glowing like the full round orb of the sun when he looks with fiery redness portending storms and tempest, rushed at his opponent. Another tremendous blow on the temple for a mo-ment staggered him, but with his face bathed in blood he grap-pled with Jack Pierce, and throwing his whole strength into an effort, heaved him upon the ground. With the chuckle of a demon he sprang upon his prostrate foe, and tried to fix his knee upon his breast, but Jack Pierce struggled so manfully that he could not accomplish his design.

It was evident, however, to all that the brute strength of Mike Fink was superior to that of Jack Pierce, and he was gradually getting his antagonist more and more at his mercy. Jack Pierce, however, managed to get the forefinger of Mike Fink's hand in his mouth, to which he held on with the tenacity of a bull-dog. This neutralized in a great measure the advantage of his antagonist, and he managed to clutch him by the throat; but with a desperate effort Mike Fink drew his lacerated finger from the mouth of Jack Pierce, and, breathing a deep curse, again hurled him to the ground. Another powerful blow from Jack Pierce, before Mike Fink had time to fetter his arms, again brought the stars before his eyes, and produced a confusion of ideas, and then with a herculean effort he succeeded in overturning him and regaining his feet, but not quicker than Mike Fink regained his; and again the combatants closed, and again Jack Pierce would have been thrown, but he thought of turning the hardness of his head to some account, overmatched as he was in the combat. With both hands he caught Mike Fink by the ears, and brought his forehead against his three times in quick succession, the blows sounding like a maul upon timber. The knees of Mike Fink trembled, his head drooped, his hands relinquished their hold, and when his adversary released his grasp he fell senseless upon the ground, sputtering white froth and blood from his mouth. He, however, did not die. He recovered, but Jack Pierce had gained the victory. . . .

Jack Pierce and his associates whilst working kept up a brisk conversation, which at last turned on ram-fighting, and one of the men said that he had heard a man say that he would give twenty dollars to witness a man fight with a ram, ram-fashion.

"Let him put up his money," said Jack Pierce, "and I will fight any ram that bleats, and kill him too. Twenty dollars would be easier made that way than chopping wood," continued he, laughing, "and just now I should like to have that much money so as to make the old woman as comfortable as possible."

That night, after his supper, and when his mother had fallen asleep, Jack Pierce went to the little public-house where he was sure to meet always some of his friends, and again the conversation turned on the fights which he had with the rams. Just then two persons entered the little tavern, when one of Jack Pierce's associates said, "Here is the man, Jack Pierce, who will give twenty dollars to see you fight a ram," pointing at the same time to one of the strangers who had entered, and who had come to St. Louis from New Orleans for the purpose of buying negroes.

"I will be as good as my word," rejoined the stranger, "and I'll plank down the twenty dollars at any time to see a fight between a man and a ram, ram-fashion."

"I'll take you up, my hearty," said Jack Pierce, advancing towards him, "and I'll engage not only to fight any ram you may pick out, but to kill him to boot."

During this conversation all the persons in the little barroom collected around Jack Pierce and the stranger. It was agreed that on the next day, about ten o'clock in the morning, Jack Pierce should fight a large ram which had been brought from Canada, and belonged to Colonel Auguste Chouteau. . . .

At the appointed hour, a large crowd assembled at the pasture in which was Colonel Auguste Chouteau's ram, to witness the fight between the animal and Jack Pierce, who was in the most jovial spirits. He approached the ram, who at first was frightened and fled, but by walking on all fours and occasionally bleating, the ram began to move more slowly away from him, and to show symptoms of anger at his approach. Jack Pierce then took a sheep's skin with the wool upon it, and wound it around his neck, and again commenced to bleat. The animal then showed a dauntless front, and remained immoveable as Jack Pierce cautiously approached him. Jack Pierce again bleated, and the ram, furious with rage, with an angry bleat, ran back a few rods, then in full gallop came towards Jack Pierce, and some feet distance, so as to give greater momentum to his force, bounded in the air, aiming his blow directly at the head of Jack Pierce, who suddenly stooped his head, as was his custom; but, unfortunately, a stubble stuck in his nostril, which caused him to jerk up his head, and he received in the crown of his head the full stroke of the furious ram. There was a crash heard, and the body of Jack Pierce was stretched quivering upon the ground. The brains were spattered all around, and the horns of the animal were crimsoned with his blood.

THE STEAMBOAT CAPTAIN WHO WAS
AVERSE TO RACING

GEORGE P. BURNHAM

[*The predilection of river captains to show off the power of their boats was often commented on by travelers. George P. Burnham of Roxbury, Massachusetts, writing in the New York* Spirit of the Times *over the pseudonym "The Young 'Un" (May 14, 1846) has produced one of the classic sketches of an experience with a captain who was absolutely "averse to racing." A volume of* Gleanings from the Portfolio of the Young 'Un *was published in Philadelphia in 1848.*]

Early in the spring of the present year, a magnificent new steamer was launched upon the Ohio river, and shortly afterward made her appearance at the Levee, opposite the flourishing city of Cincinnati. Giltedged covers, enveloping the captain's "respects," accompanied with invitations to "see her through," upon her first trip down the river, were forwarded to the editorial corps in that vicinity; the chalked hats were "numerous" on the occasion. It was a grand affair, this *debut* of a floating palace, which has since maintained her repute untarnished as the "crack boat," *par excellence*, upon the Western waters. Your humble servant was among the "invited guests"—and a nice time he had of it!

I found myself on board this beautiful craft in "close communion" with a score of unquestionable "beauties." The company proved to be a heterogeneous conglomeration of character—made up of editors, lawyers, auctioneers, indescribables, and "fancies" —with a sprinkling of "nonesuch's." There was a stray parson, too, in the crowd—but as his leisure time "between meals" was spent in trading horses, we dispensed with his "grace before meals."

We left our moorings an hour before sunset, upon a clear

cold afternoon, and passed rapidly down stream for a considerable distance, without experiencing any out-of-the-way occurrence. The "sons of temperance," and the parson aforesaid, amused themselves over a smoking whisky toddy—the "boys" were relieving each other of their superfluous dimes and quarters at euchre, when a tall gentleman, who was "some," (when he was sober), stepped suddenly into the cabin, and imparted the information that a well-known "fast boat" had just hove in sight, at the mouth of the Kentucky river. The cards were "dropt" instanter—the punches disappeared—and the "mourners" were soon distributed in knots upon the promenade deck, to watch the progress of events.

Our "bully" boat sped away like a bird, however, and the craft behind gave us early evidence that she should offer no child's play. The "fat was in the fire" at once—a huge column of black smoke curled up in the clear atmosphere—*an extra turn or two* was visible upon our own boat, and away we went! A good deal of excitement existed among the party, as the rival steamer was clearly gaining upon us. A craft like ours, with such a company, and such a captain, mustn't be *beaten*.

As the boat behind us fell in under our stern, and we could "count her passengers," a sort of impression came over us, that, by some mistake, we had got upon the wrong boat! At least, such was the expressed opinion of the parson, as he threatened to "go down stairs" and take another drink. Our captain was a noble fellow—he paced the deck quietly, with a constant eye to wind'ard; but he said nothing. A bevy of the mourners stepped up to him, with—

"What speed, cap'n?"

"Fair, gentlemen; I may say very *fair*."

"Smart craft, that, behind," ventured one.

"Very," responded the captain, calmly, as he placed his hand upon a small brass knob at the back of the pilot house. This movement was responded to by the faint jingling of a bell below, followed immediately by a rush of cinders from the smoke-pipes, and an improved action of the paddles.

"Now we move again."

"Some," was the response, and a momentary tremor pervaded the boat as she "slid along" right smartly.

But the craft in our rear moved like our shadow on the calm

waters, and as we shot down the river, it seemed as if we had her
"in tow," so calmly and uniformly did she follow in our wake.
The excitement of the congregation upon deck had by this time
become intense, and it was pretty plain that the boats must
shortly part company, or "split something!" The rascal behind us
took advantage of a turn in the channel, and "helm a-starboard!"
was clearly heard from the look-out of our rival, as she "hove off,"
and suddenly fell alongside us! The parson went below at once, to
put his threat into execution, as we came up into the current
again, "neck and neck"; and when he returned we were running a
twenty-five-knot lick, the steam smack on to 49!

"She's going—goin' go—," muttered an auctioneer to
himself.

"A perfect nonsuit," remarked a lawyer.

"Beaten, but not vanquished," added a politician; and away
we scudded side by side for half an hour.

"Wouldn't she bear a *leetle* more?" meekly asked the
parson.

"She's doing very well," replied the captain. "Don't get excited, gentlemen; my boat is a new one—her reputation and mine
is at stake. We mustn't rush her—*racing always injures a boat*,
and I am averse to it"; saying which he applied his thumb and
finger to the brass knob again—the bell tinkled in the distance—
and our rival pilot shortly had the opportunity to examine the
architecture of our rudder-post!

I was acquainted with the engineer. I stepped below (believing we should be beaten at our present speed), and entering the
engine-room—

"Tim," said I, "we'll be licked—give her another turn,
eh?"

"I rayther think she moves some as it is," said Tim.

"Yes: but the C——— is hard on us—give her a little, my
boy—just for—"

"Step in here a moment," remarked Tim; "it's all 'mum,' you
know—nothin to be said, eh? Quiet—there!—don't she tremble
some?"

I noticed, for the first time, that our boat did labour
prodigiously!

"But come round *here*," continued Tim; "*look there*!—*mum's*
the word you know."

I stepped out of that engine-room (Tim said afterwards, that I "sprang out at one bound"; but he lied!) in a hurry. *The solder upon the connection-pipe had melted and run down over the seams in a dozen places*, from the excessive heat—a crow-bar was braced athwart the safety-valve, with a "fifty-six" upon one end—and we were shooting down the Ohio, under a head of steam "chock up" to 54 40!!

My "sleeping apartment" was well aft. I entered the state-room—got over upon the back side of my berth—and, stuffing the corners of the pillow into my ears, endeavoured to compose myself in sleep. It was out of the question. In attempting to "right myself," I discovered that *my hair stuck out so straight, it was impossible for me to get my head within six inches of the pillow*!

I tossed about till daylight, in momentary expectation of being landed in Kentucky (or somewhere else!), but we got on finely. We led our rival half an hour into Louisville; and I immediately swore upon my nightcap that I would never accept another invitation, for a pleasure trip, from *a steamboat captain who was averse to racing*!

STOPPING TO WOOD

JOSEPH M. FIELD

[*Joseph M. Field, actor, manager, play doctor, and play-wright with the Ludlow-Smith theatrical company on the New Orleans-Mobile-St. Louis circuit, was a contributor to the New Orleans* Picayune *and one of the founding editors of the St. Louis* Reveille *as well as a frequently met writer in the New York* Spirit of the Times. *This river-life sketch is taken from his* The Drama in Pokerville . . . *and other* Stories (*Philadelphia, 1847*), *pp. 173–76.*]

In spite of the magic changes which have been wrought in the "way of doing things" upon the western waters, the primitive mode of "wooding" from the bank remains unaltered—as a sort of vagabond Indian in the midst of a settlement—as the gallows does in the light of civilization. The same rude plank is "shoved" ashore, the same string of black and white straggle through the mud to the "pile," the same weary waste of time exists as was the case twenty years ago. Steamers have grown from pigmies to giants, speed has increased from a struggle to a "rush," yet the conception of a ready loaded truck, or a burden-swinging crane— despatching a "cord" for every shoulder load, appears not to have entered the head of either wood dealer or captain.

At the same time, though the present mode is to be con-demned as "behind the time"; as tedious, slovenly, and unneces-sary, there are occasions when "stopping to wood" is an event of positive interest and excitement. Passed over be the fine sun-shin*ey* morning when, jogging along—nothing behind—nothing before, the passengers lounging about—heels up, or heads down— the unnoticed bell gives the signal for "wood," and the boat draws listlessly alongside of the "pile." Equally unregarded be the rainy day, when, mud to the knees and drenched to the skin, the steam-ing throng, slipping and plashing, drop their backloads, with a "*whew!*" and fail to find, even in the whisky barrel, a laugh or a "break down." But *not* so the star-lit evening in June, when, the water at a "good stage," and out for a "brag trip," with a rival boat behind, and the furnaces roaring for "more" the more they are fed, the signal is given and a faint flicker on the distant bank beacons the hungry monster towards its further supply of fuel. From New Orleans thus far on the trip up, the two boats, of nearly equal speed, have alternately passed each other during the stop to "wood," showing no gain of consequence on the part of either, and the grand struggle has been as it at present is, to "rush" the operation so as to get a start before being overtaken. The bank is reached—the boat made fast—gangways are formed —"Lively! men, lively!" cries the mate, and while the upper cabins pour out their crowds upon the boiler deck, the "hands," and the swarms of wild-looking passengers below (obliged by contract) dash ashore among the brush. Now ensues a scene that tasks description! The fire, augmented by piles of the driest wood, crimsons the tangled forest! Black and white, many of them stripped to their waist, though others, more careful, protect their skins by ripping and forming *cowls* of empty salt sacks, attack the lengthened pile, and amid laugh, shout, curse, and the scarcely intermitting scream of the iron chimneys, (tortured by the still making steam,) remove it to the boat.

"Lively, men, lively!" rings the cry, and lively, lively is the impulse inspired by it! See that swart, gigantic negro, his huge shoulder hidden beneath a pyramid of wood, hurl to the deck his load, cut a caper along the plank, and, leaping back, seize a flaming brand to whirl it round his head in downright enjoyment! "Lively! lively!" Laugh, shout, whoop, and the pile is rapidly disappearing, when a cry is heard from the "hurricane deck"—

"Here she comes, round the point!"

'Tis the rival steamer, sure enough; and once more she will pass during this detention. Now dash both mate and captain ashore to "rush" the matter. The bell is struck for starting, as if to compel impossibility; the accumulated steam is let off in brief, impatient screams, and the passengers, sharing the wild excitement, add their cries.

"Passed again, by thunder!" "We've got enough wood!" "Leave the rest!" &c. In the mean time, round the point below, sweeps the up-comer—all lights and sparks—moving over the water like a rushing fire-palace! Now her "blow" is heard, like a

suppressed curse of struggle and defiance, and now, nearing the
bank where lies her rival, a sort of frenzy seizes on the latter—

"Tumble it in!" "Rush her!" "D——n the rest!" "You've got
enough!" *Ra-a-a-s-h!* goes the steam; the engine, "working off,"
thunders below;—again, the bell rings, and the hurly burly on
shore is almost savage. At length, as the coming boat is hard on
astern, the signal tap is given, "all hands aboard!" The lines are
let go, the planks are shoved in by the negroes who are themselves
drawn from the water with them, and amid a chaos of timber, a
whirl of steam, and a crash of machinery, once more she is under
weigh. The struggle is to leave the bank before she can be passed,
and fuel, flame, and phrensy, seemingly unite to secure the object;
barrels of combustibles are thrust into the furnaces, while, before
the doors, the "firemen," naked and screaming, urge their wild
efforts!

"Here she is, along-side!" and now the struggle indeed is
startling; the one endeavouring to shoot out from the bank across
the bows of the other, and *she*, authorized by river custom, holding her way, the consequences of collision resting alone on her
imprudent competitor. Roar for roar—scream for scream—huzza
for huzza—but now, the inner boat apparently gaining, a turn of
her antagonist's wheel leaves her no option but to be *run into* or
turn again towards the bank! A hundred oaths and screams reply
to this manoeuvre, but *on she comes*—on, on,—a moment more
and she strikes! With a shout of rage the defeated pilot turns her
head—at the same moment snatching down his rifle and discharging it into the pilot-house of his opponent! Fury has now seized
the thoughts of all, and the iron throats of the steamers are less
hideous than the human ones beneath them. The wheel for a
moment neglected, the thwarted monster has now "taken a sheer
in the wild current," and, beyond the possibility of prevention, is
driving on to the bank! A cry of terror rises aloft—the throng rush
aft—the steam, every valve set free—makes the whole forest
shiver, and, amid the fright, the tall chimneys, caught by the
giant trees, are wrenched and torn out like tusks from a recoiling
mastadon.

"That's a stretcher," will cry out some readers, and such a
scene is not likely to be witnessed *now*, but the writer will not
soon forget that such he bore a part in, some ten years ago, and
that the captain, when asked what he thought of it, replied,
"Well, I think we've got h——ll, any how!"

THE SECOND ADVENT!

Tom Bangall, the Engineer, and Millerism

JOHN S. ROBB

———

[*John S. Robb wrote for the St. Louis* Reveille *and the New York* Spirit of the Times *over the pen name "Solitaire." His* Streaks of Squatter Life and Far-West Scenes (*Carey and Hart, Philadelphia, 1847*) *has lately been reprinted by Scholars Facsimiles & Reprints, Gainesville, Florida, 1962. "The Second Advent," inspired by William Miller's prediction of the end of the world for April 25, 1843, is found on pp. 148–56.*]

About the period fixed upon by Father Miller, for the general blowing up of the world, some of the engineers upon our western waters, who had been used to blowing up its inhabitants, became a little frightened by the prospect of having to encounter, in another world, the victims of steamboat disaster. Among these was Tom Bangall, the engineer of the *Arkansas Thunder*. Tom was a rearing, tearing, *bar* state scrounger—could chaw up any single specimen of the human race—any quantity of tobacco, and drink steam without flinching! A collapsed flue had blown him once somewhere in the altitude of an Alpine height, but dropped him unharmed into the *Arkansas*, and he used to swear that after the steam tried to jerk him apart and found it couldn't do it, why, it just dropped the *subject*, as the stump speakers say, by dropping him into the "drink"—he therefore incontinently set water, hot or cold, at defiance. Tom was, withal, a generous, open-hearted, whole-souled fellow, and his cheering words to the emigrants on the boiler deck, and many a kind act to a suffering passenger, proved that beneath his rough exterior he had a heart open to gentle influences. As a further proof of this, Tom had a wife, a good wife, too, and what's more he tenderly loved her; but she in vain tried to cure him of drinking and swearing. Tom swore that he would swear, that a steamboat wouldn't work without some swearing, and if a fellar didn't drink he'd bust, and, therefore, it was necessary to take a *bust* now and then to keep out of danger. "There is no use," he would say, "in blowing off steam from your 'scape-pipe agin it, for it has to be *did*!"

One day on Tom's return home, he found Mrs. Mary Bangall weeping bitterly, and Tom became, instantly, correspondingly distressed.

"Why, Polly," inquired he, "What's the matter, gal? what's hurt you? is anythin' broke loose that can't be mended? what the thunder makes you take on so? Come, out with the cause, or I shall git a blubberin' too."

"Only look here, Tom," said Mary, "here's a whole account of how the world is going to be destroyed this April. Every thing has been counted up by Father Miller, and the sum total's a general *burn*! Now, Tom, don't swear, nor drink any more or you won't be able to stand the fire no more than gunpowder!"

Tom indulged in a regular guffaw at her distress, and told her she was a fool to be frightened at that—it was all moonshine —humbug—smoke—that Father Miller was an old granny, and it warn't possible—anyhow he warn't afraid of fire, so it might *fire away*!"

"But, Tom," continued Mary, "let me read to you the proof —it's irresistible, Tom—the *times* and the *half times* are so correctly added up that there can be no mistake, and if you don't make some preparation we will be separated for ever."

The idea of a separation from Mary troubled Tom, but full of incredulity he sat down to listen, more to please her, and find something in the adding up of the catastrophe that would upset it. Mary commenced reading, and Tom quietly listening, but as she read the awful evidences of a general conflagration, the signs of the times, the adding up of the times, the proof of their meaning, and the dreadful consequences of being unprepared—with ascension robes, Tom grew serious, and at length looked a little frightened. He didn't want Mary to see its effect upon him, and so assumed an over quantity of indifference, but it was useless for him to attempt hiding his feelings from her prying eyes—she saw Miller's doctrine was grinding a *hopper* of fear in Tom's heart, and felt glad to see its effect. When she ceased he remarked, with a half-frightened laugh, that Father Miller ought to be burnt for thus trying to frighten people, and, "as for them eastern fellars, they are half their life crazy any how!"

Having tried thus to whisper unconcern to his troubled spirit, Tom set out for the boat, with the firm resolve, if he caught a Millerite to save him from the threatened burning by drowning him, for disseminating any such fiery doctrines. When he got on board he told the captain what had transpired at home, how his wife had got hold of a Miller document from a travelling disciple, and, as well as he could, rehearsed the awful contents which she had read to him. The captain, observing the effect they had produced on Tom, seriously answered the matter looked squally, and he was afraid them documents were all too *true*.

"True!" shouted Tom, "why, you aint green enough to swallow any such yarn—its parfectly rediculous to talk about burnin' every thing up. I'd like to see old Miller set fire to the Mississippi!"

"It's no funny matter, Tom," replied the captain, "and if you keep going on this way you will find it so."

"Here, give us somethin' to drink!" shouted Tom to the barkeeper, (he began to get terrified at the serious manner with which the captain treated Millerism) "come, Bill," said he, addressing the clerk, "let's take a drink."

The clerk, who was a wag, saw through the captain's joke in a minute and when he winked at him, refused to taste, adding as an apology that "on the eve of so awful an event as the destruction of the world, he couldn't daringly indulge as he formerly did, so he must excuse him."

"Well, go to h—ll, then," says Tom, half mad.

The captain sighed, and the clerk put his hand upon his heart, and turned his eyes upward, as if engaged in inward prayer for his wicked friend. Tom swallowed his glass, and bestowing a fierce look upon the pair remarked, that "they couldn't come any of them thar shines over him, he wasn't any of that *chicken breed!*"

"Poor fellow," muttered the captain.

"Alas! Thomas," chimed in the clerk.

Tom slammed the cabin door after him as he went out to descend below, swearing at the same time that all the rest of the world were turning damned fools as well as old Miller.

Steam was raised and the *Thunder* started. For a time Tom

forgot the predicted advent, but every time he came up to the bar
to get a drink, the serious look of the captain and the solemn phiz
of the clerk, threw a cold chill over him, and made him savage
with excitement. Every passenger appeared to be talking about
Millerism, besides, a waggish friend of the captain's, a passenger
on board, having been informed of the engineer's state of mind,
passed himself off as a preacher of the doctrine, and talked
learnedly on the prophecies whenever the engineer was nigh. It
was comic to see the fierce expression of their victim's countenance, and how, in spite of himself, he would creep up to the
circles where they were discussing the Second Advent, and listen
with all ears to the rehearsal of its terrible certainty, then making
for the bar, take another drink, and thrusting his hands deep into
his pockets start down to the engine, with a scowl upon his swart
countenance that would almost start a flue head from its
fastenings.

"I'd quit this boat," said Tom to his assistant, "if it warn't so
near 'the 25th of April'—cuss me if I'd stay aboard another minit,
fur captain and all hands are a set of cowardly *pukes!*"

"Why, what's the 25th of April got to do with your leavin',
Tom?" inquired his partner.

"Nothin' particular, but if this confounded blow up or burn
up should come off on that day, I want to be on the river—its
safer: but if I should leave now I couldn't get on another boat by
that time, and then I'd be in a *hot* fix."

Here was a tacit confession by Tom, that he thought there
was danger, and that there might be some truth in old Miller's
prediction. The fact of his fears was forthwith communicated to
the captain and clerk by Tom's partner, and his sufferings became
increased—he could hear no sounds but—*advent—Miller—blow-
up—dreadful destruction*—until his suspense became so horrible,
that he wished for any termination so it would put an end to his
dread. His partner ventured to increase his uneasiness by talking
to him on the subject, but Tom threatened to brain him if he said
anything about it in his presence—he remarked that "the noise of
the engine was his only peace, and no frightened, lubberly sucker
should disturb it by talking Millerism—if Miller was a goin' to
burn the world, why, let him burn and be ———— (here, Tom for
the first time checked an oath, and finished the sentence with)
never mind, just let him burn, that's all."

Starting up to the bar, without looking to right or left, he

presented a bottle, had it filled with liquor and retreated, resolved
to go as little as possible near either captain or clerk, for their
solemn looking faces were contagious—they looked disaster.

At length the 25th of April dawned, and with its advancing
hours Tom got *tight*, that is to say, so near intoxicated that he
could only move around with extreme difficulty—he knew what he
was about, but very little more. Sundry muttering which he gave
voice to, now and then, proclaimed the spirit at work within, and
it would say:

"Burn, ha! burn up, will it? goin' to take a regular bust and
blow itself out! Great world, this!—g-r-e-a-t world, and a nice
little fire it *will* be!" Then, thinking of Mary, he would continue
—"Poor Mary—what a shock it will be to her, but she's on the safe
side, for she belongs to meetin'; "and then he would get wrathy—"
Let the old world burn, and go to splintered lightnin'—who cares?
The captain and clerk's got on the safe side, too—they're afraid of
the fire, eh?" Then he would cautiously emerge from his place by
the engine, and peep out upon the sky, to see if the work of
destruction was about to commence, and then returning, take
another pull at the whiskey, until, by his frequent libations, he not
only got *blue*, but everything he looked at was multiplying—he
was surrounded by a duplicate set of machinery—even his fist,
that he shook at the intruding cylinder and piston rod, became
doubled before his eyes, and all assumed the color of a brimstone
blue! Tom became convinced, in his own mind, that the first stage
of the general convulsion had commenced!

"Hello! back her!" shouted the captain, "give her a lick
back! starboard wheel, there!"

"It's all up, now," muttered Tom, "let's see you *lick* her back
out of this scrape," and staggering towards the steam valves, to
try the amount of water in the boilers, he fell sprawling; at that
moment the boat struck the bank with a bang that shook every
timber in her; the concussion, also, injured a conducting steam-
pipe just enough to scald Tom's face and hands severely, without
endangering his life. As the steam of hot vapour hit him, he rolled
over, exclaiming:

"Good God!—it's all up, now!" and soon became utterly
insensible.

Tom was picked up and carried into the Social Hall, where
restoratives were administered to recall him to consciousness, and

remedies applied to heal his burns. All gathered in silence and anxiety around his pallet, watching for returning sensibility, the captain and clerk among the number, really grieved at the mishap, which they had no doubt was caused by their jest. While all breathlessly looked on, Tom gave manifestations of returning consciousness: of course, with sensibility returned feeling, and his burns appealed, most touchingly, to that sense. Twisting himself up, and drawing his breath through his teeth, he slowly remarked:

"Jest as I thought—the d——l's got me, *s-l-i-c-k* enough, and I'm burnt already to a cinder!"

There was no resisting this—all hands burst into a roar of laughter. Tom couldn't open his eyes, but he could hear, and after they had done laughing, he quietly remarked:

"These *imps* are mightily glad because they've got *me!*"

Here followed another roar, and when it subsided, the captain approached him, and called his name—

"Tom, old fellow," said he, "you're safe!"

"What, *you* here, too, captain? I thought you had jined meetin' and saved your bacon. So they've got you, too—well, a fellar aint alone then."

Here the clerk spoke to him.

"What, you, too Bill?—well, 'there's a party of us,' any how, but it's so confounded dark I can't see you, and its hotter than ——(here he checked himself with a shudder, and added,) Yes, I'm certain we're *thar!*" sighing heavily, he murmured— "Poor Mary—Oh, my Mary."

By the efforts of the captain and clerk Tom was made to understand the true state of the case, and through their kindness and attention, was soon able to return to duty, and though he would after[wards] laugh at a jest about old Father Miller, yet he was never again known to drink whiskey. When irritated now, Tom always shuts his lips tight, and chokes down the rising oath. Mary is gratified with the change, although she wept at the severity of the means by which he was converted.

GLIMPSES OF NEW ORLEANS IN 1819

BENJAMIN H. LATROBE

[*Arriving in New Orleans in January, 1819, to complete some building contracts the noted architect Benjamin H. Latrobe yet had time to keep an extensive diary in which he set down his impressions of the town as he first saw it. Some of the passages describing scenes which would have caught the eye and interest of any river traveler have been extracted here from John H. B. Latrobe's* The Journal of Latrobe (*New York, Appleton, 1905*), *pp. 160–63, 179–82, 220–24, 230–32. Any reader interested in New Orleans or Latrobe will want to see the beautifully printed* Impressions Respecting New Orleans by Benjamin Henry Boneval Latrobe Diary & Sketches 1818–1820, *edited with an introduction and notes by Samuel Wilson, Jr., New York, Columbia University Press, 1951.*]

On arriving at New Orleans in the morning, a sound more strange than any that is heard anywhere else in the world astonishes a stranger. It is a most incessant, loud, rapid, and various gabble of tongues of all tones that were every heard at Babel. It is more to be compared with the sounds that issue from an extensive marsh, the residence of a million or two of frogs, from bullfrogs up to whistlers, than to anything else. It proceeded from the market and levee, a point to which we had cast anchor, and which, before we went ashore, was in a moment, by the sudden disappearance of the fog, laid open to our view.

New Orleans has, at first sight, a very imposing and handsome appearance, beyond any other city in the United States in which I have yet been. The strange and loud noise heard through the fog, on board the *Clio*, proceeding from the voices of the market people and their customers, was not more extraordinary than the appearance of these noisy folk when the fog cleared away and we landed. Everything had an odd look. For twenty-five years I have been a traveler only between New York and Richmond, and I confess that I felt myself in some degree again a cockney, for it was impossible not to stare at a sight wholly new even to one who has traveled much in Europe and America.

The first remarkable appearance was that of the market boats, differing in form and equipment from anything that floats on the Atlantic side of our country. We landed among the queer boats, some of which carried the tricolored flag of Napoleon, at the foot of a wooden flight of steps opposite to the center of the public square, which were badly fixed to the ragged bank. On the upper step of the flight sat a couple of Choctaw Indian women and a stark naked Indian girl. At the top of the flight we arrived on the levee extending along the front of the city. It is a wide bank of earth, level on the top to the width of perhaps fifty feet, and then sloping gradually in a very easy descent to the footway or banquet at the houses, a distance of about one hundred and fifty to two hundred feet from the edge of the levee. This footway is about five feet below the level of the levee, of course four feet below the surface of the water in the river at the time of the innundation, which rises to within one foot, sometimes less, at the top of the levee. Along the levee, as far as the eye could reach to the west, and to the market house to the east, were ranged two rows of market people, some having stalls or tables with a tilt or awning of canvas, but the majority having their wares lying on the ground, perhaps on a piece of canvas or a parcel of palmetto leaves. The articles to be sold were not more various than the sellers. White men and women, and of all hues of brown, and of all classes of faces, from round Yankees to grizzly and lean Spaniards, black negroes and negresses, filthy Indians half naked, mulattoes curly and straight-haired, quadroons of all shades, long haired and frizzled, women dressed in the most flaring yellow and scarlet gowns, the men capped and hatted. Their wares consisted of as many kinds as their faces. Innumerable wild ducks, oysters, poultry of all kinds, fish, bananas, piles of oranges, sugarcane, sweet and Irish potatoes, corn in the ear and husked, apples, carrots, and all sort of other roots, eggs, trinkets, tinware, dry goods, in fact of more and odder things to be sold in that manner and place than I can enumerate. The market was full of wretched beef and other butcher's-meat, and some excellent and large fish. I cannot suppose that my eye took in less than five hundred sellers and buyers, all of whom appeared to strain their voices to exceed each other in loudness. A little farther along the levee, on the margin of a heap of bricks, was a bookseller, whose stock of books, English and French, cut no mean appearance. Among others, there was a well-bound collection of pamphlets printed during the American war, forming ten octavo volumes, which I must get my friend Robertson of Congress, if here, to buy. . . .

In going up St. Peter's Street and approaching the Common, I heard a most extraordinary noise, which I supposed to proceed from some horse-mill—the horses tramping on a wooden floor. I found, however, on emerging from the house to the Common that it proceeded from a crowd of five or six hundred persons, assembled in an open space or public square. I went to the spot and crowded near enough to see the performance. All those who were engaged in the business seemed to be blacks. I did not observe a dozen yellow faces. They were formed into circular groups, in the midst of four of which that I examined (but there were more of them) was a ring, the largest not ten feet in diameter. In the first were two women dancing. They held each a coarse handkerchief, extended by the corners, in their hands, and set to each other in a miserably dull and slow figure, hardly moving their feet or bodies. The music consisted of two drums and a stringed instrument. An old man sat astride of a cylindrical drum, about a foot in diameter, and beat it with incredible quickness with the edge of his hand and fingers. The other drum was an open-staved thing held between the knees and beaten in the same manner. They made an incredible noise. The most curious instrument, however, was a stringed instrument, which no doubt was imported from Africa. On the top of the finger board was the rude figure of a man in a sitting posture, and two pegs behind him to which the strings were fastened. The body was a calabash. It was played upon by a very little old man, apparently eighty or ninety years old. The women squalled out a burden to the playing, at intervals, consisting of two notes, as the negroes working in our cities respond to the song of their leader. Most of the circles contained the same sort of dances. One was larger, in which a ring of a dozen women walked, by way of dancing, round the music in the center. But the instruments were of different construction. One which from the color of the wood seemed new, consisted of a block cut into something of the form of a cricket bat, with a long and deep mortise down the center. This thing made a considerable noise, being beaten lustily on the side by a short stick. In the same orchestra was a square drum, looking like a stool, which made an abominable, loud noise; also a calabash with a round hole in it, the hole studded with brass nails, which was beaten by a woman with two short sticks. A man sung an uncouth song to the dancing, which I suppose was in some African language, for it was not French, and the women screamed a detestable burden on one single note. The allowed amusements of Sunday have, it seems, perpetuated here those of Africa among its former inhabitants. I have never seen anything more brutally savage and at the same time dull and stupid, than this whole exhibition. Continuing my walk about a mile along the canal, and returning after sunset near the same spot, the noise was still heard. . . .

Before I went to church this morning I had occasion to go to the upper end of the Faubourg St. Mary. A Sunday in New Orleans may be pretty well understood by recounting the various sights that occur in such a walk. For instance:

After taking leave of two friends who accompanied me as far as the levee, and conversed on the relative merits of the different flags which were flying on board the numerous ships along the shore, I bought three oranges for a bit (twelve and a half cents) of a black woman, and watched the mooring of a market boat which carried the broad pennant of Napoleon. Out of the boat came ashore a basket of pecan nuts, twenty or thirty wild ducks of different sorts, rather too late in the season, a great quantity of carrots, and some sugar cane. The boat was principally loaded with corn. On the cabin was a coop, well filled with poultry, and in it two black women in madras turbans, and gowns stripped with scarlet and yellow. Round their necks a plentiful assortment of bead necklaces—in fact, they were in full dress. The man who seemed to be the owner was an old sunburned creole, slovenly in his whole appearance; and two old black men, in blanket frocks with pointed hoods (capots), were the navigators, and were carrying the cargo ashore, with many a curse at being so late at market (ten o'clock). A little farther on were three drunken Indians who afforded sport to several boys that surrounded them. Then half a dozen Kentuckians, dirty, savage, and gigantic, who were selling a horse or two to a group of genteel-looking men, who spoke English. Being now arrived near the steamboats, ev-

erything like business seemed suspended, and the levee was full
of persons, well dressed, without any apparent object but to take
the air. I left the levee and walked along the houses on the old
levee. Here some sailors were buying, in a French shop, of a black
shopwoman, slops, and trying on their pantaloons, she helping
them. Many shops shut up, but some open and doing business. At
last, as the houses became thinner, I reached my destination,
which was to call on a gentleman by appointment. I stayed some
time with him, during which we sat in the gallery and saw two
ships come to at the levee—a very beautiful view. Returning, to
avoid the dust, into Magazin Street, I called, in passing, at Mr.
Brand's to inquire after Mrs. Brand, who is sick. I found him
going to church, with some others. Passing Mr. Morgan's, I
overtook another church party. On the steps of a store, a little
farther on, lay two boatmen, drunk and half-asleep, swearing in
English at some boys who were teasing them. Going along the
Levee Street, I encountered a large group of colored gentlemen
and ladies, who seemed to be about to separate. I stopped for a
moment to listen to a pretty loud conversation, and found that a
blackish sort of mulatto was discussing the merits of a new priest
who has a very fine voice. A cream-colored lady differed from
him, and gave the preference to one of the other priests, "*qui a la
voix si forte et si haute comme une cloche; mon Dieu! come une
cloche, si haute.*" Other opinions were given in creole French, and
were unintelligible to me. These folks, then, came from church;
and, by the bye, these singers, or musical reciters, had treated
them to a chapter or two of Latin. The voice, therefore, was the
only subject of discussion, for to them it was certainly *vox, et
praeterea nihil.*

It was now eleven o'clock, and I went myself to Mr. Hull's
church, following many a group who were directing their steps
thither also. The church service was just beginning; the prayers
always excellent; the music more than tolerable, and the sermon
very well composed and delivered. The church was just full. I left
the church with the congregation. In Bourbon Street, passed a
cooper who was at work with some mulatto boys. He was scolding
them in very good English. A little farther along, passed a shoemaker's. The house had a door, and a wide window on each side
of it. All were well open. Opposite to one window sat a broad-
faced, dark mulatto, on his bench. His sleeves were rolled up to

his elbows, and he sat with a very large draughtboard on his
knees; and facing him, on another shoemaker's bench, sat a good-
looking, well-dressed white man, apparently eighteen or nineteen,
with his hat on, who was playing at draughts with him. They
seemed to be arguing, on terms of perfect equality, some knotty
point of the game. Opposite to the open door stood a white
woman, with a gaudily dressed child, having a large hat and
feathers on his head, in her arms. She looked as if much interested
in the discussion. The other window discovered four boys and an
enormous man, all black, hard at work at their trade.

At the corner of Bourbon and St. Louis stood a boy of about
fifteen or sixteen years old, with his fowling piece and hunting
net, and some gentlemen were examining its contents. It contained a mocking bird, a red bird (the Virginia nightingale), a
heron (Indian hen), and a number of small martins. This shooting is the common sport of the young creoles on Sunday, but it is
to be regretted that the war should be carried on at this season, to
destroy the melody of the woods and interrupt the connubial
happiness of birds that cannot be eaten.

I turned down St. Louis Street, and on coming near the
French coffee-house, I heard the blow of the cue and the rebound
of billiard balls upstairs. The coffee-house was full. I came home
then, and in a short time was called upon by three tall Kentuckians, who came to make contracts for logs; and as they were to go
up the river the next morning, I attended to their business, which
occupied me till dinner. I walked downstairs with them, and as I
stood at the gate of the corridor there passed a cabriolet, or chair,
in which was a white man and a bright quadroon woman holding
an unbrella out of the chair, the hood of which was up. A ragged
black boy sat at their feet and drove, and a girl of thirteen or
fourteen years old sat up on the trunk board behind. . . .

In going home to my lodgings this evening, about sunset, I
encountered a crowd of at least two hundred negroes—men and
women—who were following a corpse to the cemetery. Of the
women one-half, at least, carried candles; and as the evening
began to be dark, the effect was very striking, for all the women,
and many of the men, were dressed in pure white. The funerals
are so numerous here, or rather occupy so much of every afternoon, in consequence of their being, almost all of them, performed by the same set of priests, proceeding from the same

parish church, that they excite hardly any attention. But this was so numerously attended that I was tempted to follow it; and, getting just in a line with the priests, I entered the churchyard with them and placed myself close to the grave. The grave was about three feet deep, of which eighteen inches were filled with water. It had been dug in a mass of earth and bones which formed a little hillock by its side. Ten or twelve skulls were piled up upon the heap, which looked more like a heap of sticks, so numerous were the ribs and thigh bones that partly composed it. As soon as the priests, who were five in number, had entered the cemetery, preceded by three boys carrying the usual pair of urns and cruci-fix on staves, they began their chant, lazily enough, and continued it till they arrived at the grave. The coffin was then brought and immediately let down. It swam like a boat in the water. The priest began his prayers. In the meantime a great crowd of women pressed close to the grave, making very loud lamentations. At a particular passage the gravedigger, who was a little, gray-headed negro, naked, excepting as to a pair of ragged, short breeches, threw a shovelful of earth upon the coffin, and at the same instant one of the negro women, who seemed more particularly affected, threw herself into the grave upon the coffin, and partly fell into the water, as the coffin swam to one side. The gravedigger, with very little ceremony, thrust his shovel under her, and then seized her with both hands round the throat and pulled her up, while others took hold of her legs and arms, and she was presently removed. On the heap of bones stood a number of boys, who then began to amuse themselves by throwing in the skulls, which made a loud report on the hollow coffin, and the whole became a sort of farce after the tragedy, the boys throwing about the legs and thighs and hunting up the skulls for balls to pelt each other. The noise and laughter was general by the time the service was over. The women near the grave each plucked up a little grass before they returned.

I went out in the midst of the confusion and asked one of the mourners in white, who was talking intelligible French to her companions, who the person was who seemed to be so much honored and lamented by her own color. She told me that she was a very old African (Kongo) negress, belonging to Madam Fitz-gerald, and that most of those who followed her to the grave were her children, grandchildren, great-grandchildren, their husbands, wives, and companions. I asked if her granddaughter, who threw herself into the grave, could possibly have felt such excessive distress at the death of an old woman who before her death was almost childish, and was supposed to be above one hundred years old, as to be tired of her own life. She shrugged her shoulders two or three times, and then said, "*Je n'en sais rien, cela est une manière.*"

This assemblage of negroes was an instance of the light in which the quadroons view themselves. There were none that I observed but pitch-black faces.

TEN DAYS IN NEW ORLEANS, 1826

DONALD MACDONALD

[*Donald MacDonald's account of his voyage from New Harmony, Indiana, to New Orleans, March 5–13, 1826, the reader has already seen (pp. 40–47 above). His observations made during ten days at New Orleans (March 14–24) are also from his diary kept on this visit to the United States* (Indiana Historical Society Publications, *XIV* [*1942*], 345–54).]

The following morning after breakfast I landed and took up my lodging at the Planters Hotel (M^r. Elkin) a large house the resort usually of Bachelors. I called and delivered my letter from M^r. Owen to M^r. [MS blank] who was M^r. Rapp's agent & has now become M^r. Owen's. He & his partner are druggists. He afterwards invited me to tea at his father in law's D^r. Rogers where I dined once & found his wife & daughter amiable women, & himself a very intelligent person. At the Planters' I fell in with M^r. Thomas from New York, who introduced me to a variety of gentlemen; some merchants & others planters from the neighbourhood. As the house was crowded I was at first put into a small room where there were three more beds, but upon application to the clerk he removed me to another where I had but one companion who proved to be a very respectable gentleman, a judge from Feliciana, a town in the State, & who once stood candidate for the governorship. We became very friendly, and he gave me a pressing invitation to visit him. I learnt that his wife was a very amiable person, & that he had a fine family & resided in a beautiful country. I likewise met a Philadelphia Friend, and two gentlemen with whom I had crossed the ocean last summer in the *Canada*. [My fellow travellers on board the *Columbia* introduced me to their acquaintance.] Thus Every day I had one or more companions to visit the town & neighbourhood with. [It is frequently the practice of the passengers to remain on board the steamboats in which they descend the river, and as the accommodations are good, it is sometimes more convenient to do so, than to land and put up at a crowded hotel.]

The boarding is 2$ a day. Black or coloured slaves wait upon you, and at Elkin's the female slaves dress so gaudily, that I sometimes fancied a resemblance to an eastern entertainment as I sat at the dinner table. But the house is a very inconvenient one, and the attendance irregular. The weather was to me extremely oppressive, the ther'. ranging from 76° to above 80° with little wind.

The town lies on the left bank of the river, & 5 or 6 feet below the level of the high rises of the river which are about the months of April, May & June. The Levee which protects the town is covered with shells & small stones and made into a hard terrace, behind which runs a wide road, separated from the first street or row of houses by an open space of a mile in length but only two or three hundred f'. wide. On this ground stand the custom house, the large stone market houses & some warehouses. During the first half of the year trade is very brisk, the Levee being covered with bales of cotton, casks of sugar & tobacco, coffee & rice, carts driving in every direction with goods, and shipping of all descriptions lying by the river bank. While I remained at New Orleans, there were never less than 12 or 15 steamboats lying there, and several times in the course of the day, the guns of those arriving and departing were heard in every part of the town. Two steam boats are in constant employ towing vessels the sailing vessels in & out of the river, its mouth being 100 miles below the city.

Above the steamboats lye a great number of keel & flat boats & other small craft, which have brought raw materials & provisions of all kinds down the river. The cargoes of some boats are disposed of whole sale, while the tenants of the others are occupied retailing out their goods.

The river at this place is about a mile wide, and extremely deep. Within a few feet of the levee the water is 70 ft deep, and as it rolls along at the rate of 3 miles an hour in eddies & boiling up, it is quite muddy and is constantly undermining the part of the bank against which the force of the current strikes. At present the current strikes the right bank of the river a mile above the town, wearing it rapidly away; and thence crossing over runs against the left bank at the lower extremity of the city, which it is gradually forcing in, in spite of the usual attempts to protect the bank. Within a few years the city has become possessed of several acres of valuable land which the river threw up as it receded above the town towards the opposite bank, sweeping away the house & a considerable part of the lands belonging to a widow lady.

Vessels very rarely anchor in the river on account of its depth, which likewise prevents the erection of wharves or quais. Large timbers and planks are substituted, as temporary stages for loading & unloading the vessels. On the opposite bank is the powder magazine, & place where the shipping are repaired. A Columbian Brig of War lay there while I was in New Orleans. As New Orleans was both the possession of the French & Spaniards before being sold to the United States, the styles of building are very various. Facing the levee, are a square with a Catholic church in it, a large barrack of stone, and the Arsenal inclosed within a stone wall, all built by the Spaniards, and a row of houses, shops below & dwelling rooms above, in the Spanish and Moorish style of architecture. The streets run parallel & at right angles to the river. Only one is paved (Charters street) The rest are of earth, and consequently almost impassable in rainy weather. But every street has its two footways protected from the road by wooden gutters. Since M^r. Jefferson purchased this state from the French, a great many french left it, and as many spaniards as could dispose of their property. Americans seeking their fortunes pushed in, and became active in business. It is remarkable that not a Spaniard or Frenchman has any concern in any of the many steamboats which belong to this city & run on the river; or is, indeed much employed in the active commerce now carrying on.

At first the principal public offices were filled by frenchmen, who made the Americans rather dissatisfied by their lukewarm treatment of all their proposed improvements. This has had the effect of throwing many french out of office. An attempt to get the streets paved, succeeded so far as to have the principal one so done; But as the stones must all be brought by sea from the northern States, it is probable that several years will elapse before all the [others] are paved, or macadamized which many consider a better plan.

The state house is a small old building; much is said of building a new one.

There is a law in this state which renders all marriages between whites and persons of colour or quadroons (as all are called whose blood is in any way proved to be tainted with the negroe race) illegal, and while I was there another was passed, entirely prohibiting the introduction of slaves. This latter law was made in consequence of so many slaves of the most worthless & troublesome character having been brought into the city for sale.

Many of the quadroon families are rich, and the females handsome. As the whites are the lords of the land, the quadroon females consider it an honor to be connected with them, and as marriage is forbidden, most of them live as the companions of the white men, proving true to them, as long as they are well treated. This is the French fashion, but as the relative proportion of the French & Americans diminishes, it is probable that this demoralizing law will be altered & modified.

D^r. Rogers informed me that July, August, September & October, were the unhealthy months of the year; then cold winds from the north west and a hot sun, produce fevers. At other seasons of the year the city is remarkably healthy. During the hottest season the ther^r. rarely rises above 94°. December & January are the winter months; but frost & snow are very rarely seen. Seven years ago a severe frost in the months of Jan^y & February, destroyed all the orange & lemon trees in the state. Young trees were immediately afterwards planted, and this spring a few are beginning to bear. During the unhealthy months many persons leave the city, and every thing is at rest.

The city is rapidly extending with stores & brick houses, (the residences of americans,) up the river bank.

At the back of the city, which lies some feet lower than that part which borders on the river, there extends the marsh & cypress forest intersected by a creek. Into this marsh the waters from the city are drained. A basin has been formed and a canal connecting it with the creek. There is a project for connecting the basin likewise with the river. The creek which runs into Lake Pontchartrain, has a wooden peir & battery at its mouth, to which there is a road from the city. This is the direct communication into the State of Alabama & to the seat of the general government, and is a portion of the course of inland navigation which it is proposed to extend from S^t. Augustine across the Floridas to the Mississippi. The greater number of houses in the back streets of the city are of wood & only one story high; and the people free

negroes & quadroons. A few years ago the levee many miles above
the city, being neglected, gave way. The river spread through the
marshy forest and filled the back streets where it remained 3 or 4
f'. deep for many weeks. On the falling of the river the water ran
off & dried up, and a most sickly season followed. Great penalties
are now attached to any neglect in the repair of the embankment.

There are two theaters in the city, a french & an American.
The former is large, and handsome and in every respect superior
to the latter, which has only been built three or four years. But as
there is every prospect that the English Americans will daily
encrease in numbers, while the natives of other nations will
remove, the french theater will be badly supported.

After the war in France, and the revolution in S'. Domingo,
many french families came to this place; but the society of the
Americans, the Constitution of the States, and the climate, have
all tended to drive as many of them away, as could afford to
remove.

The Levee is a place of lounge for strangers, and it is the
common practice, to ramble from steam boat to steam boat. The
captains therefore have their cabins in fine order, & spirits &
water at the service of those who come on board to admire their
boats, I saw several very large boats superbly fitted up. Among
the number were the *George Washington, Philadelphia, Feliciana, Hibernia,* & *Caledonia,* all remarkably swift boats and
constructed on so large a scale as to afford accommodations which
quite surprise a stranger.

The sale rooms for slaves are in the principal streets, & open
into them. Passing along one day I entered a room round which I
saw about 20 black men women & children seated. I quietly
examined their countenances, which bore on them a dull expression of carelessness. A middle aged French lady was examining
one of the women whom she made stand up and turn round. She
then looked at her hands, felt her arms & shoulders, and asked her
if she could wash, sew & cook. The seller was a tall stout well
dressed American. He was in conversation with two or three
strangers, to whom I heard him say pointing to a part of the room
where three children and two females sat; you shall have all five
for a bill for 1000$ payable next January. While this bargaining
was going on, some of the slaves seemed to be without thoughts
or feelings on the subject, while others endeavoured to appear to
advantage.

I was introduced to a young man an assistant judge in the city. He was remarkably attentive to me. We walked together about the town, & crossed the river in a ferry boat and visited a sugar plantation. I drank tea at his house and was introduced to his wife & mother in law. He likewise introduced me to a captain of Engineers and some officers of the line. I once went to a morning parade of two companies in the barrack yard. The men were tall, stout & steady in the ranks. They exercised correctly, but in every movement I thought them too slow. I learnt that the rest of the reg'. was stationed high up the Mississippi at a Fort above S'. Louis. The captain of the Engineers, has the direction of Forts erecting at the mouth of the river and on the shores of the lake. He gave me a letter of introduction to his lieutenant who superintends the work constructing at the mouth of the river.

The exchange coffee house is the principal resort of the french. Here I found newspapers. There is a great fancy in most of the cities & towns for oyster suppers, and a traveller whatever may be his taste, can as little avoid them as the system of grog drinking.

I heard that the Duke of Saxe Weimar had been living for the last six months in the city at a boarding house and that he was much in French society. As far as I could learn, his talents are not so highly rated as his genteel & social manners. From New Orleans he intended going to S'. Louis & through the Western States.

A gentleman planter who had served in the militia during the last war, accompanied me in a hack to visit the famous lines, where the British received a check. As he was on duty in them, he explained the situation completely to me. The lines were about four miles below the city. The road to them runs by the side of the Levee, the other or left hand side of the road being occupied in the front by fine gardens and country houses and in the rear by plantations as far back as the cypress marshy forest. The right end of the lines touched the levee & was rounded into a redoubt. The left ran into the wood & marsh. The line was nearly straight and about half a mile long. It consisted of a thin parapet & small ditch in front, which filled with water as soon as cut, being in part the ditch to drain the land. The whole was quickly finished by the militia which General Jackson has [sic] collected in haste. These were spread along in rear of the lines, where they were a few days previous to Sir Edward Packenham's attack, and after it until they heard of his embarkation, when they withdrew. A few pieces of Artillery were placed at each end, and in a few places along the line. On the opposite side of the river, a work something similar was raised, though not so well made or defended. It likewise extended from the river across a plantation to the wood on the right, and a few men were sent across the river to man it.

The Americans were for three or four days quite at a loss to guess why they had not been attacked, & the wild backwoodsmen began to think the British feared their rifles. It was in the month of Jan[y] and cold frosty weather, when early one morning just as the Eastern horizon was lighting up, the sentries placed a few hundred yards in front on the flat arable land, fired their rifles and retired. It was then perceived from within the lines that two columns were advancing, the one column along the borders of the forest, and the other from behind some farm buildings under cover of the river bank. The most expert markmen were placed in front on the step in rear of the parapet, while the remainder of the militia stood below prepared to load & hand them rifles as fast as they fired.

As the columns approached rapidly, a fire of rifles and field artillery was soon opened upon them, and day throwing light around, its destructive fire was distinctly seen from the lines. The redoubt on the right was entered by the British, but they were afterwards driven back with great loss. The column on the left advanced steadily without firing, carrying fascines or bundles of sticks to throw into the ditch; but the loss experienced in killed & wounded was so great that they could not reach it in compact numbers. Many however jumped into the ditch, & were shot endeavouring to scramble up the parapet; while others when they reached the edge of the ditch cried out for quarter & threw themselves flat on the ground, where they remained till the column finally retired and left them prisoners. In the mean time success had attended another part of the British forces, which had crossed the river in boats, and taken the lines on the right bank, where they awaited orders to advance.

But the loss sustained by the British induced them to retire after burying the dead.

General Jackson had experienced some want of zeal or suspected as much & inclination among the inhabitants of New Orleans to aid him in his defensive arrangements. This induced him to declare martial law in the place and enforce the daily attendance at parade in the city of every inhabitant bound by the terms of the militia law. Several persons who absented themselves were brought into the ranks by files of soldiers. The rich & proud planters did not much relish thus being compelled to drill in the ranks with all sorts of people; and a strong feeling of dislike was felt towards General Jackson whose conduct was characterized as being extremely arbitrary. All would however have terminated to his satisfaction, had martial law ceased the moment it was known that the British had embarked; but the General by continuing it a few days longer induced his enimies to bring an action against him, in the U. States Court, and he was cast in damages which the people offered to pay but he refused to allow. The wounded men were brought into the city. The officers were invited out, as soon as they began to recover from their wounds; but as the warm weather had commenced, and a vessel lay in the river waiting for them, they quitted the scene of their disaster as soon as all could with safety be carried on board.

As I could not find any vessel bound direct to Charleston, the trade of these two places being very similar, I determined to go by the way of Havana, with which place a considerable trade is carried on. M^r. [MS blank] got me a letter to Messrs. Castillo & Black, & M^r. Brock gave me one to Colin Mitchel. As I was advised to get a passport, I called on the Spanish consul, who asked my name & that of the vessel I was to go in. Not having quite decided, I left my name and went away to make enquiries for the one which would first leave the port. On my return the consul inserted the name of the vessel (Brig *William*) & I signed the passport printed in Spanish which was already filled up, without reading it. I afterwards found that I was described as a native of the United States, which error though it did not appear to me at first of any consequence, induced me while in Havana to be very cautious not to attract the slightest notice, people's minds being in such a state of distrust and suspense.

I left New Orleans on the evening of the 24th. In the Brig *William*, Captn. Crowell, and in company with the New York packet ship *Talma*, & a french merchant ship; we were towed down the river by a steamboat. At daylight in the morning we were near the mouth [of] the river, which divides into two or three narrow channels between sand banks where vessels are

often wrecked or injured. [About 150 miles up the river there is
another channel at a bend of the river, which runs into a large
lake to the South West & thence into the gulf.] The land around
is flat marshy & covered with long grass & bushes. On the right
bank is a small settlement where the pilots reside. The buildings
are of wood supported above the water by strong piles. Some
years since the buildings at this place were washed away during a
hurricane, which drove the sea in. This port is called the Balise,
the name given to bouyes which mark the channel. As the wind
was fair, and we set sail as soon as a pilot came on board & the
tow-rope was thrown off, I could not go on shore to deliver to the
Lieutenant the letter of introduction from his captain & see the
sight of the intended fort.

CARNIVAL IN NEW ORLEANS, 1846

CHARLES LYELL

[*Charles Lyell, the noted English geologist, who arrived in New Orleans just before Lent in 1846, included in his* A Second Visit to the United States of North America (*2 volumes, New York, 1849*), *II, 90–97, pictures of the Carnival, the theater, and other aspects of life of perennial attraction to the curious tourist on a visit to this ever-fascinating river-sea port.*]

Next morning at daylight we found ourselves in Louisiana. We had already entered the large lagoon, called Lake Pontchartrain, by a narrow passage, and, having skirted its southern shore, had reached a point six miles north of New Orleans. Here we disembarked, and entered the cars of a railway built on piles, which conveyed us in less than an hour to the great city, passing over swamps in which the tall cypress, hung with Spanish moss, was flourishing, and below it numerous shrubs just bursting into leaf. In many gardens of the suburbs, the almond and peach trees were in full blossom. In some places the blue-leaved palmetto, and the leaves of a species of iris (*Iris cuprea*), were very abundant. We saw a tavern called the "Elysian Fields Coffee House," and some others with French inscriptions. There were also many houses with porte-cocheres, high roofs, and volets, and many lamps suspended from ropes attached to tall posts on each side of the road, as in the French capital. We might indeed have fancied that we were approaching Paris, but for the negroes and mulattoes, and the large verandahs reminding us that the windows required protection from the sun's heat.

It was a pleasure to hear the French language spoken, and to have our thoughts recalled to the most civilized parts of Europe by the aspect of a city, forming so great a contrast to the innumerable new towns we had lately beheld. The foreign appearance, moreover, of the inhabitants, made me feel thankful that it was possible to roam freely and without hindrance over so large a continent, no bureaus for examining and signing of passports, no fortifications, no drawbridges, no closing of gates at a fixed hour in the evening, no waiting till they are opened in the morning, no custom-houses separating one state from another, no overhauling of baggage by gens d'armes for the octroi; and yet as perfect a feeling of personal security as I ever felt in Germany or France.

The largest of the hotels, the St. Charles, being full, we obtained agreeable apartments at the St. Louis, in a part of the town where we heard French constantly spoken. Our rooms were fitted up in the French style, with muslin curtains and scarlet draperies. There was a finely-proportioned drawing-room, furnished a la Louis Quatorze, opening into a large dining-room with sliding doors, where the boarders and the "transient visitors," as they are called in the United States, met at meals. The mistress of the hotel, a widow, presided at dinner, and we talked French with her and some of the attendants; but most of the servants of the house were Irish or German. There was a beautiful ball-room, in which preparations were making for a grand masked ball, to be given the night after our arrival.

It was the last day of the Carnival. From the time we landed in New England to this hour, we seemed to have been in a country where all, whether rich or poor, were laboring from morning till night, without ever indulging in a holiday. I had sometimes thought that the national motto should be, "All work and no play." It was quite a novelty and a refreshing sight to see a whole population giving up their minds for a short season to amusement. There was a grand procession parading the streets, almost every one dressed in the most grotesque attire, troops of them on horseback, some in open carriages, with bands of music, and in a variety of costumes—some as Indians, with feathers in their heads, and one, a jolly fat man, as Mardi Gras himself. All wore masks, and here and there in the crowd, or stationed in a balcony above, we saw persons armed with bags of flour, which they showered down copiously on any one who seemed particularly proud of his attire. The strangeness of the scene was not a little heightened by the blending of negroes, quadroons, and mulattoes in the crowd; and we were amused by observing the ludicrous surprise, mixed with contempt, of several unmasked, stiff, grave Anglo-Americans from the north who were witnessing for the first time what seemed to them so much mummery and tom-foolery. One wagoner, coming out of a cross street, in his working-dress, drove his team of horses and vehicle heavily laden with cotton bales right through the procession, causing a long interruption. The crowd seemed determined to allow nothing to disturb their good humor; but although many of the wealthy Protestant citizens take part in the ceremony, this rude intrusion struck me as a kind of foreshadowing of coming events, emblematic of the violent shock which the invasion of the Anglo-Americans is about to give to the old *regime* of Louisiana. A gentleman told me that, being last year in Rome, he had not seen so many masks at the Carnival there; and, in spite of the increase of Protestants, he thought there had been quite as much "flour and fun" this year as usual. The proportion, however, of strict Romanists is not so great as formerly, and to-morrow, they say, when Lent begins, there will be an end of the trade in masks; yet the butchers will sell nearly as much meat as ever. During the Carnival, the greater part of the French population keep open house, especially in the country.

New Orleans, February, 1846 – Walking first over the most ancient part of the city, called the First Municipality, we entered the Place d'Armes, and saw on one side of the square the old Spanish Government House, and opposite to it the Cathedral, or principal Catholic church, both in an antique style of architecture, and therefore strikingly unlike any thing we had seen for many months. Entering the church, which is always open, we found persons on their knees, as in Catholic countries, although it was not Sunday, and an extremely handsome quadroon woman coming out.

In the evening we went to the French Opera, and were much pleased with the performance, the orchestra being the best in America. The audience were very quiet and orderly, which is said not to be always the case in some theaters here. The French creole ladies, many of them descended from Norman ancestors, and of pure unmixed blood, are very handsome. They were attired in Parisian fashion, not over dressed, usually not so thin as the generality of American women; their luxuriant hair tastefully arranged, fastened with ornamental pins, and adorned simply with a colored ribbon or a single flower. My wife learnt from one of them afterward, that they usually pay, by the month, a quadroon female hairdresser, a refinement in which the richest ladies in Boston would not think of indulging. The word creole is used in Louisiana to express a native-born American, whether black or white, descended from old-world parents, for they would not call the aboriginal Indians creoles. It never means persons of mixed breed; and the French or Spanish creoles here would shrink as much as a New Englander from intermarriage with one *tainted*, in the slightest degree, with African blood. The frequent alliances of the creoles, or Louisianians, of French extraction, with lawyers and merchants from the northern states, help to cement the ties which are every day binding more firmly together the distant parts of the Union. Both races may be improved by such connection, for the manners of the creole ladies are, for the most part, more refined; and many a Louisianian might justly have felt indignant if he could have overheard a conceited young bachelor from the north telling me "how much they were preferred by the fair sex to the hard-drinking, gambling, horse-racing, cock-fighting, and tobacco-chewing southerners." If the creoles have less depth of character, and are less striving and ambitions than the New Englanders, it must be no slight source of happiness to the former to be so content with present advantages. They seem to feel, far more than the Anglo-Saxons, that if riches be worth the winning, they are also worth enjoying.

The quadroons, or the offspring of the whites and mulattoes, sat in an upper tier of boxes appropriated to them. When they are rich, they hold a peculiar and very equivocal position in society. As children, they have often been sent to Paris for their education, and, being as capable of improvement as any whites, return with refined manners, and not unfrequently with more cultivated minds than the majority of those from whose society they are shut out. By the tyranny of caste they are driven, therefore, to form among themselves a select and exclusive set. Among other stories illustrating their social relation to the whites, we were told that a young man of the dominant race fell in love with a beautiful quadroon girl, who was so light-colored as to be scarcely distinguishable from one of pure breed. He found that, in order to render the marriage legal, he was required to swear that he himself had negro blood in his veins, and, that he might conscientiously take the oath, he let some of the blood of his betrothed into his veins with a lancet. The romance of this tale was, however, greatly diminished, although I fear that my inclination to believe in its truth was equally enhanced, when the additional circumstance was related, that the young lady was rich.

Some part of the feeling prevailing in New England, in regard to the immorality of New Orleans, may be set down to the fact of their theaters being open every Sunday evening, which is no indication whatever of a disregard of religion on the part of the Catholics. The latter might, with as much reason, reflect on the Protestants for not keeping the doors of their churches open on week-days. But as a great number of the young mercantile men who sojourn here are from the north, and separated from their families, they are naturally tempted to frequent the theaters on Sundays; and if they do so with a sense that they are violating propriety, or acting against what in their consciences they think right, the effect must be unfavorable to their moral character.

During our stay here we passed a delightful evening in the St. Charles theater, seeing Mr. and Mrs. Kean in the "Gamester" and in "The Follies of a Night." Her acting of Mrs. Beverley was perfection; every tone and gesture full of feeling, and always lady-like, never overwrought, in the most passionate parts. Charles Kean's acting, especially in Richard, has been eminently successful during his present tour in the United States.

While at New Orleans, Mrs. Kean told my wife she had been complimented on speaking English so well; and some wonder had been expressed that she never omitted or misplaced her h's. In like manner, during our tour in New England, some of the natives, on learning that we habitually resided in London, exclaimed that they had never heard us confound our v's and w's. "The Pickwick Papers" have been so universally read in this country, that it is natural the Americans should imagine Sam Weller's pronunciation to be a type of that usually spoken in the old country, at least in and about the metropolis. In their turn, the English retaliate amply on American travelers in the British Isles: "You don't mean to say you are an American? Is it possible? I should never have discovered it, you speak English so well!" "Did you suppose that we had adopted some one of the Indian languages?" "I really never thought about it; but it is wonderful to hear you talk like us!"

Looking into the shop-windows in New Orleans, we see

much which reminds us of Paris, and abundance of articles manufactured in the northern states, but very few things characteristic of Louisiana. Among the latter I remarked, at a jeweler's, many alligators' teeth polished and as white as ivory, and set in silver for infants to wear round their necks to rub against their gums when cutting their teeth, in the same way as they use a coral in England.

The tombs in the cemeteries on the outskirts of the town are raised from the ground, in order that they may be above the swamps, and the coffins are placed in bins like those of a cellar. The water is seen standing on the soil at a lower level in many places; there are often flowers and shrubs round the tombs, by the side of walks made of shells of the Gnathodon. Over the grave of one recently killed in a duel was a tablet, with the inscription— "Mort, victime de l'honneur!" Should any one propose to set up a similar tribute to the memory of a duelist at Mount Auburn, near Boston, a sensation would be created which would manifest how widely different is the state of public opinion in New England from that in the "First Municipality."

Among the signs of the tacit recognition of an aristocracy in the large cities, is the manner in which persons of the richer and more refined classes associate together in the large hotels. There is one public table frequented by bachelors, commercial travelers, and gentlemen not accompanied by their wives and families, and a more expensive one, called the Ladies' Ordinary, at which ladies, their husbands, and gentlemen whom they invite, have their meals. Some persons who occupy a marked position in society, such as our friend the ex-senator, Mr. Wilde, often obtain leave by favor to frequent this ordinary; but the keepers of the hotels grant or decline the privilege, as they may think proper.

A few days after the Carnival we had another opportunity of seeing a grand procession of the natives, without masks. The corps of all the different companies of firemen turned out in their uniform, drawing their engines dressed up with flowers, ribbons, and flags, and I never saw a finer set of young men.

INDEX

Alton, Illinois, xii

Audubon, John James: steamship experiences of, xvii–xviii, xxiii

Banvard, John: youth of, 113–14; first river journey, 115–17; attacked by Murell gang, 117–18; second river journey, 118–20; panorama of Mississippi River described, 121, 126–36; exhibits panorama, 123–24; testimonials for panorama, 136–39

Baton Rouge, Louisiana, 57

Bertrand, Maréchal Simon, xxi

Biddle, Thomas, xxi

Bloody Island (near St. Louis), xxi

Boatmen (other than steam): life of, xxviii–xxix, 5–6, 41, 235–36; fight at Natchez-under-the-hill, xxxii, 19. See also Banks Finch, Mike Fink, Nigger Jim, Jack Pierce

Boats (other than steam): variety of, xxvii–xxviii, 3–9; romantic appeal of, xxviii–xxix, 5–6; perils of travel on, xxix, 13–14, 148–54, 163, 187–90

—types of: Barges, xxii, xxvii, 3–4; Canoes, 4; Dug-outs, 4; Flatboats (arks, Kentucky flats, ferry flats, broadhorns), xxvii–xxviii, 4, 5, 7–9, 14–15, 16, 41, 52, 115–18, 149, 163, 279; Horseboats, 4; Keelboats, xxii, xxvii, 4, 5, 41, 169, 149–50, 169, 187–89, 279; Mackinaws, xxvii, 4; Pirogues (periogues), xxvii, 4; Skiffs, 4

Bodmer, Karl, xxi

Brotherton, Mr. (Sheriff of St. Louis): arrests Fairchild, 96–98

Bryant, William Cullen, xxi

Campbell, Lieut. David H.: kills Finch, 21–24 passim

Casey, Capt. Thomas J. (Capt. of General Pratte): heroism of, 170–77

Chapman, William: showboat of, xxx–xxxi

Chenal du Diable. See Devil's Channel

Chester, Illinois, 74

City Hotel (St. Louis), xx

Clifton, J. W.: swindles man, 200–201; punished, 201–4

Creole: meaning of term, 290

Creoles of New Orleans, 288–92 passim

Devil's Channel (in Mississippi River): earthquake at, 150–53

Dickens, Charles, xxi

Donalds (Donnel), Samuel (Pilot of *General Pratte*): heroism of, 171, 172, 174, 176

d'Otrante, Count, xxi

Earthquake: at New Madrid, 75–76, 154; at Devil's Channel, 150–53

Fairchild, Oliver (Engineer of *General Pratte*): heroism of, 171, 172, 174, 176

Field, Matt, xvii, xxx

Finch, Banks (boatman): death of, 20–25

Fink, Mike (boatman): shoots Negro's foot, xxi; character of, 236–38; insults Proud Joe, 239–41; kills Joe, 245–47; encounters Pierce, 250–52; beaten by Pierce, 254–55

Flint, Timothy: describes river craft, xxviii, 3–12; difficulties ascending river, 187–89; wife gives birth, 189–90; baby dies, 190; encounters "Pilgrims," 191–95

Flower, George, 42

Frémont, Capt. John C., xviii–xix

Gambling: on boats, xx, 65–69, 94, 101, 107–11, 204–8, 209–13, 258; at Natchez-under-the-hill, 197–99, 201–4

Green, Jonathan ("the reformed gambler"): mentioned, xxi; tells how gamblers cheat suckers, 200–208

Hall, William C.: cheated by gamblers, 197–99

Hamilton, Capt. Thomas S.: accused of misconduct, 92–100; defended, 101–2

Herculaneum, Missouri, 72

Hobart, Nathaniel: letter quoted, xxv, xxviii

Indians: musicians at Natchez-under-the-hill, xxxii–xxxiii, 16–18; at Chickasaw Bluffs, 148–50; renegades taunted by Fink, 238–39; Choctaws at New Orleans, 271

Irving, Washington, xxi

Jackson, Andrew: at Battle of New Orleans, 283–85

Jefferson Barracks, Missouri, xxii, 72

Joinville, Prince de, xxi

Kaskaskia, Illinois, 73

Kean, Charles, xxi, 291

Kean, Mrs. Charles, xxi, 291

Klinefelter, Capt. (Capt. of *Pennsylvania*): heroism of, 179–84 *passim*

Lafayette, Marquis de, xxi, 42

La France,—: interprets for Bradbury, 148, 149

Lennox, Lord William, xxi

Lind, Jenny, xxi

Ludlow, Noah, xxi

Lynchers: punish murderer, 219–20

Marryatt, Frederick, xxi

Mathew, Father (temperance crusader), xxi

Maximilian, Prince of Neu-Wied, xxi

Memphis, Tennessee, 42, 56, 104

Miller, Henry: tells of steamboat travel, xxvi

Miller, Parson William, xxx, 264
Mounds, Indian: near Natchez, 19

Natchez, Mississippi: described,
44–45, 218; Miller reaches, 86;
hurricane at, 159–60
Natchez-under-the-hill, Mississippi:
Indian musicians at, xxxii–xxxiii,
16–18; described, 45, 56, 217–
18; gamblers at, 196–99, 200–
205, 218; Lynchers at, 219–20
National Hotel (St. Louis), 96
Nauvoo, Illinois, xxii
New Madrid, Missouri: described,
148; earthquake at, 154
New Madrid Bayou: character of,
6–7
New Orleans: character of, xxxiii,
287–88; levee at, 271–72, 273–
74, 279–80, 282; African
dances at, 272–73; Negro funeral at, 275–77; slaves at, 279,
282; quadroons of, 281, 290;
Battle of, 283–85; parades at,
288–89, 292; creole ladies of,
289–90; cemeteries of, 292
Nigger Jim (boatman): defeated
by Pierce, xxi, 248–50

Paducah, Kentucky, 92
Pettis, Spencer, xxi
Pierce, Jack (boatman): defeats
Nigger Jim, xxi, 248–50; re-
fuses to fight Fink, 250–52;
fights ram, 253; beats Fink,
254–55; killed by ram, 256
"Pilgrims": fanaticism of, xxxiii,
191–95
Plantations, southern, xxxiii, 45–
46, 57, 85
Planters Hotel (New Orleans), 278
Planters House (St. Louis), xviii,
xx
Plumb Point: Murell gang attacks
at, 117–18

Prophet, the, leader of "Pilgrims,"
192–93, 194
Proud Joe (Cherokee Indian):
insulted by Fink, 239–41; killed
by Fink, 245–47

Quadroons: at Natchez, 45; at New
Orleans, 281, 290

Royal, Mrs. Anne, xxi

St. Louis: levee at, xvii–xxiii, 70;
flood at, xxii
Ste. Genevieve, xxxi, 73
Saxe-Weimar-Eisenach, Duke of,
xxi, 283
Schultz, Christian: at Ste. Gene-
vieve, xxxi, on flatboat, 13–15 at
Natchez-under-the-hill, 15–19
Selkirk, Earl of, xxi
Selleck, Rev. Mr.: criticizes Capt.
Hamilton, 92
Shawneetown, Illinois, 116
Showboats, xxx–xxxi
Shreve, Capt. Henry M.: inventor
of machine to raise snags, 75
Slaves: on boat, 52–53; at New
Orleans, 279, 282
Smith, Dalzell, 97
Smith, Sol, xxi
Spanish burying, game of, 202–4,
218
Squatters, 41, 42, 51–52, 90
Steamboats: disasters on, xviii, xxii,
xxix–xxx, 28–29, 159–60, 167,
170–77, 178–86; life aboard,
xviii, xxiii–xxvi, 11–12, 29–36,
52–53, 60–61, 63–69, 84–85,
88–89, 103–4, 107–11; captains
of, xix, 70–71, 88–90, 92–102,
105, 111, 257–60, 266, 268,
269; passengers on, xxii, xxiii,
xxv–xxvi, 33–35, 36–38, 40,
44, 45, 49, 52, 60–61, 63, 70–

71, 77–82, 83–84, 103–4, 107–
11, 222–23, 257–58; construction of, xxiii–xxv, 27–29, 48,
58–59, 76, 88; crews of, xxvi,
30, 36, 262–63; difficulties of
travel on, xxix–xxx, 29, 40–41,
54–56, 91–92, 155–58, 167–
69; eastern and western contrasted, 27; wooding, 35–36, 90,
261–63; racing, 105–6, 258–60
Steamboats:
—*Alton*, 83; *Ambassador*, xxix;
Annawan, 167; *Arkansas Thunder*, 264; *Caledonia*, 282;
Casket, 92–102; *Cavalier*, 26;
Cleo, 270; *Columbia*, 40, 42;
Diana, 181; *Duke of Orleans*,
xxix; *Eclipse*, xvii; *Emperor*, 89–
90; *Far West*, 155; *Feliciana*,
282; *Felix Grundy*, xxix; *Florida*,
11; *Gallant*, xviii, xxiii; *General
Bernard Pratte*, xxiii, 170–76;
General Jackson, 42, 47; *George
Washington*, 11, 282; *G. Clark*,
157; *G. Gilman*, xxv; *Harry of
the West*, 59; *Helen McGregor*,
59; *Hibernia*, 282; *Huntress*, 50;
Indian, 158; *Invincible*, 223;
J. M. White, xviii; *John Aull*,
xix; *Julia Chouteau*, xviii; *Kate
Frisbee*, 181; *Lady of the Lake*,
11; *Missouri*, xxiv, 58; *Monsoon*,
70; *Omega*, xviii, xix; *Paragon*,
40, 42, 47; *Pennsylvania*, 178–
86; *Philadelphia*, 11, 282;
Prairie, xxix, 159–60; *Romeo*,
85; *Shepherdess*, xxii; *Tippecanoe*, 205; *Weston*, xviii
Stewart, Sir William Drummond,
xviii

Thackeray, William Makepeace,
xxi
Thimblerig, game of, 209–11

Vespucci, America, xxi
Virginia Hotel (St. Louis), xx
Vuides-poches (Carondelet), Mis-
souri, 156

Washington, Mississippi, 86
Webster, Daniel, xxi
Whiston, Nathaniel J.: letter
quoted, xxix–xxx
Wilcox, Capt. I. D.: tries to quiet
Finch, 20–25 *passim*
Woodworth, S. E.: describes Ban-
vard's panorama, 120–22
Wright, Frances, 42, 63, 67